I0145799

Critical Epistemologies of Global Politics

EDITED BY

MARC WOONS & SEBASTIAN WEIER

E-INTERNATIONAL
RELATIONS
PUBLISHING

E-International Relations
www.E-IR.info
Bristol, England
2017

ISBN 978-1-910814-22-2 (paperback)
ISBN 978-1-910814-23-9 (e-book)

This book is published under a Creative Commons CC BY-NC 4.0 license. You are free to:

- **Share** – copy and redistribute the material in any medium or format
- **Adapt** – remix, transform, and build upon the material

Under the following terms:

- **Attribution** – You must give appropriate credit, provide a link to the license, and indicate if changes were made. You may do so in any reasonable manner, but not in any way that suggests the licensor endorses you or your use.
- **Non-Commercial** – You may not use the material for commercial purposes.

Any of the above conditions can be waived if you get permission. Please contact info@e-ir.info for any such enquiries, including for licensing and translation requests.

Other than the terms noted above, there are no restrictions placed on the use and dissemination of this book for student learning materials / scholarly use.

Production: Michael Tang
Cover Image: coffmancmu via Depositphotos

A catalogue record for this book is available from the British Library

Abstract

While the current problems of the international system have led many scholars to examine the normative values of the inter-state system and global governance, the impact of cultural border constructions and contestations are generally of second-order interest in international relations (IR) research. Civilizational borders, racial borders, or other cultural borders are often taken as constants to think from rather than internally unstable variables with a considerable crisis potential for both IR theory and practice. *Critical Epistemologies of Global Politics* combines social science and cultural studies approaches to IR, showing why contemporary Border Studies needs to be trans-disciplinary if it is to avoid reproducing the epistemological and political order that has led to contemporary global crises like the rise of ISIS, global migration, or increasing contestations of the State form as such. Gathering contributions from Gender, Black, Religious and Post-/Decolonial Studies, the volume contributes to decolonial thinking and related concepts such as *border thinking* in IR. The volume offers a critical epistemology of global politics and proposes an enriched vision of borders, both analytically and politically, that not only seeks to understand but also to reshape and expand the meanings and consequences of IR.

iv   *Critical Epistemologies of Global Politics*

Acknowledgements

The editors of this volume would like to thank the faculty and participants in the "Borders, Borderlands, Border thinking" Summer Institute that was co-organized by the University of Bremen, the University of North Carolina at Chapel Hill, and Duke University at the University of Bremen from 15-26 May 2015. They especially want to thank the German Academic Exchange Service, whose generous funding made this volume possible. Special thanks also goes to Stephen McGlinchey, Editor-in-Chief of E-International Relations, and the rest of the publishing team whose enthusiasm and support played a crucial role in seeing this project through to fruition.

Marc Woons is a Doctoral Fellow with the Fonds Wetenschappelijk Onderzoek - Vlaanderen (Research Foundation – Flanders) and the Research in Political Philosophy Leuven (RIPPLE) Institute at the University of Leuven in Belgium. He has published numerous articles on settler colonialism and Indigenous-state relations and edited *Restoring Indigenous Self-Determination: Theoretical and Practical Approaches* (E-International Relations, 2015).

Sebastian Weier is currently an independent researcher in the field of Border Studies and American Studies. He studied Political Sciences and Cultural Studies and obtained his Ph.D. from the University of Bremen for a dissertation on "Cyborg Black Studies: Tracing the Impact of Technological Change on the Constitution of Blackness".

Contents

CONTRIBUTORS   viii

INTRODUCTION
Sebastian Weier & Marc Woons   1

1.   INTERVIEW WITH WALTER D. MIGNOLO   11

2.   DECOLONIAL FEMINISM AND GLOBAL POLITICS: BORDER THINKING
     AND VULNERABILITY AS A KNOWING OTHERWISE
     Rosalba Icaza   26

3.   DECOLONISING THE ANTHROPOCENE: THE MYTHO-POLITICS OF
     HUMAN MASTERY
     Karsten A. Schulz   46

4.   COLONIAL ANIMALITY: CONSTITUTING CANADIAN SETTLER
     COLONIALISM THROUGH THE HUMAN-ANIMAL RELATIONSHIP
     Azeezah Kanji   63

5.   A POST/DECOLONIAL GEOGRAPHY BEYOND 'THE LANGUAGE OF
     THE MOUTH'
     Amber Murrey   79

6.   ONTOLOGICIDAL VIOLENCE: MODERNITY/COLONIALITY AND THE
     MUSLIM SUBJECT IN INTERNATIONAL LAW
     Pierre-Alexandre Cardinal   100

7.   MULTICULTURALISM AT THE CROSSROADS: LEARNING BEYOND
     THE WEST
     Marc Woons   116

8.   DE-EUROPEANISING EUROPEAN BORDERS: EU-MOROCCO
     NEGOTIATIONS ON MIGRATIONS AND THE DECENTRING
     AGENDA IN EU STUDIES
     Nora El Qadim   134

9.   'UNGOVERNED SPACES?' THE ISLAMIC STATE'S CHALLENGE TO
     (POST-)WESTPHALIAN 'ORDER'
     Matt Gordner   152

10. 'WHAT GOES ON IN THE COFFIN': BORDER KNOWLEDGES IN NORTH
AMERICAN LITERATURE
Astrid M. Fellner & Susanne Hamscha   171

11. THE INFORMAL COLONIALISM OF EGYPTOLOGY: FROM THE
FRENCH EXPEDITION TO THE SECURITY STATE
Christian Langer   182

12. FUGITIVITY AGAINST THE BORDER: AFRO-PESSIMISM, FUGITIVITY,
AND THE BORDER TO SOCIAL DEATH
Paula von Gleich   203

13. INTERVIEW WITH JULIANE HAMMER   216

NOTE ON INDEXING   227

Contributors

Pierre-Alexandre Cardinal graduated from Law School at the University of Ottawa in both Civil and Common law, with a previous degree in Development Studies. His current projects include the conclusion of a Master of Law degree at McGill University. His thesis is a (decolonial) inquiry into the nature of the legal relations between Persia and Europe in the nineteenth and early twentieth century. This is a first step in a larger research project questioning the underlying assumptions of Eurocentric international law, and more specifically its 'ontologicidal' ambivalences in its relations with the 'periphery' of Europe. Pierre-Alexandre is also engaging in a post-colonial and post-humanist critique of international environmental law.

Nora El Qadim, is an Associate Professor of Political Science at the University of Paris 8-Vincennes Saint-Denis, and a researcher at the CRESPPA-LabTop. She recently published a book on EU-Morocco negotiations on migration policy entitled *Le gouvernement asymétrique des migrations. Maroc-Union européenne* (Dalloz, 2015). Her research concentrates on migration policies, on the discriminations they create, and on the various forms of resistances that exist when it comes to these policies, especially in the South.

Astrid Fellner is Chair of North American Literary and Cultural Studies and Vice-President for European and International Affairs at Saarland University in Saarbrücken, Germany. After teaching at the University of Vienna, she also held the Distinguished Visiting Austrian Chair at Stanford University. Her monographs include *Articulating Selves: Contemporary Chicana Self-Representation* (2002) and *Bodily Sensations: The Female Body in Late-Eighteenth-Century American Culture* (forthcoming). She has also published a series of articles and co-edited books in the fields of U.S. Latino/a literature, Canadian literature, Gender/Queer Studies, and Cultural Studies.

Paula von Gleich is a doctoral candidate of American Studies at the University of Bremen's Department of Languages and Literatures. She is member of the Institute for Postcolonial and Transcultural Studies and of the doctoral network Perspectives in Cultural Analysis: Black Diaspora, Decoloniality, and Transnationality in Bremen. She received her master's degree in Transnational Literary Studies and the bachelor's degree in

English-Speaking Cultures at the University of Bremen. The past recipient of a Bridge scholarship from the University of Bremen, she currently receives a doctoral fellowship from the German foundation *Evangelisches Studienwerk*. Her dissertation focuses on border concepts in contemporary African American theory and narratives of captivity and fugitivity since slavery until today. Her broader research interests include African American and Black diasporic literature and theory, critical race studies, and postcolonial and transnational literary studies.

Matt Gordner is a Tunis-based doctoral student in the University of Toronto's Department of Political Science and a 2016-2017 American Political Science Association (APSA) Middle East and North Africa Civil Society Fellow specializing in comparative and development politics with a regional focus on the Middle East and North Africa. His work, published in a number of academic journals, including *Middle East Topic and Arguments (META)*; *In-Spire: Journal of Law, Politics, and Societies*; *Illumine: Journal of the Centre for the Study of Religion*; and the U.N.-sponsored *Global Education Magazine*, examines the politics of democratization and authoritarianism, social movements, civil society activism, and youth empowerment. A Trudeau Scholarship (2012-2016) and a University of Toronto Graduate Award of Excellence (2015) supported his research in this volume.

Juliane Hammer is an Associate Professor and the Kenan Rifai Scholar of Islamic Studies in the Department of Religious Studies at the University of North Carolina at Chapel Hill. Her interdisciplinary work of the last decade has focused on women, gender and sexuality, and Qur'anic interpretation in contemporary Muslim contexts, especially within American Muslim scholarly production and communal life. Hammer is the author and editor of several books and academic articles in Religious Studies and Middle Eastern Studies and lectures widely on women, gender and sexuality in Islam. After publishing *American Muslim Women, Religious Authority, and Activism: More than a Prayer* (2012), she has turned to two related book projects. The first focuses on American Muslim efforts against domestic violence, which traces religiously framed efforts in Muslim communities to raise awareness of domestic violence. The second approaches discourses and practices regarding marriage and family in Muslim communities in the United States at the intersection of marriage ideals, religious discourses and interpretations. It also looks at the ways in which Muslim practices as well as ideas are simultaneously framed by American marriage debates and Muslim reevaluations and reinterpretations of religious tradition and normativity.

Susanne Hamscha works at the Austrian Fulbright Commission. Previously, she was Assistant Professor in American Studies at the University of Graz and Adjunct Lecturer at Saarland University. In 2014/15, she was a Visiting Scholar at the Department of English and Comparative Literature at Columbia University where she conducted post-doctoral research on the American freak show tradition and the aesthetics of the disabled body. Her publications include the monograph *The Fiction of America: Performance and the Cultural Imaginary in Literature and Film* (2013) and the co-edited volume *Is It 'Cause It's Cool? Affective Encounters with American Culture* (2014).

Rosalba Icaza is a Mexican feminist academic-activist who conducts research and teaches on social movements, epistemic justice, and indigenous people resistance and autonomy. Her pedagogical practice has been focused on making the classroom a space to share ideas-as-incarnated-experiences about the academy as a colonizing institution and/or emancipatory possibility. She is Senior Lecturer in Governance and International Political Economy at the Institute of Social Studies, Erasmus University of Rotterdam.

Azeezah Kanji received her Juris Doctor from the University of Toronto's Faculty of Law, and LLM from the School of Oriental and African Studies, University of London. She serves as Programming Coordinator at Noor Cultural Centre, a Muslim academic and cultural institution in Toronto. She is also a regular contributor to Canadian media on issues of race and law, including in the *Toronto Star*, the *National Post*, and *Rabble*. Azeezah delivered University of Toronto's 2016 Hancock Lecture on national security, Islamophobia, and settler colonialism in Canada.

Christian Langer is a doctoral candidate in Egyptology at the Free University of Berlin. His doctoral dissertation looks at deportations in ancient Egyptian history between 3000 BCE and 332 BCE. For the academic year 2016/17, he is an ERASMUS visiting research student with the Institute of Archaeology at University College London. His research interests include political and social history, political theory, imperialism and colonialism, ideology, foreign and domestic policy, unfree labour and forced migration in pharaonic Egypt, and the colonial heritage of Egyptology and its impact on modern Egyptian society. His notable publications include his MA thesis on 'Aspekte des Imperialismus in der Außenpolitik der 18. Dynastie' and the article 'The Political Realism of the Egyptian Elite: A Comparison Between the 'Teaching for Merikare' and Niccolò Machiavelli's *Il Principe*' on the theoretical similarities between ancient Egyptian and Machiavellian political thought.

Katie Merriman is a PhD Student in Religious Studies at the University of North Carolina at Chapel Hill and has been involved in civil rights work in Arab and Muslim communities in the United States and Jordan. She has written and presented on African American Muslim theology, Islam in New York City, and transnational Muslim anti-colonial discourse of the twentieth century. Her dissertation focuses on charitable giving in American Muslim communities, at the intersection of race, class, and moral subjectivities. She is also the founder and guide for Muslim History Tour New York City.

Walter D. Mignolo is William H. Wannamaker Professor and Director of the Center for Global Studies and the Humanities at Duke University. He is associated researcher at Universidad Andina Simón Bolívar, Quito since 2002 and an Honorary Research Associate for CISA (Center for Indian Studies in South Africa), Wits University at Johannesburg. Among his publications related to the topic are: *The Darker Side of the Renaissance. Literacy, Territoriality and Colonization* (1995, Chinese and Spanish translation 2015); "Delinking: The Rhetoric of Modernity, the Logic of Coloniality and the Grammar of Decoloniality" *(in Cultural Studies,* 2007, translated into German, French, Swedish, Romanian and Spanish); *Local Histories/Global Designs: Coloniality, Subaltern Knowledges and Border Thinking* (2000, translated into Spanish, Portuguese, and Korean); and *The Idea of Latin America* (2006, translated into Spanish, Korean, and Italian).

Amber Murrey has held academic posts at Boston College and Clark University in the United States as well as Jimma University in Ethiopia. She earned her PhD in Geography and the Environment from the University of Oxford and researches and writes on transformations of life and place amidst structural, development, and colonial violence(s); the dynamics of social and political resistance and co-optations of that resistance by state and corporate actors; and hegemonic and counterhegemonic intellectual practices. Her research on oil politics and resistance in Central Africa as well as her collaborative work on the Pan-African legacy of Thomas Sankara is shaped by a decolonial impetus and conviction that scholarship be active, attentive, accessible, decolonized.

Karsten Schulz is a Postdoctoral Research Fellow with the Governance and Sustainability Lab at the University of Trier, Germany, where he works on the political ecology of climate change adaptation and urban water use in West Africa. He completed his M.A. in Political Science at the University of Bonn, and his Ph.D. in Political Geography at the Center for Development Research (ZEF). He has previously published on a variety of topics such as climate change adaptation, urbanization, changing nature-society relations, and sustainability transformations. He is also a Research Fellow with the Earth System Governance Project. His latest publication is "Decolonizing political ecology: ontology, technology and the enchantment of nature" (*Journal of Political Ecology*).

Introduction

Border Thinking and the Experiential Epistemologies of International Relations

SEBASTIAN WEIER & MARC WOONS

In the first ten months of 2016, 6,155 migrants worldwide died trying to cross borders (Missing Migrants, 2016) — 4,663 of them in the Mediterranean alone (UNHCR, 2016). Long merely a statistic in government deliberations, these dead have become increasingly humanized as their mementos travel globally, crossing fatal zones and in some cases earning the dead post-mortem citizenship. Photographs such as that of 3-year-old drowned Syrian boy Alan Kurdi lying face down in the sand on a Turkish beach and 5-year-old Omran Daqneesh sitting in an ambulance covered in a layer of blood and dust have become iconic in a spreading paradigmatic debate concerning how important it is to highlight the personal dimensions of the international. Amid a renewed wave of interest and available funding driven by current global events, Border Studies is being reshaped in debates on the respective importance of, on the one hand, individuals with names and, on the other hand, mere statistics. These debates map onto existing tensions between macro- and micro-level oriented research that sometimes becomes misconstrued as embodying tensions between social sciences and the humanities. The texts collected here seek to overcome these tensions, showing why contemporary Border Studies needs to be trans-disciplinary, less they reproduce the epistemological and political order that has led to current global crises such as those faced by refugees, Indigenous peoples, and planet Earth itself. Beyond a focus on either 'cold' statistics or hyper-personal experiences, this volume argues for an epistemological critique of and within Border Studies that considers Borders and International Relations through the lenses of the individual, their experiences, and their cultures as well as simultaneously through the lenses of the imaginary, the international, and the imperial.

Critical Epistemologies of Global Politics combines approaches to borders as global political superstructures, envisioning borders as internalized patterns of affect and subjectivity inspired by disciplines such as Chicana/Chicano

Studies and theoretical approaches such as Post-Marxism and Decolonial thinking. While (post-)Marxist thinkers since Louis Althusser have detailed the interwoven character of power and knowledge, as well as culture and political economy, decolonial thinkers have refused to accept as given an international system formed in and through histories of colonialism and empire, thus keeping open the possibilities of radically contesting borders and the modern nation-state form as such. Starting from an analysis of the lived experience of the Mexican-American borderlands or from the constitutive connections between coloniality and modernity, authors such as Gloria Anzaldúa, Aníbal Quijano, and Walter Mignolo have pointed out that it is necessary to stop simply thinking *about* borders and move to a mode of *border thinking*. Borders are not simply an object of reflection; they shape and inflect subjectivities. Such approaches to borders as formations — of both politico-economic structures and subjectivities — challenge exclusively state or system focused approaches to studying borders for being insufficient.

Instead of considering border deaths and displacements as necessary collateral damage to securing systemic wealth and stability and burying the border power's disposable others in abstract anonymity, Border Studies seeks to understand experiential epistemologies as central to its hermeneutic project and its political implications. This understanding must be more than just recovering a name (United Against Racism, 2012) and an origin, as do DNA identification programs such as that run by the Greece Police's Criminology DNA Lab (Petrakis, 2016) or by the University of Milan's Labanof forensics laboratory (Scammell, 2015). It must also be more than an attempt to retrace tragic events as exceptional rather than structural, as do new research disciplines such as forensic architecture (Forensic Architecture, 2016). If Dr. Cristina Cattaneo from Labanof Laboratories can describe her vision as "Our battle is not to lose the dead" (Povoledo, 2015), *border thinking* seeks to propose an understanding of borders that lays bare the power structures that produce and even require these dead in the first place. Thus, Border Studies within this volume proposes more than just improved border management, offering instead an inherently political vision of radically different and potentially de-bordered modes of thinking, living, being, and sense-making.

Arising out of a Summer School titled *Borders, Borderlands, Border thinking* held in May 2015 at the University of Bremen in cooperation with the University of North Carolina at Chapel Hill and Duke University, the present volume seeks to address global border issues from a *border thinking* platform. While the current problems of the international system have led many scholars to examine the normative values of the inter-state system and global governance, the impact of cultural border constructions and contestations are generally of second-order interest in IR research. Civilizational borders, racial borders, or other cultural borders are often taken as constants to think from rather than internally unstable variables with a considerable crisis potential both for International Relations and IR Theory. The terms borders, border thinking, and borderlands will not only be approached in their immediate political and physical sense, but also as tropes of thinking. Gathering contributions from (and beyond) Gender, Black, Religious and Post-/ Decolonial Studies, the volume offers various border-critiques rooted in these fields.

Instead of recuperating the dead beyond the borders, the epistemic critique proposed in the following pages questions both the existence of these borders and sciences' complicity in upholding them. Critical self-interrogation of various academic disciplines is a major thread of the volume. Traditional dichotomies between researcher and object or between scientist and politician are reconsidered, both multiplying the number of analytical dimensions and refuting the notion of both qualitative and scalar differences between approaches to borders in humanities and social science-inflected IR theory. In so doing, the contributions move beyond separations between inside and outside, self and other, critically engaging their own bordering logics to trace a mode of epistemological, ontological, and corpo-real interweaving and continuity with reference to the border.

Borders cannot be understood separate from the bodies they affect and form. The geopolitics of knowledge cannot be separated from the lived experience of borders. These are two decolonial perceptions that recur in the book and show why IR cannot understand contemporary border phenomena and formations without Cultural Studies, and *vice versa*. Beyond both biopolitics and realpolitik, the following contributions seek to delink from Euro-centrism and Western hegemony within Border Studies.

The volume begins with an interview of Walter Mignolo, who introduces readers to the concepts of decoloniality and border thinking. Calling on scholars of IR and beyond to "delink" from Western modernity and its colonialist implications, Mignolo emphasizes the role of non-state actors in contemporary global politics and critical academia. In researching borders, one must not approach them simply as geopolitical entities and intellectual problems, but consider their experiential dimensions and engage with how they shape the life and death of individuals everywhere. To perform *border thinking*, contemporary IR would have to move from overemphasizing the macro-politics of inter-state relations to include more prominently micro-political contestations and re-inventions of the political. Researchers would have to move away from the position of an assumed abstract rational observer and consider how that position as well as their very own subjectivities are defined by the political trajectories of their fields. Mignolo insists that special attention must thus be paid to epistemologies and how they determine the realm of the thinkable and, consequently, the realm of the doable as key to decolonizing IR.

Rosalba Icaza proposes re-thinking IR by considering how modernity (as an international regime of knowledge) and coloniality (as an international regime of power) are mutually constitutive. Decolonizing IR, her contribution shows, would require a fundamental departure from Western epistemological paradigms such as the un-bodied rational choice actor, proceeding both from non-Euro-centric systems of thinking (i.e., Indigenous cosmologies) and different modes of knowing and being, such as the corpo-realities created through experiences of vulnerability. Following Maria Lugones, Icaza argues for 'dwelling in the border,' for 'an emphasis on a knowing that sits in bodies and territories and its local histories in contrast to disembodied, abstract, universalist knowledge that generates global designs.' Offering field notes from research trips along the Mexican migrant trail with her students, Icaza reflects on practical examples of such a decolonial approach to IR through the epistemologies of affect and the corporeal.

Karsten Schulz focuses on epistemic and ontological 'borders' between humans and the more-than-human environment by inviting readers to 'decolonis[e] the Anthropocene.' By engaging 'the role of myth and mythical narratives in shaping today's ecological crisis,' Schulz delivers an example of a decolonial perspective that takes the Anthropocene concept and its underlying notion of 'anthropos' as its main targets of critique. Schulz approaches the Anthropocene as a new political paradigm, both in IR and beyond. This new paradigm, he argues, is still influenced by older mythical substrata that carry with them the 'grand narratives' of human mastery, anthropocentrism, and Euro-centrism. The 'mytho-politics' of the Anthropocene, Schulz maintains, must therefore be taken seriously in their capacity to shape contemporary societal processes.

Azeezah Kanji combines the theoretical decolonization of Euro- and anthropocentrism to formulate a critique of settler-colonialism. Kanji shows how the naturalization of the concept of the 'nation-state' in legal thought both founds and veils the settler-colonial nature of Canadian jurisprudence and discourse. The constitution of a nation's borders is enmeshed with the constitution of a human/non-human divide, she argues, that intersects with the dehumanization of Indigenous peoples and its legal consequences (e.g., the right for settler Canadians to appropriate Indigenous lands and alienate Indigenous peoples from them). Recognition of the settler-colonial legal system's right to grant 'Aboriginal rights' with respect to animals (such as hunting and fishing rights) legitimates the system and its ontological and epistemological understandings of the human/non-human divide. Discourses on Aboriginal and animal rights must thus be read as entwined within Canadian settler-colonialism in so far as the notion of rights and recognition is fundamentally embedded within its jurisprudence. Being at the basis of the Canadian nation, matters such as 'colonial animality' thus translate into inter-*national* law and IR and point to dynamics of dehumanization and (mis-) recognition as inherent to the formations and potential transformation of geopolitical borders.

Amber Murrey also focuses on how localized and relational critical epistemologies emerge in struggle with global structures by looking at the ways knowledge is created and expressed in small towns in Cameroon that have experienced multidimensional and multigenerational dispossessions as a result of their proximity to the Chad-Cameroon Oil Pipeline. Writing from the knowledge shared with her during her research in and near Nanga-Eboko and Kribi, Murrey considers how such instances of global capital embark upon highly publicized promotional practices of supporting local education that often turn out to be little more than the construction of empty structures tagged as 'schools.' The text borrows the expression 'the language of the mouth' from a local woman to theorize such performative acts as empty and purely symbolic social acts with little material effect. 'The language of the mouth' thus describes a decolonial methodology and critical epistemology through which the 'knowledge' or 'facts' produced by oil companies are read critically and which permits Murrey to 'argue for a decolonial research consciousness that is foremost attentive to the productions, circuits, policing(s) and geopolitics of knowledge within socially, culturally, psychologically destructive forms of imperial development and extraction.' Like those chosen by other authors in the volume, Murrey's approach values individual experiences over the consideration of systemic imperatives in thinking IR, arguing for the necessity of considering the international in terms of its local formations and potentially destructive effects.

Pierre-Alexandre Cardinal's contribution combines the questions of epistemology and ontology touched upon in preceding contributions with more traditional subjects of IR research by considering the 'ontologicidal violence' of International Law. Projecting Western modes of enlightenment rationality as the only possible legal logic, while at the same time excluding non-Europeans from partaking in that logic, Cardinal argues that International Law is inherently designed to disallow the existence of the non-European. Considering the example of imperial capitulations in the Ottoman Empire, he considers this as being a form of 'legal Orientalism' that makes impossible 'Muslim subjectivity,' while at the same time undermining traditional border concepts. The international, in as far as it is 'national' can only claim universal validity by forcefully erasing non-European modes of social organization — of being, doing, thinking, and sense-making. Cardinal traces such erasures with a focus on the coloniality of 'secularism' as the necessary foundation for both legible and legitimate International Law. At the same time, his engagement with capitulations shows how International Law extends Western sovereignty beyond its territorial borders by giving special legal status to Western nationals even beyond their state's borders.

Marc Woons looks at multiculturalism in Canada and Azerbaijan in an effort to dissect Euro-centric power dispositives inherent to the concept. While Western states increasingly question multiculturalism, Azerbaijan has been more active in terms of implementing its own version. As opposed to the 'liberal multiculturalism' designed as a redemption narrative that attempts to permit settler-colonial nation-states to deal with their post-colonial heritage, multiculturalism in Azerbaijan has served to create common ground in a complex society, after the country's independence from, first, Tsarist Russia and, later, the Soviet Union. In comparing Azerbaijan with Canada, Woons offers a decolonial re-reading of the political epistemologies underpinning multiculturalism. By considering the concept's realities in a region some see as a borderland between Europe and Asia, Woons shows how the internal logics of such policies determine their outcomes. While liberal multiculturalism always tries to reconcile the decolonization of states with continued Western epistemological hegemony, multiculturalism in Azerbaijan seems to do better in avoiding such hegemony by any one group making it more likely that political and cultural negotiations can occur among equals.

Nora El Qadim's contribution offers a decolonial alternative to the prevalent Western-/Euro-centrism in IR research. Thinking from the border instead of just about the border, El Qadim analyzes the pro-active agency of the Moroccan State in migration policy negotiations with the European Union. In so doing, she not only chooses to work from a perspective stressing non-European agendas, but she also emphasizes the necessity of considering non-European primary material such as Moroccan sources. El Qadim complements this by taking into account decision factors that cannot be understood through modern-colonial epistemologies. El Qadim stresses 'the importance of symbolic and affective dimensions of international relations, which are often minimized in accounts highlighting a rationalist logic of international actors.' She specifically considers the role of 'dignity and (self-) respect as important motivations' in Moroccan negotiations with Europe, and the perception of European visa regulations as a humiliation imposed by European institutions on the people of Morocco.

Matt Gordner looks at how the Islamic State challenges the Euro-centric

Westphalian international order. Starting with a critique of the colonial nature of the international State system, Gordner refutes the notion the regions held by the Islamic State are in fact 'ungoverned.' He shows how indeed the Islamic State offers many key characteristics of a State (such as regular income, military power, unified ideology), except for sharing the Westphalian notion of borders and exclusive sovereignty within the territory specified by these. Indeed, the Islamic State is marked by 'the erasure of the border' and its attempt to create a 'transnational Islamic polity,' thus questioning the fundamental tenets of the Westphalian international order. The Islamic State 'refus[es] to recognize the sovereignty of other states' in terms of proposing a radically different model of the state rather than simply in terms of conquest and taking control of other states. It therewith undermines the reification of the nation-state model as the 'natural' model of human political organization and forcefully questions the centrality of both the state and the status of borders in IR.

Astrid M. Fellner and Susanne Hamscha trace constitutive and hidden histories of death in settler-colonial culture and history or, as they put it, 'a silence and inaction, a failure to articulate a conflict or crisis, to which death is offered as a pragmatic resolution.' Such epistemologies of death and erasure, Fellner and Hamscha argue, have repeatedly been engaged with through the metaphor of the coffin, which indicates a haunting absence, but does not (yet) permit its decoding and the (re-)appearance of the antagonism it suspends. In order to theorize this presence of erased or suppressed absences, the authors offer a form of border thinking that they call a 'cripistemology of the coffin.' This is developed through close-readings of the figure of the coffins in Alvar Núñez Cabeza de Vaca's *La Relación* and Herman Melville's *Moby-Dick*. Like Rosalba Icaza's take on physical vulnerability, Fellner and Hamscha's cripistemology seeks an epistemology of crisis to subvert the coloniality/modernity dispositive and, implicitly, the IR it shapes. In engaging subjugated knowledges through cripistemology, questioning what constitutes legitimate and legible knowledge. Thus, the power inherent in the ability to decide who or what is admitted to the inter-national or not (in their case, Indigenous peoples) is implicitly revealed as the modern-colonial *a priori* bias of IR.

Christian Langer shows how an erasure of non-European forms of knowledge and social organization are adopted by post-colonial local elites to legitimize their own power. Tracing the development of Egyptology from Napoleon's military forays into the region to the present day, Langer argues that the field's almost exclusive engagement with Egypt from the time of the Pharaohs erases the country's Muslim past and present. Instead of truly engaging Egyptian society, culture, and history, Egyptology has from its beginnings mutilated these by reading them into pre-existing European categories of knowledge and power. Langer's contribution to this volume seeks to show how this same narrative, as well as its tools, have been picked up by the various military regimes in recent decades to legitimize and consolidate their own 'paternalist rule' using a process he refers to as 'informal colonialism.'

Paula von Gleich looks at the epistemic erasure of non-white forms of agency in her chapter on border crossing and social death in the figure of the fugitive slave. Slave fugitivity is, according to von Gleich, both an act of stealing the captive body and a mode of epistemic disobedience, or even resistance, to modern-colonial categories such as that of The Human that ensures the persistence of black social life. Crossing the border becomes not simply a movement across territory but an act of resisting socio-epistemic ascriptions and the power relations that they imply. Black fugitivity recognizes neither a naturalized difference between national territories, cultures, and populations, nor the notions of Human and non-Human they found or the border-mechanisms that uphold them. Thus withdrawing from IR's defining concepts and modes of knowing, decolonial acts such as fugitivity radically question both the theory of the contemporary world order and the order itself.

Katherine Merriman's interview with Juliane Hammer ends the volume by giving insights into questions of normativity and authority in Islamic Studies, with a special focus on Gender and Feminism. The chapter demonstrates the multi-layered character of borders, which do not fit neatly into just one academic discipline. Critically engaging the epistemic dominance of Western academia, Hammer traces the tension between the dangers of a 'reductive reading of women writers according to their personal biography' on the one hand, and how the significance of personal relations in border thinking prohibits the notion of dis-engaged research, thus creating a difficult but necessary interweaving of academia and activism, on the other.

This tension between the necessarily personal of *border thinking* and the universalist aspirations of Western academia runs through the volume. Border Studies has expanded the concept of the border beyond that of territory to include questions of subjectivation and subjectivities, though they still define themselves and their fields of research in relation to such territorial borders. International relations, as the contributions show, may be radically rethought and dewesternized by considering the personal in the international and including alternative epistemologies and the experiential dimensions of borders. In so doing, however, these borders are not denied or forgotten, but continue to serve as the determining factors in the world and politics *border thinking* engages. *Border thinking* does not replace one model of global politics or borders with another, but multiplies border dimensions and international relations. To combine social sciences with the humanities in researching borders, then, is not to offer an alternative model but to expand the existing concepts and methodologies of engaging Global Politics within and beyond IR. Such a multiplication of border dimensions requires a multiplication of conceptual and methodological dimensions in researching and understanding borders, which is what this volume hopes to offer. *Border thinking*, as a critical epistemology of global politics, offers an enriched vision of borders. Analytically and politically, it is a vision that does not simply seek to understand – but also to reshape and expand the meanings and consequences of *International Relations*.

References

Forensic Architecture. (2016, Aug. 23). The Left-to-Die Boat. *Forensic-Architecture.org.* Available at: http://www.aljazeera.com/indepth/features/2015/12/identifying-refugee-victims-mediterranean-151221102203683.html

Missing Migrants Project. (2016, Nov. 25). Available at: http://missingmigrants.iom.int

Petrakis, M. (2016, Apr. 5.) Athens DNA lab helps trace those Lost at Sea on Aegean Crossing. *UNHCR.org.* Available at: http://www.unhcr.org/news/latest/2016/4/5703bd576/athens-dna-lab-helps-trace-lost-sea-aegean-crossing.html

Povoledo, Elisabeth. (2015, Oct. 2.) Italian Lab Battles 'Not to Lose the Dead' from Migrant Ship. *NYTimes.com.* Available at: http://www.nytimes.com/2015/10/03/world/europe/italian-lab-battles-not-to-lose-the-dead-from-migrant-ships.html?_r=0

Scammell, R. (2015, Dec. 23). Identifying the Refugee Victims of the Mediterranean. *AlJazeera.com.* Available at: http://www.aljazeera.com/indepth/features/2015/12/identifying-refugee-victims-mediterranean-151221102203683.html

Spiegel Online. (2013, Oct. 9.) Fortress Europe. How the EU turns its Back on Refugees. Available at: http://www.spiegel.de/international/europe/asylum-policy-and-treatment-of-refugees-in-the-european-union-a-926939.html

UNHCR. (2016, Nov. 25). Refugees/Migrants Emergency Response. Available at: http://data.unhcr.org/mediterranean/regional.php

United Against Racism (2012, Nov.1.) *List of Deaths.* Available at: http://www.
unitedagainstracism.org/pdfs/listofdeaths.pdf

1

Interview with Walter D. Mignolo

Where do you see the most exciting research happening in your field?

To start with, I am not sure how I would define my 'field.' Perhaps my field involves borders all over. Not as a 'field of study' but as places of dwelling. I do not dwell in every border but I know that there are billions of people on the planet that do. Billions of them are still repressed by territorial epistemologies, religious and secular, and by the virus of the nation-state that invaded the planet over the past two hundred years. If I had to identify myself, I would say that I am a decolonial thinker today. So, in the past 20 years, my 'field' has been the analytic of modernity/coloniality and exploring decolonial venues of thinking, doing, and living. That is not a 'field' in the traditional academic sense, though it certainly is a 'field' at large, where people inside and outside academia are searching for something the State, the corporations, the banks and, in some case, religious institutions cannot offer. Once people understand the universal fictions of modernity and the logic of coloniality enacted in order to advance the promises of modernity, the question of how to delink from that bubble becomes the main driving factor of decoloniality.

This delinking is not something that is done by the State, the banks, the corporation, or religious institutions, although it could be in some cases. Religion could be a liberating or a regulatory belief system. It has to be done by people taking their/our destinies into their/our own hands. This is by far the most exciting of activities rather than research in 'my field.' Research and knowledge are needed — decoloniality concerns those too — but not in the academic sense. Decoloniality is beyond academic research; it does not require grants from the Mellon or Volkswagen Foundations.

How has the way you understand the world changed over time and what (or who) prompted the most significant shifts in your thinking?

I would say that there have been four stages. During stage one, from the University of Cordoba to Paris, semiotics, discourses analysis and literary theory guided my intellectual pursuits. The second stage began in the United States, when I 'discovered' what being Hispano or Chicano meant. That sent me back to the sixteenth century and the conquest and colonization of the Americas. My book entitled *The Darker Side of the Renaissance: Literacy, Territoriality and Colonization* (1995) came out of that research. It was a historical research project, theoretically articulated in search of myself, of understanding how I came to be who I was not as an individual but in the frame of the Argentinian, French, and American societies that I inhabited. For this, border thinking was the necessary tool. Indeed, *The Darker Side of the Renaissance* was influenced very much by Gloria Anzaldúa's *Borderland/La Frontera: The New Mestiza* (1987).

The third stage was initiated by the encounter with the concept of *coloniality* and the awareness that coloniality is constitutive of — i.e., not derivative of — modernity. That was one of my central theses in *Local Histories/Global Designs* (2000) that was extended to *The Idea of Latin America* (2005) in a more specific geo-historical mode of research. And the fourth stage emerged after the publication of these two books, as I devoted more time to thinking about the current profile of modernity/coloniality. This was the moment when my academic research and my activities in the public sphere became one. This is the moment when disciplinary boundaries became meaningless to me, in which you see the 'disciplines' as what the word itself says they are: something that disciplines you. Perhaps my article entitled 'Epistemic disobedience, Independent Thought and Decolonial Freedom' (2009a) offers the most concise formulation of this fourth stage. It involves many activities including directing a non-academic publication in Argentina devoted to promoting decolonial thinking, working with journalists also in Argentina, working with artists and curators in Colombia, the United States, and Europe (mainly in Berlin and Copenhagen), co-directing and teaching Summer Schools like the one in Middelburg (the Netherlands) and the Bremen-UNC-Duke Summer Institute, doing many interviews in Spanish and English, writing op-ed essays for online publications and newspapers, and running workshops in South America, Africa, Asia, and Europe. All of that is what motivates me rather than simply just being attentive to what researchers are doing in my field. Perhaps then, to come back to the first question, my fields are the social sciences and the humanities related to modernity/coloniality.

You often refer to the idea of 'border thinking' in your work. How would you define border thinking?

Indeed, the subtitle of *Local Histories/Global Design* is 'coloniality, subaltern knowledges and border thinking.' And as a matter of fact, this book is devoted to border thinking. What is this and why it is so prevalent in my argument? First of all, border thinking implies dwelling in the border, not crossing borders. That is, border thinking is not an impersonal algorithm, but a conceptualization of the experience of living in the border. One of the chapters of Frantz Fanon's *Black Skin, White Mask* was translated into English as 'The fact of blackness,' but the original French title was 'L'expérience vécu des noirs' — the 'lived experience of black people.' Fanon theorized about this from his lived experience of being black (see Fanon 1952; 1967). I theorize border thinking from my experience of dwelling in the borders: as the son of immigrants in Argentina, as métèque in France, and as hispano/latino in the United States. It was Gloria Anzaldúa's *Borderland/La Frontera* that made me realize that I was dwelling in the border without being aware of it. *Borderland/La Frontera* is border thinking in action. Anzaldúa is not 'studying' borderlands. She inhabits them.

Dwelling in the border brings a particular type of consciousness. Anzaldúa herself certainly makes this clear, but so does W. E. B. Du Bois with his idea of double consciousness, which also expresses the experience of inhabiting the border (Du Bois 1903). So does Frantz Fanon using the important concept of *sociogenesis* and its function for the consciousness of being seen as *a Negro.* The border here is between Fanon's self-consciousness and the moment he realized that although he *knew of course that his skin was black, he did not know he was a Negro.* He realizes that he is a Negro when he realizes that he is seen as a Negro. You will hardly find a trace of border-consciousness in Edmund Husserl's theory of consciousness, which is totally incompatible with how Anzaldúa conceives of a 'conciencia de la mestiza' as 'a new consciousness.' 'La conciencia de la mestiza' and 'double consciousness' emerge from the enactment of border thinking and not as a territorial description of something that is 'outside' the very act of conceiving it.

Not everyone inhabits the border, and it is not necessary to do so. Not everyone inhabits the territory; those who inhabit the borders do not. But borders (they called them 'frontiers' in the advance of civilization) were traced by actors inhabiting the territory and guarding it from 'foreign' forces. The problem is that modern Western epistemology is territorial, and territorial epistemology presupposes 'the frontier' rather than the border. On the other side of the frontier exists the void, namely space to be conquered or civilized.

Territorial epistemology (modern and postmodern) cannot be decolonial; it is an imperial epistemology. Modern epistemology was built precisely to make sense of, justify, and legitimize coloniality. Post-modern epistemology is an in-family critique of modern epistemology but remains within the rules of the game. Decolonial thinking is always-already border thinking; although not all border thinking is always already decolonial thinking.[1] Furthermore, decolonial border thinking implies epistemic disobedience and delinking from modern and post-modern epistemology, including Marxist post-modern versions.

In decolonial theories, the contemporary nation-state model of international relations is usually considered a product of European modernity that became globalized through colonialism and imperialism. Could you explain why that is the case and what decolonial alternatives to this model might look like?

We could certainly talk about 'decolonial theories,' but to avoid putting decoloniality in the box of 'modern theories' (and thus make border thinking one more modern 'us' when border thinking is in fact a delinking from a territorial 'us'), I prefer talking about border thinking and doing — for thinking is doing and doing is thinking. This formulation also allows me to delink from the pernicious distinction between theory and practice (another modern pre-judgment or prejudice).

Decolonially speaking (that is, thinking and doing), the nation-state was a powerful tool of Western expansion. The modern nation-state was, as we know, the form of governance created by the bourgeois ethno-class that took over the Church and the monarchies in Europe, after the Glorious Revolution in England and the French Revolution. It was powerful in two different ways. On the one hand, it emerged out of the ruins of such crumbling State formations as the Austro-Hungarian Empire and the Ottoman Sultanate after World War One. On the other hand, the nation-state was also the form of governance that emerged in Asia and Africa after decolonization. That is, geopolitical decolonization sent the colonizer home, but it also adapted and adopted their structure of governance: the nation-state. That is how the nation-state became globalized and encouraged not only the legal formation called the State but also the civil formation called the nation. Thus, if the State became the legal form of governance, the nation became the sensing, the feeling that connects people of the 'same nation,' the nationals, the citizens.

---

[1]   I have explored these issues extensively in the already mentioned book *Local Histories/Global Designs: Coloniality, Subaltern Knowledge and Border thinking*. For a more recent, shorter version, see Mignolo (2011).

Today, the State form is crumbling and becoming unsustainable. The first step in thinking a decolonial alternative would have to be imagining *alternatives to the State form,* and thinking about the many and rich possibilities of *governance.* What I mean is that we must not confuse the State form with the variegated forms of governance that are open to people. What is unsustainable — and indeed an aberration — is the pyramidal form of the State that, on the one hand, in a capitalist economy, leads to corruption and to dynasties, and, on the other, leads to manipulation of the voting population through money being poured into the media and advertising.

One decolonial alternative to the State form of governance has been advanced by the Zapatistas. The creation of the Caracoles after the agreements of San Andrés (2003) — agreements that were not respected by the Mexican State — is one way into the future: a form of governance, based on indigenous past experiences and legacies, that consists in governing and obeying at the same time. In this form of governance there is no place for corruption, for dynastic formation, or for manipulation of the voters by the media and advertising.

Now, it is crucial here not to understand this according to modern/Western epistemology and political theory. If you attempt to understand what the Zapatistas are trying to do from the perspective of Western cosmology, you would not understand. It is necessary to approach what the Zapatistas are trying to do by bracketing Western and secular cosmology. It is crucial not to think that Zapatismo as it exists today constitutes a universal model. That expectation is very modern and provincial. Zapatismo is teaching two things: a) that people need to delink from the State form (secular and bourgeois, like in Germany, Mexico, France, or the United States) by organizing themselves; and, b) that a form of autonomy and self-governance by the people and delinking from the State form is possible. We may not see people organizing themselves and taking their destiny into their own hands any time soon, but the process has begun, and it is irreversible.

Now, what we have to keep in mind is that the world order is already multipolar and increasingly so. Multipolarity refers to inter-State relations, not to the people of one or another nation. The question to be asked here is how do inter-State relations impinge on domestic lives. Take for example out-sourcing corporations, or immigration and refugees in Europe right now. These displacements are in a way 'forced' by inter-State relations and the differential of power between states.

You mentioned 'delinking' as one possible decolonial intervention against the current system of international relations. Could you

elaborate on this concept? How is it useful for (border)thinking?

Delinking from the system of inter-State relations is one sphere of delinking. The other sphere is people/us delinking from the colonial matrix of power that includes our relations with the State. I have touched upon the idea of delinking from the State in talking about the Zapatistas. Delinking in the sphere of inter-State relations requires what I describe as dewesternization. Iran, China, Russia, and other BRICS-member States are currently the most imminent forces of dewesternization.

Delinking from the colonial matrix of power is what I call decoloniality, but this is not a task that States could enact. States are a fundamental dimension of the colonial matrix of power. Consequently, decolonizing the State (or democratizing the State as others would say) is non-sense because, as I said, the State is one domain — the domain of institutional politics — interconnected with the other domains (epistemic, economic, racial, sexual, aesthetics, religious, ethical, and subjective) of the colonial matrix. Decolonial delinking starts from knowledge and being, that is, delinking from the ways of knowing and the ways of being that trap us into the promises of modernity and the tentacles of coloniality.

Suppose that you are Zapatista or a decolonial Muslim or decolonial South African or a Maori or belong to one of the First Nations in Canada. You have recourse to other languages, memories, histories, sensibilities, and so on, that modernity told you to despise. So you are in between the experiences that shaped you when you came into this world and that came to you through non-European languages, non-European memories, non-European religions and, on the other hand, the presence in your local of European memories, European languages, European religions. You are in between those; you dwell in the border. You cannot become European even if you wished to do so. You can pretend and you can be successful in passing as European. Or you can decide to affirm yourself in the memories, languages, and ways of being that European modernity told you to abandon should you want to become modern. If your choice is the second option, you are dwelling in the border and engaged in border thinking, doing, and being. You are in the process of delinking from Western modernity and European cosmology.

Post- and decolonial writing has shifted the focus of the analysis of power from geopolitical territories to populations and infrastructure, in the process rethinking 'borders' between separate entities into 'borderlands' of hybrid interbeing. How would a decolonial reading of territories and populations explain contemporary border-crises such as those on the European continent as seen, for instance, in Ukraine?

Decolonial interpretations of current events or processes are based on the analytic of the colonial matrix of power (or the analytic of coloniality of power for short). International law emerged in the sixteenth century to regulate appropriation and expropriation of land and territorial control. Carl Schmitt's work is very helpful on this. But his story of 'global linear thinking' from the sixteenth to the mid-twentieth century, when he finished writing *The Nomos of the Earth in the International Law of the Jus Publicum Europaeum,* is only half of the story (see Schmitt 2003[1950]). The reason for this is that, as he clearly states, international law was a Euro-centred legal technology; according to Schmitt, it was created with Europe's interests in mind. So his story does not provide — and he certainly did not have to provide — any information about those non-European people and territories who were subjugated to the power of the movement of 'linear thinking' and who responded to it. And of course there were such responses! But up until recently, global linear thinking and international law was created, changed, managed, and controlled by Western European imperial states and, lately, the United States. To illustrate what I am saying, I could refer to several studies in the twentieth and beginning of twenty-first centuries on decolonizing international law. Decolonizing international law means to show that it is neither neutral nor democratic, but that it is a legalization of imperial delinquency. One example of someone who tells the missing half of the story is Siba N. Grovogui (2006) in 'Regimes of Sovereignty'.

What does that imply for a decolonial reading of the border conflict in Ukraine? Following the analytic of coloniality, interstate law was created and managed by actors and institutions promoting, defending, and advancing imperial interests. Ukraine was and remains a very strategic location for the United States, with European Union support, in terms of advancing territorial control beyond the line traced by Samuel Huntington in his article on 'The Clash of Civilizations' before he published the book by that name (see Huntington 1993; 1996).[2] So, the United States supported the Ukrainian extreme right to debunk an elected President allied with Russia — President Viktor Yanukovych. Vladimir Putin knew, as did the leaders of the United States and the European Union, that there was more to the Ukrainian uprising than a call for democracy, and whatever may have been an honest concern of the Ukrainian people was taken up in the long lasting struggle for control of the 'line.' Advancing the line was justified in the nineteenth century in the name of civilization. Now it is justified in the name of democracy, so you depose an elected President that is allied with a strong State (Russia) that you would like to 'contain' (in order to advance NATO to the new line that is Ukraine). You resort to the rhetoric of modernity to advance, and hide, coloniality. If myself and others like me, who do not have access to inside

---

[2]   For the map, see Huntington (1993: 30).

information, understood this dimension of inter-State containment in the 'popular' uprisings, how would it be possible for Vladimir Putin not have seen that they were part of a re-westernization process?

Some political and social theorists argue that the Market is replacing the State as the plane from which bio-political governance emerges. This has long been a tenet of decolonial thinking concerning the role of the slave trade and its aftermath in the formation of capitalism and racism, which you have engaged with in your work on dispensable and bare lives (Mignolo 2009b). How do you see this relation between the State, the Market, and the (trans)formation of race developing in the near future?

I can tell you how we (the modernity/coloniality collective) could respond to your question based on the history of formation, transformation, and management of the colonial matrix of power since the sixteenth century.

First, let's start with two basic assumptions in the formation of the colonial matrix of power: (a) there is no world system before the invention (some said discovery) of America understood as the integration of America to the political, economic, and cultural European imaginary starting at the end of the fifteenth century. This is obvious, nobody knew (except God) that there were two masses of land disconnected until that moment. And, (b) the Americas were not integrated to an already existing capitalist economy. There could not have been a capitalist economy without the Americas. Assumptions (a) and (b) imply that there is no capitalist economy without a world system. And the world system goes hand in hand with the triumphal narratives of modernity.

Second, there is no economic theory until the mid-eighteenth century with the physiocrats in France and Adam Smith in Scotland. There is no antecedent in the political theory of Greece or Rome. Why? Because political economy needed an interconnected world led by Atlantic European monarchies first and secular nation-states later, even if economic practices and relations always existed. As we all know, markets were all over the planet since at least the axial age,[3] but 'capitalist' markets were not.

Third, from the formation of the world-system economy of accumulation until World War Two, the economy had always been one dimension of society or, if you wish, of the colonial matrix of power. For the British and the French, for instance, the civilizing mission and the more abstract idea of progress

---

[3]   Coined by Karl Jaspers (1953), the term 'axial age' refers to the period from the eighth century to the third century B.C.

(understood not only in economic terms) were crucial domestically and in inter-State relations. Civilizing abroad was related to domestic progress, and the idea of domestic progress justified the civilizing mission abroad. But after World War Two, the United States took the lead of the global order and Harry Truman translated 'progress' into development. During the second half of the twentieth century the relations within the domain of the colonial matrix of power changed. Up to World War Two, the economy was integrated into society. Since 1950 society began to be increasingly integrated into the economy.

Where is racism in this picture? Well, I go to Aníbal Quijano in linking the emergence of racism with the emergence of capitalism. Racism consists in the racialization of ethnicities (see, e.g., Quijano 2007). *Ethnos* is a Greek word translated to Latin as *natio.* But there was also the terms *religio* and *relegere* in Latin that refer also to community building; the former by re-linking (re-ligare) and the second by memories (re-legere). That is, ethnos and natio refer to what a community of people share in living together and recognizing themselves/ourselves in their/our memories, languages, symbols, shared knowing, and emotions, while race refers to an asymmetrical power relation between ethnicities or nations.

The inter-State relations of the sixteenth century that served as the historical foundations of today's international state system and international law also established a hierarchy of ethnicities. Thus, existing ethnicities (religious and/ or national communities of faith or/and birth) around the planet became racialized by one ethnicity (Christian/European) that moved from being one among many to being the one who controls knowledge and classification. For racism is nothing else than epistemic and it depends on the institutions and languages that control knowledge.

The bottom line concerning the relation between the State, the market, and race is thus as follows: (a) a world-system or, in other words, an interconnected world order emerged in combination with Western Catholic Christianity and shaped the world until the eighteenth century, after which Western Protestant Christians took the lead and secularized theological knowledge to the degree of eliminating Christian theology from international relations; (b) during this emergence and transformation of the westernized world-system, knowledge became controlled by Western European languages and map making. Map making was crucial to this emergence because it produced the idea of a unified world order of land and water masses; and, (c) this world-system included the creation of a global ranking of ethnicities and continents: Asia, Africa, and the America were constructed as inferior to Europe by European global powers, and so on. That is racism. How can one overcome it? It is crucial to decolonize knowledge and liberate sensibilities.

How does decolonial theory respond to the proliferation of digital or cyber territories, borderlands, and conflicts?

Digital or cyber territories are one thing; borderlands and conflicts are another. They are related, but not the same. Let's start with borderland and conflicts.

Borderlands are a consequence of the linear global thinking mentioned above, and global linear thinking refers to the enactment of international law that emerged in the sixteenth century and not before; de Vitoria in Salamanca, Grotius in Holland, and Locke in England set the rules of the game. The Berlin Conference of 1884, which saw Africa parcelled out and distributed among European States, was yet another chapter. One side of the border marked the march of Western Civilization, while the other side of the border marked people to be civilized and land to be appropriated and expropriated. This lasted until people on 'the other side of the border' began to raise their voices and resist. One recent example is Russia stopping the march of Western civilization and 'taking' Ukraine; another example is China stopping the United States and its allies from infringing on their jurisdiction. But borders are also financial: the China Development Bank stopping the International Monetary Fund and the World Bank in their attempt to 'develop' the world. And, of course, borders can also be subjective as is the case when it comes to racism and sexism. Borders, then, can be found at all levels: personal, economic, aesthetic, political, etc. And because people at all those levels began to say 'Basta' to the Western juggernauts, we now must face the global disorder that we find ourselves in. The juggernauts work with the idea of *frontiers*. Frontiers mark the limits of civilization. Beyond that there is barbarism, of all kinds. The *frontiers* could be within a territory; sexual frontiers for example are intra-territorial. However, when the *barbarians* on the other side of the frontier began to talk, and talk the language of civilizations, but from the experience and knowledge and memories that civilization despises, that is the moment in which *borderlands and border thinking emerges. Border thinking is thinking of and by the barbarian. This is precisely what I am doing in this interview and all my work: barbarian theorizing that arises from dwelling in the borderland.*

Cyber-territoriality is just an extension of global border thinking. First came the sovereignty of land and seas, where machines and men could move and conquer. Then it was the turn of airspace, when machines began to fly. And now, it is the cybernetic control of space. Remember that the foundational book of all of this was Norbert Wiener's *Cybernetics or Control and*

Communication in Animals and Machines (1948). 'Control' is the key word here that connects with your question. We (the modernity/coloniality collective) operate from the basic assumptions that the colonial matrix of power is a structure of management and control operated by human beings through specific institutions. Cyber-territorialities are not (yet) made by cyborgs, but by humans who both manage and are controlled by the colonial matrix of power. So cyber-global-linear-thinking is just an extension of global linear thinking and what Carl Schmitt (1950) called the *Jus Publicum Europaeum* that has now been taken up by the United States.

So, what are decolonial takes on such cyber-territorialities? Politically, they are not different from all previous versions of global linear thinking — that is a game from which it is necessary to delink through decoloniality. Cyber-territoriality is a new dimension of inter-State struggle. Civil society does not engage in cyber-territoriality. Under international law, which is a fundamental component of the colonial matrix of power, cyber-war is one more aspect of inter-State wars which are no longer just military but hybrid as 'experts' say — financial, mediatic, military, diplomatic, political, and cyber. The world order, including cyber space, is still regulated by the colonial matrix of power, even now that there are no longer *frontiers* that Western States could expand but *borderlands (spaces)* where there are people who do not want to be ruled and rolled over. *Cyber-war is a war between rewesternization and dewesternization.* Decoloniality does not have much to say about it other than to analyse it and delink from it.

Will international relations (IR) remain a colonialist discipline as long as it seeks to analyse the inter-*national* instead of proposing the abolition of all borders and the creation of a new world order?

Well, IR was invented just for that: to make possible and legitimize arrangements among sovereign states and to appropriate and expropriate territories, as can clearly be seen with the Berlin Conference of 1884. IR will remain a colonialist discipline as long as there is the inter-State system that was created in the sixteenth and seventeenth centuries. So, I see two ways of responding to your question.

(a) The emergence of decolonial approaches to IR, something that goes under the rubric of 'decolonizing IR.' Work on this has proliferated lately. I already mentioned the pioneering work of Siba N Grovogui. There is also the most recent work of Nigerian Christian N. Okeke (2015), Australian scholar Anthony Anghie (2005), and Afro-Brit Robbie Shilliam (2015) among others. All these works look at IR from the perspective of colonial histories and legacies. Minimally, considering this decolonial IR work means that it does not get caught up in the European half of the story (mentioned with Schmitt above), it starts from the impact of international law on the colonies. That was after all the job of European IR as Schmitt clearly saw it. These are all arguments engaging border thinking for the simple reason that the starting point focuses on the experiential legacies of colonialism rather than the Western half of the story of imperialism.

(b) The radical decolonial view summons the moment in which IR will no longer be necessary because coloniality would be over. As long as coloniality is not over, but all over, IR will remain a colonialist discipline entrenched in coloniality and contested by both decolonial and dewesternizing thinkers, even if with different aims. Decolonial thinkers argue for the end of the nation-state as the form of governance entrenched with capitalism, while dewesternizing thinkers in places like China, Russia, and Iran — where none of these countries question yet the State-form although they may pursue different styles of governance depending on the local histories of each country — argue for bending IR so they can no longer 'be instructed on what to do' and grow their ability to instead expose their own interests.

What is the most important advice you could give to young scholars of borders, borderlands and border thinking?

That is a tough question, the hardest one in this conversation. I would start by inviting young scholars to distinguish borderlands as a place where things happen (the State tracing border, immigrant crossing borders, disputing borders) and the *study of borderlands* from any of the existing disciplines — economy, political sciences, international relations, literature, art, inter-disciplinarily, or even trans-disciplinarily — from *dwelling in the borderland.* Studying the borderland means that whomever does the study places themselves outside the borderland while whomever dwells in the borderland *reflects* on themselves and their experiences of living in the border. I mentioned the examples of Anzaldúa and Fanon. We could add W. E. B. Du Bois, Steve Biko, Sylvia Wynter, and others to the list. All these thinkers are un-disciplinary: they do not study, they think and their thinking is border thinking because they think from their body and not from the 'mind,' as modern and secular (Cartesian if you wish) disciplines do. Disciplines separate the known from the knower. Horkheimer (1972) corrected this and argued rightly that in critical theory the knower invents, constructs the known. The difference between Horkheimer and the thinkers mentioned previously is that Horkheimer did not experience colonial forms of racism. Granted, as a Jew he experienced European internal colonial racism. But that is different from the experience of a lesbian Chicana, a black Caribbean woman, a Caribbean man in France or an Afro-American born in the American borderland.

Concerning borders, I already talked about distinguishing them from frontiers. Let me add here that borderlands as well as border thinking, living, and the use they foster are not academic but lived experiences. I 'learned' through this that prior to being an academic, I am a person located in the colonial matrix of power, and the colonial matrix of power cannot be observed externally because there is no outside. We are all within the colonial matrix. The challenge is to think and learn from where we are located.

Not all of us on the planet dwell in the border. For the border to exist there has to be a line and two sides with respect to the line. On one side dwell the *humanitas* and on the other side the *anthropos*. This line dividing the borderland between the humanitas and the anthropos was invented and traced by the humanitas in the process of constituting itself in their own territory. As a third world person, I belong to the anthropos and I began to assume it with pride. That was my decolonial moment. Before that I wanted to be on the side of the humanitas and for that reason I went to study in France.

So, my advice is to be aware that there are people on both sides of the border and be aware of what side you dwell in. You have not chosen it; you came to the world when the world was already delineated by international relations, global linear thinking, racism, sexism, and so on. If pedagogically you want to understand critical theory à la Horkheimer and border thinking (or border theory if you would like a modern rather than a decolonial vocabulary), you could think of their points of origination and all their consequences; critical theory originated in Europe at the crossroads of Jewish European history and Marxism, while border thinking and decoloniality originated on the 'other side of the border,' in the Third and Second World. You have to be aware of the geo- and body-political dimensions of knowledge and understand them as the energy fuelling both border thinking and decoloniality.

This interview was conducted by Sebastian Weier

References

Anghie, A. (2005) *Imperialism, Sovereignty, and the Making of International Law*. Cambridge: Cambridge University Press.

Anzaldúa, G. (1987) *Borderlands/La Frontera: The New Mestiza*. San Francisco: Aunt Lute.

Du Bois, W. E. B. (1903) *The Souls of Black Folk.* New York: Bantam Classic.

Fanon, F. (1952) *Peau Noire, Masques Blancs*. Paris: Les Éditions du Seuil.

Fanon, F. (1967) *Black Skin, White Masks*. New York: Grove Press.

Grovogui, S. N. (2006) *Beyond Eurocentrism and Anarchy: Memories of International Order and Institutions*. New York: Palgrave Macmillan.

Horkheimer, M. (1972) *Traditional and Critical Theory.* New York : Herder & Herder.

Huntington, S. P. (1993) 'The Clash of Civilizations?' *Foreign Affairs* 72(3): 22–49.

Huntington, S. P. (1996) *The Clash of Civilizations and the Remaking of World Order*. New York: Simon and Schuster.

Jaspers, K. (1953) *The Origin and Goal of History*. Translated by M. Bullock. New Haven: Yale University Press.

Mignolo, W. D. (1995) *Darker Side of the Renaissance: Literacy, Territoriality, and Colonization*. Ann Arbor: University of Michigan Press.

Mignolo, W. D. (2000) *Local Histories/Global Designs: Coloniality, Subaltern Knowledges, and Border Thinking*. Princeton: Princeton University Press.

Mignolo, W. D. (2005) *The Idea of Latin America*. Hoboken: Wiley-Blackwell.

Mignolo, W. D. (2009a) 'Epistemic Disobedience, Independent Thought and Decolonial Freedom.' *Theory, Culture & Society* 26(7): 159–181.

Mignolo, W. D. (2009b) 'Dispensable and Bare Lives. Coloniality and the Hidden Political/Economic Agenda of Modernity.' *Human Architecture: Journal of the Sociology of Self-Knowledge* 7(2): 69–88.

Mignolo, W. D. (2011) 'Geopolitics of Sensing and Knowing: On (De) Coloniality, Border Thinking, and Epistemic Disobedience.' *Postcolonial Studies* 14(3): 273–283.

Okeke C. N. (2015) 'The Use of International Law in the Domestic Courts of Ghana and Nigeria.' *Arizona Journal of International and Comparative Law* 32: 371–430.

Quijano, A. (2007) 'Coloniality and modernity/rationality.' *Cultural Studies* 21(2–3):168–78.

Schmitt, C. (2003[1950]) *The Nomos of the Earth in the International Law of the Jus Publicum Europaeum*. Translated by G. L. Ulmen. New York: Telos Press.

Shilliam, R. (2015) *The Black Pacific: Anticolonial Struggles and Ocean Connections*. London: Bloomsbury Academic Press.

Wiener, N. (1948) *Cybernetics or Control and Communication in the Animal and the Machine*. Cambridge: MIT Press.

2

Decolonial Feminism and Global Politics: Border Thinking and Vulnerability as a Knowing Otherwise

ROSALBA ICAZA

For more than two decades, the vast production of post-structuralist/post-positivist feminist critique and postcolonial feminist thinking within the field of International Relations (IR) and, more recently, Global Politics (GP) has prompted critical investigations on their modern and colonial foundations (for examples, see, Sylvester 1993; Pappart and Marchand 1995; Gruffyd Jones 2006; Shilliam 2010). In doing so, different epistemological positions have been deployed in attempts to destabilize narratives that (re)produce dominant ideas about 'the international' and 'global politics.' Today, these contributions constitute a fruitful background to the current wave of academic interest focused on critically understanding the epistemic foundations of IR and GP as disciplines responsible for thinking about how power operates in international and global spheres.[1]

---

[1]   International Relations is understood in this text as a discipline mainly concerned with the understanding of nation-states (i.e., unified rational actor, sovereign entities, etc.), the operations of power between nation-states, the nature of this power (i.e., as domination, relational, etc.), and the system or environment in which they operate (e.g., anarchical, cooperative, complex interdependent, etc.). Meanwhile, Global Politics is taken here as a field of analysis in its own right that contests the narrowness of state-centric approaches (i.e., their methodological nationalism) for thinking power operations in political economic structures, institutions, actors, and discourses under complex conditions of supraterritoriality or globalization. I am using the term *otherwise* following Arturo Escobar's seminal article 'Worlds and Knowledges Otherwise' in which he speaks of the modernity/coloniality program as crossing the borders of thought, as 'a

Decolonial thinking has recently played a key role in this critical endeavour (Icaza 2010; 2015; Taylor 2012; Icaza and Vazquez 2013). Belonging to a different geo-genealogy[2] than that of post-colonial studies, decolonial thinking takes as its point of departure the acknowledgement that there is 'no modernity without coloniality' (Quijano 2000; Mignolo 2003; 2013; Walsh 2007; 2010; 2011; 2012; Lugonés 2010a; 2010b; Vazquez 2009; 2011; 2014). For the purposes of this text, the relevance of this affirmation is that coloniality as the underside of modernity constitutes an epistemic location from which reality is thought. This locus of enunciation, following Mignolo, means that hegemonic histories of modernity as a product of the Renaissance or the Industrial Revolution are not accepted but challenged in order to undo the Eurocentric power projection inherent to them. Precisely, in seeking to avoid becoming just another hegemonic project, decolonial thinking is also understood as an *option* — in contrast to a paradigm or grand theory — among a plurality of options.[3]

Furthermore, from the perspective of this option, 'Western modernity' constitutes a dominant civilizational project that claimed universality for itself at the moment of its violent encounter with 'the Other' and the subsequent concealment of this violence. This seminal encounter traces its origins back to 1492 when *Abya Yala* (the Americas) was conquered through the genocide of Indigenous peoples, their knowledges, and ways of being in the world (Quijano 2000; Mignolo 2003).

Early writings on modernity/coloniality understood it as a co-constitutive binomial and a structure of management that operates by controlling the economy, authority (government and politics), knowledge and subjectivities, gender, and sexuality (Quijano 2000; Mignolo 2013). From this perspective the 'coloniality of power' highlights 'the basic and universal social classification of the population of the planet in terms of the idea of "race" is introduced for the first time' with the Conquest of the Americas (Lugonés 2010a: 371). This analysis 'has displayed the heterogeneous and transversal character of the modern/colonial system' (Vazquez 2014: 176) counterpoising racial domination to Eurocentric Marxist theories of class exploitation.

---

decisive intervention into the very discursivity of the modern sciences in order to craft another space for the production of knowledge, another way of thinking, *un paradigma otro*, the very possibility of talking about "worlds and knowledges otherwise"' (Escobar 2007: 179).

[2]   Vázquez explains the relevance of geo-genealogies for decolonial critique in order to stress the site of enunciation. In his view, a geo-genealogy is a genealogy that acknowledges its relationship to a geographically situated origin (Vázquez 2014).

[3]   Argentinean Cultural Historian Zulma Palermo (2008) connects the relevance of understanding decolonial thinking as an 'option' to a border epistemology.

More recently, it has been argued that modernity/coloniality is the binomial around which decolonial thinking gravitates, which has as a departure point the acknowledgment of the limits and exteriority of modernity (Vazquez 2014). This is in contrast with thinking centred in the Western philosophical tradition, in which modernity in its different facets (i.e., unfinished modernity, plural and hybrid modernities, postmodernities, globalization, capitalisms, and so on) is assumed to be the totality of reality. 'For decolonial thinking modernity (with its modernities) cannot claim to cover all the historical reality. There is an outside, something beyond modernity, because there are ways of relating to the world, ways of feeling, acting and thinking, ways of living and inhabiting the world that come from other geo-genealogies, non-Western and non-modern' (Vazquez 2014: 173, my translation). From this perspective, awareness of modernity's underside (coloniality) provides a decolonial understanding of one's own perspective which allows for thinking and sensing situated in the exteriority of 'modernity' (ibid.; Dussel 2001). Furthermore, the binomial of modernity/coloniality as an epistemic position seems to question categorical separation in two main ways: specific categories (e.g., men-women, civilized-primitive) and also separation as a heuristic operation to represent, and hence appropriate, reality. For some thinkers, this later operation constitutes a key characteristic of Euro-centrism (Lugonés 1990; Vazquez 2014). But what seems more relevant for my purposes is that modernity/coloniality expresses a *duality*, which is not to be conflated with a binary[4] or a dialectic.[5] In short, modernity cannot be thought, sensed, and experienced without its underside: coloniality. From this perspective, the analysis of global development (either sustainable or 'green') cannot be done without unpacking its ethno-centrism. In the same way, the analysis of international human rights cannot be done without the analysis of the epistemic violence of monoculturalist and imperialist understandings of justice (Icaza 2010; Walsh 2011). Therefore, to think 'global politics' or 'international relations' from this perspective carries an inseparable duality.

This duality has recently been explained as two different historical movements or forms of relationship with reality to highlight their different loci of enunciation. For example, the historical movement of modernity from which hegemony and privilege has named reality, for example, refers to *Abya Yala*

---

[4]   One of the key contributions of feminist anti-essentialist approaches reveals the complex and multiple operations of power in binary thinking. But, what happens when duality is thought from a different geo-genealogy to that of feminist anti-essentialist approaches? The thought of Gloria Anzaldúa and Maria Lugonés is crucial for an understanding of duality *otherwise*. In the same way, the work of Mexican ethno-historian and feminist Sylvia Marcos (2006) on Mesoamerican civilizations' eroticism and spirituality reveals an exteriority to Western feminist anti-essentialism.

[5]   When thinking duality not just as a dialectic, I have in mind a proposal by Enrique Dussel (2001) for transmodernity.

using the foreign name of Latin America. It also gives its peoples the name of 'Indians,' more recently also labelling them as 'indigenous' or 'minorities.' Meanwhile, the historical movement of coloniality is a moment in which the negation of realities and worlds that otherwise exceed the dominant modern geo-genealogy of modernity takes place when, for instance, normative systems outside or in the margins of the nation-state are denied validity (Vazquez 2014; Icaza 2015).

To understand this duality in relation to time is central for the identification of a third movement: the decolonial option. In this third movement, trajectories in knowledges and cosmovisions that have been actively produced[6] as backward or 'sub-altern' by hegemonic forms of understanding 'the international' and 'global politics' become politically visible (Santos et al. 2007). This has been explored in relation to sumak kawsay ('the good living') and global trade politics in South America (Walsh 2011). I have also explored this in relation to customary law, the monocultural perception of 'human' rights, and global social dissent (Icaza 2015).

Decolonial thinking precisely introduces *border thinking* as an epistemological position that contributes to a shift in the forms of knowing in which the world is thought from the concrete incarnated experiences of colonial difference and the wounds left (Icaza and Vazquez 2016).[7] Moreover, through border thinking, the violence of the dominant epistemology grounded on abstract universality as 'a zero point' of observation and of knowledge is seen as disdainful by all other perspectives and forms of knowing (Mignolo and Tlostanova 2006; Mignolo 2010). As such, border thinking is seen as a 'fracture of the epistemology of the zero point' and as a possibility for a critical re-thinking of the geo and body politics of knowledge, of the modern/colonial foundations of political economy analysis, and of gender (Mignolo and Tlostanova 2006; Grofoguel 2007; Lugonés 2010a; 2010b). However, Argentinean feminist philosopher Maria Lugonés' interpretation of Gloria Anzaldua's *Borderlands* allows us to fully consider the epistemic contribution of border thinking as an *embodied consciousness* in which dualities and vulnerability are central for a decolonization of how we think about the geo and body politics of knowledge, political economy and, of course, gender in IR and GP (see Lugonés 1992). This will be the focus of the remainder of this

---

[6]   I am using 'produced' in an active sense, hence not an accident or natural circumstance following Santos. He speaks of the historical power asymmetries *produced* by European cultural imperialism and capitalism, which have led to the imposition of epistemologies and ways of knowing at the expense of other existing knowledges (Santos et. al. 2007).

[7]   Inspired by Maria Lugonés' decolonial feminism, I am thinking here of the colonial wound not only as a cultural expression, but also the physicality of the enslavement, racialization, rape, and dehumanization of some bodies.

chapter.

In what follows, I am particularly interested in addressing the invitation of the editors of this volume to consider the centrality of border thinking as one that sits in an embodied consciousness to 'show how the corporeal, fleshly, material existence of bodies is deeply embedded in political relations' including coloniality (Harcourt, Icaza and Vargas 2016). Likewise, I am also interested in understanding what happens when, in the process of that critical rethinking, 'the self-ascribed privileges of the West *knowing subject* are laid bare'. In so doing, I introduce auto-ethnographic reflection in a *dialogical* format as developed by Mexican anthropologist Xochitl Leyva (2013) as a kind of praxis of research of *co-labor* (collaborative research). From this perspective, the written text is a dialogue with the spoken and written word, with visuality, with past and present experiences and, with an imagined horizon of autonomy (Leyva 2013; Barbosa et. al. 2015; Icaza 2015).

This 'method' provides a way of imagining the world's 'self-ascribed' *epistemic* privileges of interpretation and representation as well as the state of vulnerability that implies un-learning them and refusing to accept them as the only possibilities to think/sense global and international politics. I am driven by the following questions: Is this un-learning a possibility of knowing *otherwise? For whom and for what purposes?*

These ideas are developed with the help of Lugonés' powerful interpretative analysis of Anzaldua's *Borderlands*. As such, this text has the following sections. The first introduces central elements in Lugonés' interpretative analysis of Anzaldua's *Borderlands*: border subjectivity, duality, and vulnerability. The following section presents three vignettes of different extensions and formats introducing places in the cartography of contemporary violence in Mexico: Las Patronas Veracruz, Ixtepec Oaxaca, and Ayotzinapa Guerrero. The vignettes are presented as dialogical auto-ethnographic reflections in which the global politics of migration and drug-cartel related violence are thought/sensed not from a zero-point of observation but from the embodied experience of the vulnerability that carries the un-learning and/or refusal to reproduce epistemic privileges of a 'subject' interpreting and representing reality. The final section offers some initial reflections about the questions considered throughout this chapter.

Borderlands and Vulnerability in International Relations

Elsewhere, I have argued that Lugonés' work constitutes a powerful perspective for a critical re-thinking of the global politics of resistance to neoliberalism (Icaza 2010). In particular, Lugonés' feminist decolonial thinking contributes to a critical re-thinking of IR and GP by highlighting the dominant modern/colonial epistemology that informs these disciplines as disembodied, masculinist, and placeless when producing analysis about global or transnational resistance (Icaza 2015; 2016).

To avoid such dominant forms of knowing, feminist IR thinker Christine Sylvester already insisted in 1993 that 'We [who study IR] develop ourselves, our research skills, our capacities to see with less arrogance, by negotiating knowledge at and across experiences, theories, locations and words of insight and relationships' (Sylvester 1993: 271). Inspired by Anzaldua's *Borderlands. The New Mestiza* and Lugonés' border dwelling approach to knowledge, Sylvester (1993: 270) tells us about 'the need to see and theorize the domestic shadow lands around us.' But, what Sylvester does not tell 'us' is what might happen to the way 'we' think in IR and GP if *border thinking* is to be understood as an embodied consciousness and not just a discursive strategy to destabilize dominant narratives over 'the international.'

Ann Fausto-Sterling's work on the construction of the body offers some elements that help to address this question by telling us that 'as we grow and develop, we literally not just "discursively" (that is, through language and cultural practices) construct our bodies, incorporating experience into our very flesh. To understand this, we must erode the distinctions between the physical and the social body' (Fausto-Sterling 2000: 20).

However, it is Lugonés' decolonial feminism grounded in African-American, Chicana, and women of colour feminisms whose *border thinking* as an *embodied consciousness* of dualities and vulnerability brings to the fore the racialized body as an historical one produced in the colonial encounter, as the one that did not reach the standards of 'humanity' in order to be enslaved, raped, and exploited. In short, Lugonés' thinking from an embodied experience of enslavement and racialization invites us 'to think from the ground up, from the body, therefore averts the generalizations that are common to abstract modern/colonial thought' including dominant epistemologies in IR and GP (Icaza and Vazquez 2016: 69). Moreover, this embodied thinking can also help us to understand 'the limits of feminist anti-essentialist discourses that praise the performativity of identity as holding the only possibilities for desestabilization and resistance' (ibid.: 63). This is developed in what follows.

The self-in-between, border subjectivities, and embodied dualities

For Lugonés, Anzaldua's *Borderlands* 'captures both an everyday history of oppression and an everyday history of resistance ... Her culture, though oppressive, also grounds her resistance' (Lugonés 1992: 32). This expresses, for Lugonés, two states of the self being oppressed and resisting — hence, the self as multiple. This is an important realisation that has informed my own work of re-thinking the one-dimensional view of the actors in social resistance that are prevalent in accounts of civil society and social movements against global capitalism in IR and International Political Economy (Icaza 2010).

Following Anzaldua's notion of mestizo consciousness, Lugonés tells us that 'there is the self oppressed in and by the traditional Mexican world; the self oppressed in and by the Anglo world; and the self-in-between — the Self — herself in resistance to oppression, the *self in germination* in the borderlands. If the self is being oppressed, then she can feel its limits, its capacity for response, pushed in, constrained, denied. But she can also push back' (Lugonés 1992: 32, my emphasis).

Lugonés' analysis also tells us about *Coatlalopeuh*, an early Mesoamerican creator goddess that embodies both a dark aspect (Coatlicue) and a lighter side (Tonantsi). Through this, Lugonés not only brings to the forefront the duality of thinking about the social (or in our case the international and the global), but an *embodied duality* that invites us to transcend the abstraction that is so akin to dominant masculinist thinking.

In speaking of how *Coatlalopeuh*, in Anzaldua's *Borderlands*, becomes the chaste and desexed character of the Virgin of Guadalupe by the Spanish colonizers and the Catholic Church, Lugonés focuses on an important aspect of Anzaldua's ideas of borders and borders subjectivities: Chicanos/Mexicanos as people who cross cultures are tolerant to ambiguity *out of necessity*. Lugonés characterizes these subjectivities as 'a tolerance for contradiction and ambiguity, by the transgression of rigid conceptual boundaries, and by the creative breaking of the new unitary aspects of new and old paradigms' (ibid.: 34).

Border subjectivities rooted in a tolerance for ambiguity *out of the necessity* remind us of an important element of what a border epistemology — as a way of thinking — for IR and GP could entail: border thinking as a physical sensual experience of a self-in-between that is a plural self (ibid.: 35). This means an emphasis on a knowing that sits in bodies and territories and its local histories in contrast to disembodied, abstract, universalist knowledge that generates global designs (Mignolo 2009; 2010). Recognizing that knowledge is situated implies "[seeing] the world from specific locations, embodied and particular, and never innocent" (Rose 1997: 308).

On Vulnerability, (Epistemic) Privileges, and Coalitions

Lugonés tells us that this self-in-between as a plural self 'is captive of more than one collectivity, and her dilemma is which collectivity to listen to' (Lugonés 1992: 35). In this listening, Lugonés identifies a deep sense of vulnerability: 'she effects a rupture with all oppressive traditions at the same time that she makes herself *vulnerable* to foreign ways of thinking, *relinquishing safety'* (ibid.: 35, emphasis added). A border thinking as a form of knowing otherwise is then an embodied sensual experience of vulnerability in which the safety of how one thinks/knows something is relinquished. This concerns our abstract universals, our detached and disembodied ways of knowing the international, our assumptions of objectivity to generate 'right' science, and so on.[8]

Considering the possibility of coalitional forms of resistance, Lugonés notes Anzaldua's interest in 'describing states in the psychology of oppression and liberation' that lead her to emphasize crossing-over as '*a solitary act*, an act of solitary rebellion...[hence] she does not reveal *the sociality of resistance*' (ibid.: 36, emphasis added). The sociality of resistance is central to Lugonés' interpretation of Anzaldua's *Borderlands* in her latest work (Lugonés 2003; 2010a; 2010b) to the extent that she emphasizes it in relation to a multiple self that resists and germinates in the borderlands. On this, she writes that 'unless resistance is a social activity, the resister is doomed to failure in the creation of a new universe of meaning, a new identity' (Lugonés 1992: 36).

In this way, Lugonés offers coalitions and coalitional selves as a necessary step out of that state of isolated vulnerability in which the border dweller finds herself: 'If rebellion and creation are understood as processes rather than as acts, then each act of solitary rebellion and creation is anchored in and responsive to a collective, even if disorganized, process of resistance' (ibid.: 36). The survival of the Spanish language among Chicanos/Mexicanos is an example that Lugonés brings from Anzaldua to emphasize the sociality of resistance. The over 5,000 years of struggle of original peoples in the Americas would be another example of this sociality.

This sociality of resistance is central in Lugonés as she reminds us that 'this society places border dwellers in profound isolation. The barriers to creative

---

8   Here I try to emphasize that to relinquish safety is an act of resistance to oppression. In that sense, it is a liberatory act of those selves and coalitions that delink from the confines of intelligibility, of what we are told or allowed to think/sense. As such, this liberatory act is not only a possibility or a choice for just some 'oppressed/ colonized' people, but a potential to create coalitions with those who also delink from different epistemological privileges.

collectivity and collective creation appear insurmountable. But that is only if we think of the act and of the process of creation' (ibid.: 36). To the isolation of border thinking as a form of embodied consciousness in which resistance sits, Lugonés counterpoises coalitions in order to break 'down our isolation against the odds prescribed by the confines of the normal' (ibid.: 37).

Three Vignettes in the Cartography of Contemporary Violence in Mexico

Las Patronas, Veracruz, Mexico

For almost two decades, in the town of La Patronas, Veracruz, Mexico a group of women have organized to help immigrants, mostly from Central America, passing through their town as they make their way to the United States. The story of these women that today are called '*Las Patronas*' (The Female Patrons) began in 'February 1995 when two sisters, Bernarda Romero and Rosa Romero, were standing with their groceries at a train crossing in the village, waiting for the train to pass. Migrants on the first train car began shouting, "Madre, I'm hungry"' (Sorrentino 2012). Since that day, sisters Romero have been joined by a dozen volunteer women and children from the town and elsewhere, who have cooked hundreds of daily portions of food packed in plastic bags, adding refilled water bottles to hand to the immigrants while the train is in motion.

In international media outlets and academic analyses, *Las Patronas'* actions have been framed as a form of 'motherly' solidarity and as an example of an ethics of care (Buzzone 2012; Grant 2014). What is common in this sort of analyses is their emphasis on correctly understanding *Las Patronas* and what they represent in the geopolitics of migration and diaspora. It seems to be about how 'a knowing subject' — the academic, the activist, the media correspondent — understands *them*.

> I have not stopped thinking about *Las Patronas*. I hope to never lose the steady thumping of the rushing freight train that I still feel each time my heartbeats. As I move about my days, slight motion sickness disturbs the remnants of nausea that I felt in in the heat of the glaring sun. I know the nausea I felt that day was not just a physical response to the heat (Veracruz is a state with average highs in the 90s during the month of May) but an emotional torrent pushing and pulling and grasping at my gut — still stirring in the pit of my stomach (Price 2013: 13).

The words above from Cassandra Price describe her physical state in her encounter with *Las Patronas*. In her text, featured in the Global Perspective section of Loyola University's *Women and Gender Studies Journal*, Price tells us of the high risks that migrants from Central America face on their way to the United States, which range from accidents while riding *la Bestia* or *the Death Train* to human traffickers and corrupt authorities. However, her account about migrant vulnerability turns into a reflection of her own physical vulnerability when confronted with the extenuating work of delivering food to migrants hanging from the fast-moving train as done by *Las Patronas*:

> I had reached my limit. I walked dizzily back to the bus to sit down out of the sun...I felt my condition worsening. I could hear the group sharing a beautiful meal, filled with laughter and true gratefulness. I couldn't eat...since the moment the train had passed I felt my entire body inside out begin to boil. I closed my eyes and began thinking about the way dehydration can make a person delirious. I imagined the heat of the metal... I thought of what it must take to drive a person to leave behind everything and everyone they know and love. I thought of how many people are forced to take such risks in hope of a better future for their families. I thought of my family, my friends and how I would likely never have to make such a journey. I breathe in and out slowly to the beat of the freight car still thumping in my head (ibid.: 15).

The words above aim to display what would happen if/when the experience of *Las Patronas* became/becomes the starting point from where a 'knowing subject' is questioned in their self-ascribed privileges. This could be, for example, about their objectivity and abstract universals from which Mexican women like *Las Patronas* are 'studied.' In the encounter with *Las Patronas*, Cassandra Price's words bring forward some elements to start addressing how in the (social) construction of our bodies we also incorporate 'experience into our very flesh' (Fausto Sterling 2000: 20).

Fieldwork Diary Notes on the Going Glocal Program[9]

August 7th 2013, visit to the Migrant Shelter "Hermanos del Camino"

Today, we visited the migrant shelter 'Hermanos del Camino' (*Brothers of the Road*) in Ixtepec, Mexico. We had arrived the night before in Juchitan, where we spent the night. As our visit to the shelter was previously organized, the

---

[9]   The Dutch Ministry of Foreign Affairs financed this program through a SBOS grant. See: http://www.goingglocal.nl.

volunteer staff warmly welcomed us. The residents of the shelter, mostly young men, greeted us reluctantly and with curiosity. After five minutes of awkward silence, the main coordinator of the shelter, Catholic Priest Alejandro Solalinde Guerra, appeared to welcome us. He told us that the shelter was founded in 2007 and explained that they provide temporary humanitarian aid, which includes food, shelter, medical, psychological, and legal help, to migrants from Central America.[10] We are told the residents of the shelter stay an average of three days. A female volunteer indicated that in 2012 they received a total of 11,000 people, and by June 2013 they had supported a total of 7,100 from which 90% are men from Honduras, Guatemala, and El Salvador.

Solalinde continued to explain that the place is run with the help of Mexican and international volunteers. Then, he showed us a big map on the wall of the shelter's small clinic:

> Look, most of our brothers enter through Guatemala walking around 275 kilometres to the city of Arriaga in Chiapas where they get into the train. After ten to twelve hours they arrive to Ixtepec, Oaxaca. Seven-hundred kilometres later they will arrive to Lecheria in Mexico City. From there they have to travel around 2,800 kilometres hanging in the train to reach Tijuana, Ciudad Juarez, or Matamoros which are the main entry points to the US in the border with Mexico.

A deep silence followed Solalinde's explanation. A few seconds later, the silence was broken by a female volunteer's invitation to visit the shelter's facilities. During the visit, we found a very young single mother from Nicaragua and her two-year-old daughter. They were also on their way to the United States. The mother told me that she had to stop in the shelter because her daughter became ill. While I translated this for the students, I noted that some of them were holding hands. Is this an act of mutual physical comfort? I was wondering that when Solalinde invited us to sit down and hold a conversation with the residents of the shelter.

All the residents were called and we formed a circle. Each of them shared their name and nationality. We did the same. I volunteered to do the translation from Spanish into English. One of the students asked *why they left their families and countries*. Poverty, unemployment, violence, gangs, no future were their answers.

---

[10] See http://www.hermanosenelcamino.org/english.html

After one hour, the jokes broke out. One Cuban asked me to translate: 'Tell them that I might not want to go anymore to the US, I think that I will want to go to the Netherlands.' Everybody laughs until one of the students asked what they could do to *help them*. Solalinde's reply was straightforward: 'We don't need your help here, we need your help back in Europe. You need to help migrants there.' Another man replied too: 'go back home and tell your friends and family what *you have been able to see here*'. Total silence again.

Once more the silence was broken by a warm invitation to have a meal together with all the residents of the shelter who actually had cooked the food to share with us.

On our way to the small dining room, one of our young female students collapsed. She was crying, shaking, sweating. As the only female member of the teaching team, I volunteered to take her back to the rental vehicle and to stay with her. On our way to the vehicle I thought of the food and conversations I was about to miss.

Once in the car, she couldn't stop crying. Her whole body was shaking; her pale skin had become bright red. I offered her some water, which she drank. She started to talk to me about her family and friends back home in the Netherlands. She couldn't stop talking to me. I simply listened and thought on how important it seems for her to tell me about her loved ones and how important they are to her. She fell asleep. I thought in silence that all is okay now and that she suffered the effects of the harsh heat. One hour later, the group came back. She woke up and everybody comforted her. We continued our journey to Chiapas.

Ten days later, during our final group session in Mexico, this student shared with all of us the following: 'I don't know where to start, but I always knew there were many harsh questions to ask to myself, and it is only when I came here that I realized how much I needed to ask them.'

While listening to this, I cannot stop asking myself if we have just witnessed a self in germination out of a conscious realization of her own vulnerability? Is this a form of knowing *otherwise*?

The above shared words are the notes gathered during my participation as one of the coordinators of the Dutch program of education on global citizenship in higher education entitled 'Going Glocal.' In Mexico, this program included a field trip that brought student of the University College Roosevelt in the Netherlands to meet with social activists and their communities in two prominent Mexican indigenous regions: Oaxaca and Chiapas (Vazquez 2015:

92).

In reporting about the experience, the main coordinator of the program in Mexico reflected on the idea that 'the geographical trip did not guarantee that the participants would be able to travel beyond their world of meaning, beyond their position of consumers of the world, or beyond the "selfie tourist" position' (ibid.: 95). Therefore, the trip was designed and implemented as an intercultural encounter between university students with the concrete struggles of Oaxaca and Chiapas indigenous communities and of Central American migrants on their way to the United States.

At its core, the program was grounded on a decolonial framework and the deployment of pedagogies of positionality and world traveling. The former is understood as promoting critical self-reflectivity in the students as members of the consumer society regarding their privileges (socio-economic and epistemic) as being built upon the destitution of 'others.' The later understood as providing students with (a) critical awareness of their own location as a historically situated site of enunciation, but also with (b) the option of 'relating to the world' as a place of different words of meaning, instead of a place that is there to be consumed (ibid.).

Eurocaravana 43: Thinking Through the Vulnerability of a Sick Body

On 26 September 2014, the town of Ayotzinapa, Mexico made global headlines when 42 male students at the Raúl Isidro Burgos Rural School, some of them minors and indigenous, were kidnapped and, according to Mexico's attorney general's office, killed and burned by members of the drug cartel *Guerreros Unidos*.

A few hours after these tragic events, the hashtags *#todosomosayotzinapa* (we are all ayotzinapa) and *#ayotzinapaaccionglobal* (ayotzinapa global action) began trending on twitter in Mexico. A few days after, massive street demonstrations, performances, and flash mobs were organized in different Mexican cities as well as across the United States, Europe, and Asia. Meanwhile in Europe, local human rights organizations started to organise social media campaigns to raise awareness of the events (Icaza 2016). Between 17 April and 19 May 2015, the *Eurocaravana 43*, as an international awareness-raising tour of Ayotzinapa students' representatives and their families, visited eighteen cities and fourteen European countries.[11]

---

[11]   Social media also played a significant part using Facebook (https://www.facebook.com/Caravana43) and on Twitter (with the handle of #Eurocaravana43).

In the *Eurocaravana 43* organisation process, young Mexican activists resident in the Netherlands expressed to me their concerns regarding the role that academics might want to play in the planned events: 'we think that the Ayotzinapa students' representatives and families need to play a central role, not the academics nor their institutions. We don't want that the relatives or their terrible and painful experience to be taken by academics as something to be analyzed, as an object of study'.[12] Like other conversations held with activists, these words express, in a daring and clear way, the dominant ways of working in IR and GP in which people's experiences of violence become an 'object' that is studied, but not from which one theorizes and re-learns the world (Icaza and Vazquez 2013; Barbosa, Icaza, and Ocampo 2015; Icaza 2015). But, then how can one actually do such un-learning and re-learning?

In the Netherlands, the *Eurocaravana 43* visited the city of Leiden on May 16 and Amsterdam the day after. As a feminist IR academic of Mexican background, I was invited to participate in the different academic-activist events organized to raise awareness in the Netherlands on the tragic events of September 2014 in Ayotzinapa. I had to follow the events from my bed in Twitter and Facebook, and the academic conferences through livestream.[13] An unexpected complication of undergoing cancer treatment didn't allow me and my sick body to do more. Feminist Yoanna Hedva's 'sick women theory' reflects on the modes of protest that are afforded to sick people. My participation was reduced to limited forms of distant solidarity: 'I listened to the sounds of the marches as they drifted up to my window. Attached to the bed, I rose up my sick woman fist, in solidarity' (Hevda 2015).

But in contrast to Hevda, the sense of vulnerability that sickness brought with it was an opportunity to re-think and further question the always-capable-healthy-fit-mobile-body of an academic doing research in contemporary academia on social resistance (Icaza 2015). In other words, not to be physically able to participate in the planned events of the *Eurocaravana 43* brought with it a deep sense of understanding, an embodied one, of the vulnerability of the body and of feminists analyses denouncing the epistemic violence of academic writing that stems from nowhere and is bodiless (Lugonés 2003; Escobar and Harcourt 2005; Adichie 2009). It is from that placeless/bodiless position that the histories of certain bodies as the 'normal' ones (the head of state, the male financial broker), of certain places (Washington, D.C, Brussels, Paris), and of certain events and memories (Charlie Hebdo killings) are universalized and reproduced as 'common' senses from which 'we' think in the international and the global (Icaza 2015).

---

[12]   Interview with representatives of *Eurocaravana 43*.
[13]   For the proceedings, visit https://www.youtube.com/watch?v=r9kRtzTe9fA.

Three Vignettes, Some Common Questions

The vignettes above were introduced as one possible way to present moments of vulnerability of the 'knowing subject' from which a *knowing otherwise* is in germination. What are the elements of that knowing? And in which ways is border thinking as an *embodied consciousness* central for a critical re-thinking of how we think/sense the international and the global? In this final section, I present some initial elements that I hope can help address these two questions.

First of all, it is central to understand that one of the crucial limitations of the dominant epistemology in IR and GP is grounded on a one-dimensional self: the one able to observe, scrutinize, and analyse the international, including other selves as well as their places and communities, who are there to be observed, scrutinized, and analysed.

Second, the self in germination is not only an invitation to re-think that supposedly 'unitary observant self' but also their gaze over other selves and to consider the creative force that inhabiting the borderlands entails. In other words, it is an invitation to consider what kind of selves germinate in the borderlands and what this germination tells us about supposedly unitary/ homogenous selves observing 'the international' reality. In this text, through the vignettes, I am trying to display the power that this gaze has had over the analysis of the international and the generation of knowledge, or what Mignolo calls the geo and body politics of knowledge.

Third, border subjectivities are central for a critical re-thinking of the dominant epistemologies of IR and GP not just as discursive sources that destabilize binary thinking, but as embodied epistemic sites of enunciation in their own right. This embodied episteme invites us to think seriously about selves and 'the international' that these selves inhabit in a way that implicates us/them in the global dynamics of migration and diaspora and the interconnectedness of resource exploitation to people's lives.

As such, the vignettes aim to transmit the vulnerability, even physical vulnerability, as one's way of thinking about 'reality' to countering the placeless, abstract, bodiless epistemological foundations dominant in IR and GP. This is the kind of gnosis that aims to be stressed in each vignette, of a vulnerable 'knowing subject' as a detached, objective observer. The main purpose in emphasizing this is in line with Snyman who argues for the decolonial challenge of thinking *otherwise* from a position of privilege as requiring a hermeneutic of vulnerability 'of the self as a perpetrating agent and of those who still bear the brunt of [coloniality's] aftermath' (Snyman 2015: 269).

References

Adichie, C. (2009) The Danger of the Single Story. *Ted Talk*. Available online at: https://www.ted.com/talks/chimamanda_adichie_the_danger_of_a_single_story?language=en.

Anzaldúa, G. (1987) *Borderlands/La Frontera: The New Mestiza*. San Francisco: Aunt Lute Books.

Barbosa da Costa, L., Icaza, R., and Talero, A. M. O. (2015) Knowledge about, knowledge with: dilemmas of researching lives, nature and genders otherwise. In Harcurt, W. and Nelson, I. eds. *Practising Feminist Political Ecologies*. London: Zed Books.

Buzonne, M. (2012) *Las Patronas, Clientelism and Care.* Unpublished thesis submitted in partial fulfillment of the requirements for the degree of Master of Science (Geography) at the University of Wisconsin-Madison. Available at: https://minds.wisconsin.edu/bitstream/handle/1793/67767/Bruzzone%20Mario%202012.pdf?sequence=1.

Dussel, E. (2001) Eurocentrismo y modernidad. Introducción a las lecturas de Frankfurt.In Mignolo, W. ed. *Capitalismo y geopolítica del conocimiento. El eurocentrismo y la filosofía de la liberación en el de bate intelectual contemporáneo*. Buenos Aires: Signos.

Escobar, A. (2007) World And Knowledges Otherwise. The Latin American Modernity/Coloniality Research Program. *Cultural Studies* 21(2): 179–210.

Escobar, A. and Harcourt, W. (2005) *Women and the Politics of Place*. Delhi, India: Kumarian Place

Fausto Sterling, A. (2000) *Sexing the Body. Gender Politics and the Construction of Sexuality*. New York: Basic Books.

Grant, W. (2014) Las Patronas: The Mexican Women Helping Migrants. *BBC News*. Available at: http://www.bbc.com/news/world-latin-america-28193230.

Grosfoguel, R. (2007) The Epistemic Decolonial Turn. Beyond Political Economy Paradigms. *Cultural Studies* 21(2-3): 211–223.

Gruffydd Jones, B. (2006) Introduction. International Relations, Eurocentrism and Imperialism. In Gruffydd Jones, B. ed. *Decolonizing International Relations,* Plymouth: Rowman and Littlefield Publishers.

Hevda, J. (2015) Sick Woman Theory. *Mask Magazine.* Available at: http://www.maskmagazine.com/not-again/struggle/sick-woman-theory

Icaza, R. (2010) Global Europe, Guilty! Contesting EU Neo-liberal Governance to Latin America. *Third World Quarterly* 3(12): 123–139.

Icaza, R. (2015) Testimony of a Pilgrimage. (Un)learning and Re-learning with the South. In Barahona, M. and Arashiro, Z. eds. *Women in Academia Crossing North-South Borders: Gender, Race and Displacement.* Lanham, Maryland: Lexington Books.

Icaza, R. (2016) #Yamecanse Activismo Transnacional de México en redes sociales y el feminismo decolonial, In Alejo, A. ed. *Activismos transnacionales de México: una pespectiva multidisciplinary* Mexico: Universidad Nacional Autonoma de Mexico (UNAM).

Icaza, R., Harcourt, W., and Vargas Valente, G. (2016) Thinking through embodiment and intersectionality in transnational feminist activist research processes. In Biekart, K., Harcourt, W., and Knorringa, P. eds. *Exploring Civic Innovation for Social and Economic Transformation.* London: Routledge.

Icaza, R. and Vázquez, R. (2013) Social Struggles as Epistemic Struggles. *Development and Change*, 43(6): 683–704.

Icaza, R. and Vazquez, R. (2016) The Coloniality of Gender as a Radical Critique to Developmentalism. In Harcourt, W. ed. *The Palgrave Handbook on Gender and Development: Critical Engagements in Feminist Theory and Practice.* London: Palgrave Macmillan.

Leyva Solano, X. (2013) Y/osotras ¿Mi/nuestras Luchas Epistémicas Creativas? *Obra Colegiada del Seminario Virtual Internacional.* Available at: http://www.encuentroredtoschiapas.jkopkutik.org/index.php/es/xochitl-leyva-solano

Lugonés, M. (1990) Structure/Antistructure and Agency under Oppressions. *Journal of Philosophy*, 87(10): 500–507.

Lugonés, M. (1992) On Borderlands/La Frontera. An interpretative analysis. *Hypathia*, 7(4): 31–37.

Lugonés, M. (2003) *Pilgrimages/Peregrinajes. Theorizing Coalitions Against Multiple Oppressions*. Lanham, MD: Rowman and Littlefield.

Lugonés, M. (2010a) The Coloniality of Gender. In Mignolo, W. and Escobar, A. eds. *Globalization and the Decolonial Option.* London: Routledge.

Lugonés, M. (2010b) Towards a Decolonial Feminism. *Hypathia* 4: 742–759.

Marcos, S. (2006) *Taken from the Lips: Gender and Eros in Mesoamerican Religions*. Leiden: Brill.

Mignolo, W. (2003) *Historias locales/diseños globales: colonialidad, conocimientos subalternos y pensamiento fronterizo.* Madrid: Ediciones Akal.

Mignolo, W. (2009) Epistemic Disobedience, Independent Thought and Decolonial Freedom. *Theory, Culture & Society* 26(7-8): 159–181.

Mignolo, W. (2010) Delinking: The Rhetoric of Modernity, The logic of Coloniality and the Grammar of decoloniality. In Mignolo, W. and Escobar, A. eds. *Globalization and the De-Colonial Option.* London: Routledge.

Mignolo, W. (2013) Dewesternization, Rewesternization and Decoloniality: The Racial Distribution of Capital and Knowledge. Public Lecture given at the Centre for the Humanities, University of Utrecht. May 13.

Mignolo, W. and Tlostanova, M.V. (2006). Theorising from the Borders. Shifting to Geo and Body Politics of Knowledge. *European Journal of Social Theory* 9(2): 205-221.

Palermo, Z. (2008). La Opcion Decolonial. In *Diccionario del Pensamiento Alternativo I.*   Buenos Aires, Argentina: Editorial Biblos Lexicón. Availbale at: http://www.cecies.org/articulo.asp?id=227.

Pappart, J. and Marchand, M.H. (1995). *Feminism, Postmodernism, Development*. London: Routledge.

Price, C. (2013). Las Patronas: Women and the Train of Death. *Broad. A Feminist and Social Justice Magazine,* Issue 60. Available at: https://issuu.com/broadmagazine/docs/broad_issue_60_sept_2013_linked/12.

Rose, G. (1997). Situating Knowledges: Positionality, Reflexivities and other Tactics. *Progress in Human Geography* 21: 305-320.

Sorrentino, J. (2012, August 29). Women of Las Patronas Aid Central American Migrants in Mexico. In: *Upside Down World*. Available at: http://upsidedownworld.org/main/mexico-archives-79/3596-women-of-las-patronas-aid-central-american-migrants-in-mexico.

Vázquez, R. (2009). Modernity Coloniality and Visibility: The Politics of Time. *Sociological Research Online*, 14(4). Available at: http://www.socresonline.org.uk/welcome.html.

Vazquez, R. (2011). Translation as Erasure: Thoughts on Modernity's Epistemic Violence. *Journal of Historical Sociology* 24 (1): 27-44.

Vazquez, R. (2014). Colonialidad y Relacionalidad. In: Borsani, M.E. and Quintero, P. eds. *Los Desafíos Decoloniales de nuestros Días: Pensar en Colectivo*. Neuquen, Argentina: EDUCO/Universidad Nacional de Comahuep. 173-96.

Vazquez, R. (2015). Decolonial Practices of Learning. In: Friedman,J. et. Al. eds. *Going Glocal in Higher Education: The Theory, Teaching and Measurement of Global Citizenship.* Middelburgh: University College Roosevelt. 92-100.

 Quijano, A. (2000). Coloniality of Power, Ethnocentrism, and Latin America. *Nepantla* 1(3): 533-580.

Shilliam, R. ed. 2010. *International Relations and Non-Western Thought: Imperialism, Colonialism and Investigations of Global Modernity*. Routledge, London & New York.

Snyman, G. (2015). Responding to the Decolonial Turn: Epistemic Vulnerability. *Missionalia*, 43(3): 266-91.

de Sousa Santos, B. et. al. (2007). Opening up the Canon of Knowledge and Recognition of Difference. In: de Sousa Santos, B. ed. *Another Knowledge is Possible: Beyond Northern Epistemologies*. London: Verso. xix-ixi.

Sylvester, C. (1996) The Contributions of Feminist Theory to International Relations. In: Smith, S et. al. eds. *International Theory: Positivism and Beyond.* Cambridge: Cambridge University Press. 254-277.

Taylor, L. (2012). Decolonizing International Relations. Views from Latin America. *International Studies Review* 14: 386-400.

Walsh, C. (2007). Shifting the Geopolitics of Critical Knowledge. Decolonial Thought and Cultural Studies 'Others' in the Andes. *Cultural Studies* 21(2 &3): 224-239.

Walsh, C. (2010). Development as Buen Vivir: Institutional Arrangements and (de)Colonial Entanglements. *Development*, 53(1):15-21.

Walsh, C. (2011). The (De)Coloniality of Knowledge, Life and Nature: The North America-Andean Free Trade Agreement, Indigenous Movements and Regional Alternatives. In: Shefner, J. & Fernandez Kelly, P. eds. *Globalization and Beyond: New Examinations of Global Power and its Alternatives.* Pennsylvania: Pennsylvania State University Press. 228-249.

Walsh, C. (2012). El Pluralismo Jurídico: El Desafío de la Interculturalidad. *Nueva America* 133: 32-37.

3

Decolonising the Anthropocene: The Mytho-Politics of Human Mastery

KARSTEN A. SCHULZ

Discussing the fluid boundaries between humanity and nature in light of destructive human interactions with the biosphere raises controversial issues. There is now growing consensus among many scholars that a dualistic understanding of humanity and nature as separate and monolithic entities is insufficient to describe the richness of relations 'beyond the human' and the embeddedness of humans in the interdependent web of life (Kohn 2013). Furthermore, assuming that there is no mode of social relationality that is entirely free from power differentials, it seems no longer viable to speak of a single humanity or nature in the context of the current ecological crisis. Instead, it seems more sensible to conceive of abstract concepts such as humanity or nature in terms of multiple 'biosocial becomings' (Ingold and Palsson 2013).[1]

Yet as long as the modernist paradigms of technological utopianism and economic growth are taken to represent the 'natural order of things' under global capitalism, it is necessary to place the concept of biosocial becomings in a wider context. To begin with, it seems plausible to suggest that today's biosocial relations are markedly structured by a 'capitalist world-ecology, joining power, capital, and nature as an entwined whole' (Moore 2015: 70). Moreover, a considerable body of critical scholarship has pointed out that the

---

[1]   Humans are, according to Ingold and Palsson (2013: 39), 'fluid beings, with flexible, porous boundaries; they are necessarily embedded in relations, neither purely biological nor purely social, which may be called "biosocial"; and their essence is best rendered as something constantly in the making and not as a fixed, context-independent species-being.'

capitalist world-ecological system is inextricably linked to *coloniality*, defined not only as an unjust economic model, but also as a racialised, androcentric, and class-based hierarchy of knowing and being which still marginalises non-western cultures and histories (Escobar 2004; Quijano 2007). Imagining collective becomings otherwise, in the sense of a transformation towards less destructive and more just forms of conviviality, thus means to avoid the superficial agglomeration — or a mere reshuffling — of what is presently deemed 'natural' or 'social' *within* the commodifying logic of the modern capitalist world-ecology.

At this point it is certainly interesting to note that more holistic and spiritually inclined forms of knowing and being-in-the-world are gaining renewed prominence in contemporary ecopolitical debates. In particular, there is growing awareness among scholars from various disciplines that storytelling and mythical thought have long prefigured philosophies on human-nature relations and left their traces in our collective social imaginaries (Williams et al. 2012; Vetlesen 2015). Hence, I intend to bring into sharper relief the role of myth and mythical narratives in shaping today's ecological crisis. At a time when new mystifications of human-nature relations are rapidly emerging, most notably through the increased humanisation of *geological time*, it is crucial to bear in mind that mythical narratives often come with their own (colonial) politics.

So how exactly can we imagine the scientific mystification of geological time? After all, geological epochs normally do not generate much excitement outside a narrow circle of scholars. Unlike historical epochs, commonly associated with characteristic representations of the world's meaning and the human position therein, geological epochs usually appear as the silent backdrop to the struggles of the human species. While being confronted with rapid technological change and pressing concerns such as poverty, conflict, and environmental degradation, it seems almost reassuring that humans have now been living in the Holocene for approximately 11,700 years.

Today, however, a number of leading earth scientists propose that humanity has already entered a new geological epoch, the so-called *Anthropocene*, in which humankind is seen as a geological force transforming the planet. As currently used, the term Anthropocene was introduced by Nobel Prize-winning atmospheric chemist Paul J. Crutzen in 2000. Together with the ecologist Eugene F. Stoermer, Crutzen suggested that a new epoch should be added to the geological timescale, arguing that such a far-reaching decision may be warranted based on mounting evidence for a profound anthropogenic influence on the biological, chemical, and geological processes on earth (Crutzen and Stoermer 2000). In other words, it is now assumed that unprecedented human influence has led to a situation in which the earth system as a whole is 'operating in a *no-analogue state*' (Crutzen and Steffen 2003: 253, emphasis in the original).

In view of such unsettling changes, a lively discussion has emerged among scholars from different fields regarding the historical origins of the Anthropocene. Does the Industrial Revolution of the eighteenth century and the invention of the stream engine mark the beginning of the Anthropocene (Steffen et al. 2011)? Is it the invention of agriculture around 8,000 BC that has ushered in a new epoch (Ruddiman 2013)? Or did the Anthropocene begin with the explosion of the first atomic bomb in July 1945, when techno-scientific progress paved the way for the atomic age and sparked the 'Great Acceleration' in human communication and resource use that has shaped our societies since the post-war boom period (Steffen et al. 2015)?

Debates about the origins of the Anthropocene remain inconclusive, and a decision on whether the Anthropocene should be officially recognised as a period, epoch, or age in the geological timescale has yet to be made by the International Commission on Stratigraphy. However, despite ongoing discussions on whether the Anthropocene should be considered an additional chronostratigraphic unit above or within the current Holocene epoch — and, if so, how this proposed new unit should be formally defined — the idea of a 'New Human Epoch'[2] has seemingly struck a critical chord with many scholars in the broader humanities and environmental social sciences.[3] The recent mushrooming of Anthropocene-themed journals, books, and conferences as well as the prominent use of the concept by major earth system science initiatives such as Future Earth (2013) has even prompted a number of scholars to speak of an emerging 'Anthropo-scene' dominated by the epistemic and ontological tenets of complexity science and managerial systems thinking (Castree 2015; Rickards 2015). Especially the notion of earth system science as a new 'integrative super-discipline' that is arguably best equipped to take the lead in addressing the complex entanglements between biophysical, social, and technological 'systems' has sparked a heated debate about the Anthropocene's far-reaching implications (Pitman 2005: 137).

In sum, two fundamental questions are at the heart of these ongoing discussions. The first question concerns the multifaceted relations between humans, nature, and technology in the twenty-first century. What does it mean for our understanding of these relations if we accept the scientific proposal that humanity has become a 'geological force' similar to glacial and

---

2   'Anthropocene' from Greek: άνθρωπος = human being/man, καινός = new/current.
3   For an overview, see Lövbrand et al. (2015).

tectonic processes (Dalby 2015: 3)? And secondly, what are the political, ontological, and epistemic implications of the Anthropocene concept?

If the notion of the New Human Epoch ultimately implies that 'in a very real sense, the world is in our hands' (Vitousek et al. 1997: 499), it is evident that the same idea has been formulated long before the Anthropocene became a topic of interest for both natural and social scientists. In 1873, the Italian geologist Antonio Stoppani already introduced the notion of an *Anthropozoic era*, while a number of other scientists such as G. P. Marsh, Vladimir Vernadsky, Pierre Teilhard de Chardin, and Edouard Le Roy further developed the idea of a human age. However, in spite of the fact that it now seems to be a commonly accepted view that the precedents of the Anthropocene can be traced back at least a century, this intellectual genealogy does not seem to be very precise. As Hamilton and Grinevald (2015: 59) remind us, earlier conceptions of the human age mainly focused on the human impact on the earth's surface, and not on the *earth system* as a whole, while relying on 'a progressive and linear evolutionary understanding of the spread of humankind's geographical and ecological influence, whereas the Anthropocene represents a radical rupture with all evolutionary ideas in human and Earth history, including the breakdown of any idea of advance to a higher stage.'

Explaining the lively debate about the Anthropocene among scholars from various disciplines is then not so much about the immediate relevance of the Anthropocene as a geological or natural scientific concept. Perceiving the Anthropocene as a new epoch, which suggests at least some kind of stability, may even be misleading given the fast rate of current anthropogenic change. It is rather the ambiguous notion of the *Anthropos* itself, the idea of an undifferentiated humanity that is at the heart of the concept, which might help to illuminate the success of the Anthropocene as a discursive rallying point. The notion of an undifferentiated humanity is precisely ambiguous because it raises a number of critical questions regarding the political, historical, epistemological, and ontological assumptions that undergird contemporary discussions about the human condition. What does it mean to be 'human' in the Anthropocene—and who decides? Who (and what) is included and excluded as soon as notions of a single 'humanity' are invoked?

Considering the unequal distribution of dangerous anthropogenic changes to the earth's ecosystems, as well as different degrees of responsibility for the emergence of such threads, it has become clear that the undifferentiated notion of 'humankind as the new geological agent' is inadequate to describe the politics and injustices of capitalist development (Malm and Hornborg 2014: 64). Modernity and its western global expression are still marked by historically situated lines of inequality that are drawn according to categories such as species, gender, race, class, ability, or sexual orientation. Taken together, these material-semiotic practices of *b/ordering* and *othering* also define how biosocial relations are projected, performed, and policed in everyday life.

In view of the far-reaching political implications of this state of affairs, it is indeed problematic that mainstream debates about ecology and sustainability continue to be dominated by a troubling separation between the realm of science and the realm of the political — a separation that is increasingly difficult to uphold. The Anthropocene narrative offered by earth system scientists, for example, has been heavily critiqued for its primary focus on environmental symptoms and its relative neglect of the social, political, and economic processes that are arguably at the heart of the Anthropocene 'crisis.' Whether such criticisms are entirely justified, assuming that natural science investigations have drawn political attention to environmental problems in the first place, is another question.

In any case, the framing of humanity as a geological force implies that the living environment is now shaped by (and entangled with) a complex political economy whose origins and inequalities cannot be sufficiently understood unless one realises that western-centric narratives of a single modernity are characterised by wilful abstractions, silences, and the 'wound inflicted by the colonial difference' (Mignolo 2011: 63). Yet, while particularistic and western-centric narratives of modernity are increasingly being questioned, few scholars have explored the concept of the Anthropocene from the perspective of *decoloniality*.

Decoloniality — as a perspective, conceptual lens, and political project — engages with a critical reading of modernity that is inseparably bound to the 'coloniality of power' (Quijano 1992: 437). According to Walter Mignolo (2009: 39), 'de-colonial thinking and doing emerged, from the sixteenth century on, as responses to the oppressive and imperial bent of modern European ideals projected to, and enacted in, the non-European world.' Based on the assumption that the coloniality of power can be characterised as a hierarchical system of control and oppression, coloniality is defined as a constitutive element of modernity. There is no western modernity without coloniality and its exploitative relations. Modernity and coloniality are essentially two sides of the same coin.

In this sense, decolonial scholarship differs considerably from historical studies of decolonisation, since it does not assume that colonialism has ended and can thus be historicised. Decolonial theorists would rather argue that contemporary forms of coloniality are perpetuated on a global scale through discursive-material processes of imperialism, appropriation, and unequal economic exchange. This includes ethnocentric forms of education as well as the selective application of human rights. In other words, coloniality constructs human *subjects* and less-than-human *objects* at the same time. It produces schisms within humanity by inscribing itself onto bodies, minds, and histories, while simultaneously promulgating a logic of objectification. In the words of Aimé Césaire (2000: 42), this colonial logic of objectification is based on the 'thing-ification' of so-called subaltern people and the nonhuman world. Just as the logic of coloniality denies subaltern people their full subject status as human beings and establishes a colonial difference based on an alleged *lack* (of knowledge, history, development, and so on), it also negates the subject status of the nonhuman world. The living environment and other species are not seen as subjects in their own right, but as objects that can be mastered and exploited.

Intent on counteracting the coloniality of power, being, and knowledge, decolonial scholarship also distinguishes itself from the field of postcolonial studies through, for instance, its strong emphasis on *epistemic disobedience*. By refusing to adopt the theoretical outlook of poststructuralism and postmodernism to which postcolonial theory arguably takes recourse, decolonial scholarship seeks to *delink* itself from western-centric worldviews. This process of delinking does not simply refer to a critical project within western academia, a mere deconstruction of terminologies. It describes a delinking from an epistemological frame that silences and subalternises non-western voices, knowledges, and languages within the totalising hierarchy of a single modernity (Mignolo 2007; Gutiérrez Rodríguez 2010). To this end, decolonial scholarship relies on concepts and theories that have been developed by scholars, artists and activists such as Waman Puma de Ayala, Enrique Dussel, Aimé Césaire, Frantz Fanon, Aníbal Quijano, W. E. B. Du Bois, and Gloria Anzaldúa, among others.

Yet the idea of decoloniality is *not* to celebrate a proudly defiant counter-stance that ultimately remains dependent on the totalising views and beliefs that it reacts against. Instead, the decolonial option is to develop a consciousness of *border thinking* that is able to inhabit different worlds at once, while creating new cultural and political imaginaries from a position of being-in-between (Anzaldúa 1987). In doing so, decolonial scholarship attempts to move beyond First World and Third World fundamentalisms to direct attention toward the epistemic *locus of enunciation*, the ideological, geopolitical, and body-political location of the subject that speaks. The motivation behind this approach is to avoid the fallacy of a totalising *zero-point* epistemology that 'hides its local and particular perspective under an abstract universalism' (Grosfóguel 2011: 5). Simply put, this means to change not only the epistemic rules of the geopolitical conversation, but also the asymmetric power relations which govern these very rules. What decoloniality certainly does not mean, however, is to reject the best of western science and modernity *tout court.* Decolonial scholarship is not anti-scientific. Instead, it seeks to show how particular knowledges and epistemologies are devalued, decentred and reduced as being 'traditional, barbarian, primitive, mystic' (Mignolo 2011: 46). While each of these value-laden ascriptions would certainly be worthy of investigation, I shall nevertheless limit myself to focusing on the latter aspect of *myth* and its relevance for a decolonial politics of the Anthropocene.

What exactly is a myth? On the one hand, there is an observable tendency in everyday speech and various scholarly writings to disparage content as 'myth' that appears to be false, misleading, or simply different from one's own valued convictions. On the other hand, the notion of myth is frequently invoked to designate some kind of primordial truth, sacred narrative, or imaginative way of knowing that fulfils particular adaptive, sense-making, and identity-generating functions.

Yet, to avoid getting bogged down in endless theoretical debates about the truth-value of myth, I will begin my discussion with a structuralist definition provided by the French linguist and philosopher Roland Barthes. According to Barthes, a myth is neither a concept nor an idea that is related to certain contents, but rather a *form of speech* that needs to be interpreted in a concrete social and material context. Mythology, or the study of myth, is thus described by Barthes as being partly scientific (semiotic) and partly ideological, since myth must be understood historically, in its context, which is always a subjective and ideologically charged process (Barthes 1991).

This Barthesian separation between science (semiotics) and ideology (history) leaves us with a paradoxical situation. Studying particular myths through the eyes of a scientific discipline such as semiotics normally implies that science itself can be separated from myth due to its rational and empirical approach. In other words, framing a particular worldview as mythical — which is usually done from the universalising zero-point perspective of western science and philosophy — means precisely to juxtapose the mythical with the rational, non-ideological, and factual.

Contrary to Barthes, I nevertheless maintain that science at large, and not only history, is characterised by the presence of myth and the existence of an ideological dimension that arises from the embeddedness and application of science in concrete conditions of sociality. The main question that follows from this assumption, however, is how exactly the relationship between myth and ideology may be defined vis-à-vis a western-centric politics of knowledge generation.[4]

Generally, literature on this specific topic is rather sparse. While there are large bodies of literature devoted to either the theory of myth or the conceptualisation of ideology, there has been surprisingly little exchange between the two fields of research (Flood 2002). The notional use of the term mythology as an apparent synonym for ideology, for example in the writings of Louis Althusser and Roland Barthes, illustrates this conceptual lacuna (Von Hendy 2001). It is certainly questionable whether such a vague conceptualisation of the relationship between myth and ideology is sufficient to inform a decolonial politics of delinking.

In line with a critical deconstructionist conjecture, it would of course be intuitive to assume that the ideological element of myth can be easily identified and demystified by those who know how to decipher and contextualise mythical forms of expression. However, defining the relationship between myth and ideology is not quite as easy. Barthes (1991: 143) reminds us that myth does not simply conceal or deny ideologies, but *naturalises* them: 'it makes them innocent, it gives them a natural and eternal justification, it gives them a clarity which is not that of an explanation but that of a statement of fact.'

After all, categories such as truth or falsity and even concepts like false consciousness do not apply well to myth, since myth can hardly be assessed according to principles of justified belief. Most people today would probably agree that there is no evidence for the existence of a 'real' person named Prometheus, let alone for the existence of Zeus. Nevertheless, acknowledging the powerful message of progress and mastery that is conveyed by the Promethean myth, to take just one example, shows that myth has a very distinct way of entering the sphere of the political, notably by presenting ideology as a natural condition of the world at large.

Of course, such a structuralist reading of myth and ideology has its own difficulties. Understanding myth and ideology as being largely equivalent in their meaning and omnipresence in both the structures of society as well as

---

[4]   Such a definition does not imply a desire for conceptual closure. My intention is to illustrate how western-centric (in this case, structuralist) and decolonial expositions of the relation between myth and ideology differ from each other. There are also a number of conceptual approaches to both ideology and mythology that must remain unexplored at this point, including those by Friedrich Nietzsche, Karl Marx, C. G. Jung, Mircea Eliade, Joseph Campbell, Karl Mannheim, Claude Lévi-Strauss, Enrique Dussel, and Theodor W. Adorno.

the unconscious structures of the human psyche makes it very challenging for many theoreticians of ideology to legitimise their own epistemic privilege, especially while advocating for social change. A possible solution to this predicament may be found in decolonial scholarship. Here, the push for 'neutral' or non-mythical forms of expression that drive the western-centric structuralist approach appears to be much less salient. Instead of promulgating a primarily negative view of myth-as-ideology, decolonial theorists would rather see myth as a fully legitimate way of knowing and being in the world. The creative use and re-envisioning of western as well as non-western mythical material through the lens of *border thinking* plays an important role, for example, in the writing of decolonial scholars such as Gloria Anzaldúa, where myth is described as a symbolic, poetic, and spiritual language that is in constant flux and allows for the transformation and reconstruction of seemingly monolithic realities and identities (Keating 1993).

Mytho-politics, at least as I define the concept here, then refers to a critical approach which understands the ontological and epistemological neutrality claims of western modernity/coloniality as the product of a naturalising function that the concept of 'myth' allows us to decode. Such a view emphasises the openness and integrative function of mythic cosmologies, which may be used to either naturalise or transcend particular ideologies. In other words, myths are not merely political because they narrow the scope of a societal discourse by, for instance, presenting us with binary choices ('either/or'). It is often precisely their openness and suggestiveness in the sense of an ideological 'both/and' which marks them as sites for political contestation.

To further elucidate this mytho-political perspective, I now turn to one of the most prevalent ideologies of western modernity, the idea of human mastery, the anthropocentric notion of being *above* the nonhuman world. By using this example, I will attempt to illustrate that the symbolic and conceptual structures with which 'we' are trying to make sense of the current Anthropocene condition remain firmly rooted in the European mythological tradition. I am aware that an exhaustive treatment of this topic would require a book-length study, particularly if the goal is to include a nuanced inquiry about the complex origins of 'western' or European thought. Similarly, there are various western and non-western mythologies which, at least to some extent, connote a more holistic view of the interdependent web of life. These enchanting mythologies should neither be idealised nor discarded, for they are certainly influential in their propensity to shape the outcomes of societal processes — even if they are often marginalised in today's globalised cultural fabric. For the purposes of this inquiry, I will nonetheless focus on the mythical legacy of the western-centric and anthropocentric worldview that is now commonly referred to as the *human mastery of nature*.

This being said, wide consensus exists among historians that the radical elevation of the human species over the nonhuman world by means of reflexive reason and scientific self-improvement is an idea of European origin (Leiss 1994). Moreover, there seems to be fair agreement that the idea of human mastery over nature has been progressively shaped by three influential cultural currents, the first of which is arguably the intellectual and artistic tradition of ancient Greece. In his broad historical account entitled *The Beginnings of Western Science*, David C. Lindberg (2007) illustrates that the emergence of pre-Socratic natural philosophy during the sixth century BC was marked by a distinct turn from a mythical worldview toward independent inquiry and generalised scepticism. Nature came to be understood as an autonomous object which had to be comprehended through logical reasoning.

However, the gradual change that took place in Greece from the beginning of the sixth century BC was not simply a miraculous turn from *mythos* to *logos* that signalled the end of Greek mythology. Mythical thought can be found in every period of ancient Greece for which evidence exists — to the end of antiquity and into the Middle Ages (Lloyd 1979). These influential mythical tropes certainly played their part in naturalising the ideology of human mastery within western cultural imaginaries. Aristotelian, Platonic, and Stoic philosophy as well as the works of the Greek playwright Sophocles explicitly emphasised the divinity of the world, while simultaneously asserting 'the godlike rationality and hence superiority of human beings, and the rightfulness of ruling over land, vegetable and animal life' (Wybrow 1991: 129).

Western ideas of human mastery, in other words, never developed in a historical and scientific vacuum that was entirely free from mythical thought, particularly if we turn our attention toward the second mythical tradition that played a decisive role in legitimising the human dominion over nature, the Judeo-Christian religious tradition. Decreed by divine providence, 'Man' was given *dominium terrae*, the cultural mandate to rule over God's creation. Occasionally this mandate was interpreted in the sense of a paternalistic stewardship, while in other cases it was taken quite literally as a divine decree to subdue the earth and all living things.[5]

As a dominant cultural force and frame of reference for the interpretation of what I would call 'second degree' mythical thought (mythical thought that openly disavowed any intention to make a claim of absolute truth), Christianity exerted a continuous influence throughout the entire early modern

---

[5]   Notably, the mandate of *dominium terrae* has also been misused to categorise particular groups of people as less-than-human and less-than-civilised (i.e., as *primitive* and ready to be dominated).

period — a period that witnessed the scientific revolution, the colonisation of the Americas, and the emergence of capitalism and the modern nation-state. Reinforced by technological and scientific progress taking place at a hitherto unprecedented pace, mythical themes of mastery — that 'man' and spirit stand apart from nature and that human beings rightfully exercise authority over nature — slowly blended with the modern scientific and capitalist worldview. In the seventeenth century, iconic thinkers such as Francis Bacon and René Descartes set out to conquer nature by means of philosophy, science, and technology, driven by the desire to reconcile and transmute mythical, alchemical, and Christian influences under the aegis of a naturalistic and rationalistic worldview (Leiss 1994).

Particularly the Cartesian dualism between the extended physical world and the nonphysical world of thought was seen as the definitive completion of the pre-Socratic turn from mythos to logos, when myth finally became synonymous with the subjective and the irrational (Scarborough 1994). From this point onward, myths could neither serve as cosmological narratives of the universe, nor as valid allegories of nature, for they were now fully associated with the inner realm of subjective experience and not with the outer realm of the objective physical world. In the same vein, myths had to be sharply distinguished from history as well, since history could from then on only refer to objective events.

This Cartesian schism was further exacerbated by the spread of Enlightenment thought during the eighteenth century, which celebrated the power of reason and embraced a triumphalist scientism. Even though the Enlightenment was not a unified cultural expression with a single doctrine, it nevertheless gave rise to new forms of secular modernism which gradually reduced the influence of mythical and religious thinking as a dominant cultural frame of reference. Simultaneously, the Enlightenment created its own utopian paradigm of the rational and autonomous individual who imposed upon nature as well as on herself or himself the orderly totality of a universal reason. Nevertheless, the persistence of various mythical or spiritual imaginaries in our contemporary societies certainly illustrates that such a lasting demystification of life turned out to be a rather short-lived illusion.

If we consider contemporary discussions about the Anthropocene, we can easily see that the sediments of powerful mythical narratives advancing the idea of human mastery and distinguishing mind from matter, subject from object, and nature from culture can still be found in today's political debates. A number of scientists recently suggested that the Anthropocene should be seen as an opportunity and, ultimately, as a 'good' epoch in which human ingenuity and technology will provide the means to solve the critical environmental problems of our time (see, for example, Ellis 2011).

These Promethean myths of ecomodernism, synthetic biology, and geoengineering are not only fallacies of control in the light of unprecedented changes which are currently occurring in the earth's ecosystems. They are also about to be woven into a new geopolitical master narrative that is on the verge of replacing the abstract totality of a single humanity with the abstract plurality of more-than-human entanglements. Put differently, it is important to realise that *more-than-human* or *posthuman* accounts of the Anthropocene provide the discursive background for the mytho-politics of the newly proclaimed human epoch. From the contested metaphor of *Gaia*, popularised by James Lovelock as a synonym for earth system science (and recently reworked by the French philosopher and anthropologist Bruno Latour), to animistic and pantheistic currents in western environmental philosophy and non-western thought, there currently exists an intriguing interest in imagining other possible ways of relating to the world at large.[6]

Decolonial scholars nevertheless argue that such attempts at conceptualising the relations between humans and more-than-human nature(s) must pay attention to the coloniality of power, knowledge, and being, while becoming more sensitive to the vital role that myth and mythology play in articulating alternatives to hegemonic western knowledge practices. The idea of border thinking, in particular, alerts us to the limiting modes of relationality and representation that are inherent to the anthropocentric worldview, a worldview which perceives more-than-human nature primarily as an *object* (socially produced, biophysically constituted, or both).

The gradual delinking from such a limiting perspective, and the simultaneous consideration of cosmologies which see nature as an active and 'ensouled' *subject* in its own right, so it seems, must therefore appear as one of the most radical projects imaginable vis-à-vis the epistemic hierarchy of western-centric technoscience. Quite possibly, many scholars would fervently revolt against such a proposed bridging of established science/myth, rational/ primitive or fact/value divides — particularly if such an attempt is performed without a certain ironic or subjective gesture — for it conjures up vivid images of seemingly regressive elements that have been expelled from today's dominant scholarly discourses: essence, spirit, esotericism, non-modernism, non-rationalism, romanticism, totalitarianism, and so on.

And yet it is evident that the predicaments of the Anthropocene, whether they are taken to be economic, spiritual, or sociopolitical in nature, will require a

---

[6]   For a decolonial critique of the Latourian concept of 'Gaia,' see Luisetti (2015). For a panpsychist interpretation of western environmental philosophy, see Vetlesen (2015).

cultural-cognitive and affective shift in how (many) humans relate to the world they inhabit. While imagining the possibilities for new biosocial becomings, it is crucial to realise that contemporary societies are still influenced by older mythological substrata that carry with them the sediments of the 'grand narratives' of human mastery. Such deep-seated sociocultural patterns must be taken very seriously in their capacity to shape the future outcomes of Anthropocene politics. After all, the ideology of human mastery might well survive without the much-critiqued nature/culture binary and become enshrouded in new Anthropocene myths. Advanced algorithmic or biopolitical control mechanisms and the capitalist-materialistic ethos of desire, production, and consumption are certainly well attuned to the Anthropocene rhetoric of biosocial complexity, indeterminacy, interconnectedness, and plurality (Pellizzoni 2015).

By contrast, decolonial scholarship reminds us of the liberating potential and integrative function of myth and myth-making. The concept of *mytho-politics*, which I have outlined here, thus draws attention to the complex openness and suggestiveness of myth in the sense of an ideological 'both/and.' This means that, even if the role of mytho-politics in transforming imaginaries of biosocial relations is fully recognised, it is difficult to predict how the Anthropocene debate might develop in the near future. Will the discussion become more open to different views of knowing and being? Will it include marginalised perspectives which reject the objectification of nature and point toward the need for a decolonial politics of 'delinking' and 're-learning'? Or will the debate remain entrenched in western-centric and anthropocentric ideas of planetary stewardship, managerial control, and (bio-)technological fixes? Whatever the case may be, it is clear that the discussion about the Anthropocene, has already moved beyond questions of mere geological evidence. It has become a lively debate about the principles of thought, speech, and action which provide the seemingly 'natural' foundations for the idea of unlimited human mastery over the earth.

References

Anzaldúa, G. E. (1987) *Borderlands/La Frontera. The new mestiza*. San Francisco: Aunt Lute.

Barthes, R. (1991) *Mythologies*. Twenty-fifth printing. New York: Noonday Press.

Castree, N. (2015) Changing the Anthropo(s)cene: geographers, global environmental change and the politics of knowledge. *Dialogues in Human Geography* 5(3):301–16.

Césaire, A. (2000) *Discourse on colonialism*. New York: Monthly Review Press.

Crutzen, P. J. and Stoermer, E. F. (2000) The Anthropocene. *IGBP Newsletter* 41:17–18.

Crutzen, P. J. and Steffen, W. (2003) How long have we been in the Anthropocene? *Climatic Change* 61(3):251–57.

Dalby, S. (2015). Framing the Anthropocene: the Good, the Bad and the Ugly. *The Anthropocene Review* 1–19 (published online before print). Available at: doi. 10.1177/2053019615618681.

Ellis, E. (2011). The Planet of no Return: Human Resilience on an Artificial Earth. *Breakthrough Journal* 2:39–44.

Escobar, A. (2004). Beyond the Third World: Imperial Globality, Global Coloniality and Anti-Globalisation Social Movements. *Third World Quarterly* 25(1): 207–30.

Flood, C. (2002). Myth and Ideology. In: Schilbrack, K. ed. *Thinking through Myths. Philosophical Perspectives*. London and New York: Routledge. 174–90.

Future Earth. (2013). *Future Earth Initial Design: Report of the Transition Team*. Paris: International Council for Science (ICSU).

Grosfóguel, R. (2011). Decolonizing Post-Colonial Studies and Paradigms of Political Economy: Transmodernity, Decolonial Thinking, and Global Coloniality. *Transmodernity* 1(1): 1–36.

Gutiérrez Rodríguez, E. (2010). Decolonizing Postcolonial Rhetoric. In: Encarnación Gutiérrez Rodríguez, E., Boatcă, M. & Costa, S. eds. *Decolonizing European Sociology: Transdisciplinary Approaches*. Farnham: Ashgate. 49–70

Hamilton, C. and Grinevald, J. (2015). Was the Anthropocene Anticipated? *The Anthropocene Review* 2(1):59–72.

Ingold, T. and Palsson, G. (2013). *Biosocial Becomings: Integrating Social and Biological Anthropology*. Cambridge: Cambridge University Press.

Keating, A. (1993). Myth Smashers, Myth Makers: (Re)visionary Techniques in the Works of Paula Gunn Allen, Gloria Anzaldúa, and Audre Lorde. *Journal of Homosexuality* 26(2-3): 73-96.

Kohn, E. (2013). *How Forests think: Toward an Anthropology beyond the Human*. Berkeley, Los Angeles and London: University of California Press.

Leiss, W. (1994). *The Domination of Nature*. Reprint. Montreal and Kingston: McGill-Queen's University Press.

Lindberg, D. C. (2007). *The Beginnings of Western Science: the European Scientific Tradition in Philosophical, Religious, and Institutional Context, Prehistory to A.D. 1450*. Second edition. Chicago and London: University of Chicago Press.

Lloyd, G. E. R. (1979). *Magic, Reason and Experience. Studies in the Origin and development of Greek Science*. Cambridge: Cambridge University Press.

Lövbrand, E. *et al.* (2015). Who speaks for the Future of Earth? How critical Social Science can extend the Conversation on the Anthropocene. *Global Environmental Change* 32: 211–18.

Luisetti, F. (2015). Decolonizing Gaia. Or, why the Savages shall fear Bruno Latour's Political Animism. Available at: http://www.academia.edu/20084027/Decolonizing_Gaia._Or_Why_the_Savages_Shall_Fear_Bruno_Latour_s_Political_Animism

Malm, A. and Hornborg, A. (2014). The Geology of Mankind? A Critique of the Anthropocene Narrative. *The Anthropocene Review* 1(1): 62–69.

Mignolo, W. D. (2007). Delinking: the Rhetoric of Modernity, the Logic of Coloniality and the Grammar of De-coloniality. *Cultural Studies* 21(2-3): 449–514.

Mignolo, W. D. (2009). Coloniality: the Darker Side of Modernity. In: Breitwieser, S., Klinger, C. & Mignolo, W.D. eds. *Modernologies. Contemporary Artists researching Modernity and Modernism*. Barcelona: MACBA. 39–49.

Mignolo, W. D. (2011). Epistemic Disobedience and the Decolonial Option: A Manifesto. *Transmodernity* 1(2): 44–66.

Moore, J. W. (2015). Putting Nature to Work. Anthropocene, Capitalocene, and the Challenge of World-Ecology. In: Wee, C., Schönenbach, J. & Arndt, A. eds. *Supramarkt: A micro-toolkit for disobedient consumers, or how to frack the fatal forces of the Capitalocene*. Gothenburg: Irene Books. 69–117.

Pellizzoni, L. (2015). *Ontological Politics in a Disposable World: the New Mastery of Nature*. Farnham: Ashgate.

Pitman, A. J. (2005) On the Role of Geography in Earth System Science. *Geoforum* 36(2):137–48.

Quijano, A. (1992). Colonialidad y Modernidad-Racionalidad. In: Bonilla, H. (ed.) *Los conquistados. 1492 y la población indígena de las Américas*. Bogotá: Tercer Mundo Editores. 437–49.

Quijano, A. (2007). "Coloniality and Modernity/Rationality. *Cultural Studies* 21(2-3): 168–78.

Rickards, L. (2015). Critiquing, Mining and Engaging Anthropocene Science. *Dialogues in Human Geography* 5(3): 337–42.

Ruddiman, W. F. (2013). The Anthropocene. *Annual Review of Earth and Planetary Science* 41: 45–68.

Scarborough, M. (1994). *Myth and Modernity. Postcritical Reflections.* Albany, NY: SUNY Press.

Steffen, W. *et al.* (2011). The Anthropocene: Conceptual and Historical Perspectives. *Philosophical Transactions of the* Royal *Society of London A: Mathematical, Physical and Engineering Sciences* 369(1938): 842–67.

Steffen, W. *et al.* (2015). The Trajectory of the Anthropocene: The Great Acceleration. *The Anthropocene Review* 2: 81–98.

Vetlesen, A. J. (2015). *The Denial of Nature. Environmental Philosophy in the Era of Global Capitalism*. London and New York: Routledge.

Vitousek, P. *et al.* (1997). Human Domination of Earth's Ecosystems. *Science* 277(5325): 494–99.

Von Hendy, A. (2001). *The Modern Construction of Myth*. Bloomington and Indianapolis: Indiana University Press.

Williams, L., Roberts, R.A., and McIntosh, A. (2012). *Radical Human Ecology: Intercultural and Indigenous Approaches*. Farnham: Ashgate.

Wybrow, C. J. R. (1991). *The Bible*, *Baconianism, and Mastery over Nature*: *The Old Testament and its Modern Misreading*. New York: Peter Lang.

4

Colonial Animality: Constituting Canadian Settler Colonialism through the Human-Animal Relationship

AZEEZAH KANJI

Located at the juncture of critical animal studies and decolonial theory, this analysis contemplates the connections and entanglements between settler colonialism and animality in Canadian constitutional discourse. How are coloniality and anthropocentricism — and the borders they draw between humanity, infra-humanity, and non-humanity — (re)produced with and through one another in Canadian constitutional jurisprudence and discourse? The very concepts used to understand and dispute the legal status of non-human animals (property and personhood, humanity and citizenship, rights and sovereignty) are shot through with the coloniality of their genealogies (see, for example, Anghie 2007; Isin 2012). Canadian constitutional law and legal discourse — the juridical warp and woof of the settler colonial state — therefore serves as one productive site for investigating the underexplored relationship between settler colonialism and animality, and for thinking through the mutual salience of decolonial and animal liberation projects.

This intervention is particularly motivated by the dominant strand of thinking on legal protection of non-human animals, which tends to take the nation-state for granted as the natural forum for making and adjudicating law, for deliberating on the interests of various subjects and according them appropriate legal recognition. I am especially concerned by theorists working from states like Canada, who render invisible the settler colonial constitution of the legal apparatus appealed to in the name of granting rights to non-human animals. Here I focus specifically on the work of Will Kymlicka and

Sue Donaldson. As Patrick Wolfe argues, settler colonialism should be understood as a 'structure not an event' (2006: 388) — as a political formation that continues to order relationships of power, and privilege particular modes of ontology, epistemology, and legality, rather than as a completed historical episode. Once settler colonialism is conceptualized as a field of power comprising multiple, interlocking juridico-socio-political relationships between human and non-human life-forms — and once the settler colonial state's particular investment in managing animal life and death is made visible — this inattention to the colonial nature of the state in non-human animal rights theorizing is rendered deeply problematic.

I begin by situating the figure of the animal in the context of Canadian settler colonialism. I then consider how the juridical power of the settler state is exercised through jurisprudence concerning non-human animals. This analysis of how law's power in regulating the human/non-human animal relationship is implicated in sustaining settler colonialism enables critique of projects like that of Donaldson and Kymlicka — projects which advocate for animal rights within the existing structure of the settler colonial state.

The Human and its Others in Canadian Settler Colonialism

The production of the 'human' in relation to its various infra-human and non-human others has been central to the project of European colonialism (Wynter 2003; Maldonado-Torres 2014). Indeed, the structure of settler colonialism in North America has been, and continues to be, constructed and stabilized through multiple biopolitical/necropolitical logics limning the borders of the 'human,' including race, gender, sexuality, and species. These logics intertwine and intersect, so that coloniality's hierarchies of racial, gendered, and sexual difference were (and are) understood and coded through the prism of species difference, and *vice versa* (Deckha 2006; 2008; Salih 2007).

'The biopolitical and geopolitical management of people, land, flora and fauna within the "domestic" borders of the imperial nation' (Tuck and Yang 2012: 4) was accomplished through distinctions drawn between non-Europeans and Europeans, between humans and animals, and between different types of animals ('domestic' versus 'wildlife') (Deckha and Pritchard 2016). The exertion of colonial power worked to supplant Indigenous ontologies, epistemologies, and legal orders, asserting its own set of categories as natural and universal. The failure of Indigenous societies to adhere to European ways of carving up the world for subordination, exploitation, and killing — for example, by not domesticating the proper animals for agriculture, or by hunting 'wild' animals for subsistence and not sport — was cited to justify the civilising mission using violence (Anderson 2004; Huggan and Tiffin

2010; Kim 2015). In this way, European settler colonialism in North America radically reconfigured the categorization of, and relationships between, the land's life-forms, dismantling and re-assembling human-nonhuman relationships within a matrix of Eurocentric-anthropocentric-androcentric power (Belcourt 2015; Zahara and Hird 2015).

European colonial discourse located non-European others in the liminal zone between complete humanity and animality; the Indigenous peoples of the 'New World' were represented as closer to 'nature' and 'animals,' and therefore less 'rational' and more 'primitive,' than Europeans (Plumwood 1993; Elder, Wolch, and Emel, 1998; Anderson 2000; Deckha 2008). 'Rendering Indians wild beasts of the forest proved crucial,' writes Claire Jean Kim (2015, 44),

> first, to constructing an account of why English colonists and other Europeans had a right to appropriate the land, and second, to constructing an account of why they had a right to clear the Indians out, much as they killed wolves and cleared forests, in order to make way for civilization. ... They knew Indians were men but they thought them animal-like men, ... [and] they imagined them into the human-animal borderlands in ways that decisively shaped white-Indian relations into the twenty-first century.

The exclusion of Indigenous peoples from legal personhood disqualified them from exerting property rights over non-human life and land, leaving European colonizers free to claim sovereignty over what was declared to be *terra nullius* (Arneil 1996; Miller et al 2010).[1] At the same time, the ambiguous status of Indigenous peoples — not fully included in humanity, but not always and entirely *excluded* from humanity either (and consigned to absolute animality) — enabled their interpellation as subjects of the Eurocentric-anthropocentric colonial legal order (see, for example, Anghie 1996).[2] The apparent tensions

---

[1]   Although according to John Locke, Indigenous peoples *could* claim ownership over *dead* non-human animals killed by hunting, since the act of killing constituted labour sufficient for exertion of property rights: 'this Law of reason makes the Deer, that *Indian's* who hath killed it; 'tis allowed to be his goods who hath bestowed his labour upon it, though before, it was the common right of every one' (Arneil 1996, quoting Locke).

[2]   For example, Anghie (1995: 325–326) writes, '[sixteenth-century Spanish jurist Francisco de] Vitoria's characterization of the Indians as human and possessing reason is crucial to his resolution of the problem of jurisdiction. ... [I]t is precisely *because* the Indians possess reason that they are bound by *jus gentium* [the universal natural law system used to justify Spanish colonialism]. ... While appearing to promote notions of equality and reciprocity between the Indians and the Spanish, Vitoria's scheme finally endorses and legitimizes endless Spanish incursions into Indian society.'

and indeterminacies of European colonial discourse on the human and the non-human bolstered, rather than vitiated, the efficacy of colonial power by enabling its flexible exercise in the service of racial domination and territorial accumulation.

Non-Human Animals and Aboriginal Rights in Canadian Jurisprudence

The structure of anthropocentric settler colonialism is maintained in contemporary Canadian constitutional discourse recognizing 'Aboriginal rights' involving non-human animals (for example, rights to hunt and fish). 'The existing Aboriginal and treaty rights of the Aboriginal peoples of Canada,' including hunting and fishing entitlements, have been enshrined in section 35 of the Canadian Constitution since 1982; this constitutional guarantee has sometimes been interpreted by legal actors and animal rights activists as endangering or undermining the protection of non-human animals. Reading constitutional discourse through the lenses of Glen Coulthard's critique of the colonial politics of recognition, and Samera Esmeir's analysis of the colonial production of juridical humanity, elucidates how the adjudication of Aboriginal rights to hunt and fish within the Canadian legal order entrenches the structure of settler colonialism.

In *Red Skin, White Masks: Rejecting the Colonial Politics of Recognition*, Coulthard (2014: 3) argues that

> instead of ushering in an era of peaceful coexistence grounded on the ideal of *reciprocity* or *mutual* recognition, the politics of recognition in its contemporary liberal form promises to reproduce the very configurations of colonialist, racist, patriarchal state power that Indigenous peoples' demands for recognition have historically sought to transcend.

In *Juridical Humanity: A Colonial History*, Esmeir (2012) likewise considers how colonial power has operated through selective processes of legal recognition, rather than simple exclusion, of the humanity of the colonized. Non-human animals featured significantly in the colonial production of human subjects. For British colonial authorities in nineteenth and twentieth-century Egypt (the site of Esmeir's study), the purportedly inhumane treatment of animals was one (more) sign of the colonized's inferior humanity, requiring remediation by the humanizing effect of legal reforms. 'Humane reforms for preventing cruelty to animals reveal the extent to which nonhumans marked the humanity of Egyptians ... Nonhuman animals were not the other of the human; rather, their presence facilitated the cultivation of the particular colonial humanity of the Egyptians' (ibid.: 132). Esmeir shows how the imperative of establishing properly humane relationships between humans and animals — which did not preclude all violence, but only non-instrumental cruelty (ibid.:130) — rationalized the assertion of European juridical power over both human and non-human subjects, tethering both to the colonial state.

The Supreme Court of Canada's contemporary Section 35 jurisprudence reproduces the settler colonial polity's 'configurations of ... state power' in several inter-connected ways (regardless of the success or failure of the rights claim in question in any particular case). First, the process of adjudicating Aboriginal rights in Canadian courts consolidates the authority of a judicial system predicated on the erasure of Indigenous legal and social orders. 'In Canada, the state's claims to jurisdiction over Indigenous lands assume the authority to inaugurate law where law already exists,' observes Shiri Pasternak (2014: 160). '[T]o engage in the question of what it means to decolonize law, we must ask by what authority a law has the authority to be invoked and to govern' (ibid.). While the Supreme Court has officially repudiated the colonial doctrine of *terra nullius*[3] — and acknowledges that Aboriginal rights derive from 'the fact that aboriginals lived on the land in distinctive societies, with their own practices, traditions and cultures'[4] — it continues to implicitly rely on the idea of *terra nullius* in the absence of any alternative foundation for the establishment of Canadian sovereignty (Borrows 1999; 2012; 2015; Asch 2002).

In *R v Van der Peet* (1996, para. 31), a seminal case involving Aboriginal fishing rights, the Court held that the purpose of Aboriginal rights jurisprudence was to 'reconcile[e] the pre-existence of aboriginal societies with the sovereignty of the Crown'; the unquestioning acceptance of the legitimacy of Crown sovereignty precludes critical engagement with the colonialism that is its condition of possibility. While Aboriginal rights must be proven, the state's authority to adjudicate those rights is taken as given. But as Kanien'kehaka philosopher Taiaiake Alfred (1999: 57) asks:

> To what extent does that state-regulated 'right' to food-fish represent justice for people who have been fishing on their rivers and seas since time began? ... To frame the struggle to achieve justice in terms of indigenous 'claims' against the state is implicitly to accept the fiction of state sovereignty.

Second, the legal recognition of discrete practices as Aboriginal rights dislocates activities like hunting and fishing from holistic Indigenous

---

[3]   *R v Tsilhqot'in Nation v British Columbia* [2014] SCJ No 44.
[4]   *R v Van der Peet*, [1996] SCJ No 77.

ontologies and epistemologies, instead insinuating them within the human-animal metaphysics and biopolitics of the colonial state. While the Supreme Court of Canada has defined Aboriginal rights as 'practice[s], custom[s], or tradition[s] integral to the distinctive culture of the aboriginal group claiming the right,'[5] the process of adjudication and recognition tends to pluck isolated practices, customs, and traditions from the 'cultural' fabric that imbues them with meaning. Indeed, the Supreme Court has insisted that Aboriginal rights must be 'framed in terms cognizable to the Canadian legal and constitutional structure'[6] — within which animals have the status of 'property' rather than 'persons' (Bisgould and Sankoff 2015: 115; Sankoff, Black, and Sykes 2015: 4). The absence of a complementary Court-issued requirement that the Canadian 'legal and constitutional structure' should be rendered 'cognizable' in Indigenous terms reinforces the supremacy of the settler legal *nomos*. In this largely unidirectional translation exercise, Indigenous understandings of the intricate webs of relationships linking human people and non-human people, including animals, are displaced by Canadian law's abstract, liberal framework of human persons' 'rights' over non-human animal 'property' (Bryan 2000; Metallic and Monture-Angus 2002; MacIntosh 2015). In the case of the 'wildlife' being fished or hunted, ownership effectively lies with the state before capture (Asch 1989). Thus, the recognition of Aboriginal rights with respect to the legal category of 'wildlife' reaffirms the settler colonial state's underlying entitlement to property rights over 'nature.'

This ontological and epistemological displacement entrenches the 'superior positivity' (Chakrabarty 2000: 83) of Euro-Canadian beliefs and practices as capturing the 'objective truth' about humans, animals, and the relationship between them. Within this universalized framework, Indigenous hunting practices are vulnerable to being labelled 'cruel' and a potential abuse of 'animal welfare' or 'animal rights' (see, for example, Deckha 2007; Kymlicka and Donaldson 2014; 2015), marginalizing Indigenous perspectives which do not consider killing to be necessarily incompatible with appreciation of non-human animals' personhood (Nadasdy 2007; 2011; Brighten 2011; Gombay 2014). In the staged contest between Aboriginal rights and animal rights, Canadian law is taken for granted as the arbiter between the two (Kymlicka and Donaldson 2014; 2015). This naturalizes both the liberal ontology of rights, as well as the settler colonial state as the neutral site for recognition of rights and mediation between apparently competing interests.

Third, Aboriginal hunting and fishing rights, like all Aboriginal rights, are susceptible to significant limitation by the regulatory activity of the Canadian state. In the landmark case of *Delgamuukw v British Columbia*, the Supreme

---

[5]   *R v NTC Smokehouse LTD,* [1996] SCJ No 78.

[6]   *Van der Peet,* [1996] 2 SCR 507 at para 49.

Court held that 'the development of agriculture, forestry, mining, and hydroelectric power, general economic development ..., protection of the environment or endangered species, the building of infrastructure and the settlement of foreign populations to support those aims' could all qualify as legitimate governmental purposes for infringement of Aboriginal rights (para. 165). Aboriginal rights are excised from the structures of regulation and limitation internal to Indigenous legal orders (Borrows 1997). Their exercise is instead delimited by the technological rationality of the settler state's exploitation, management, and conservation of 'its' wildlife and natural resources (Willems-Braun 1997; Schneider 2013). The Court's assurance that infringement for the sake of conservation is in fact 'consistent with aboriginal beliefs and practices'[7] disguises the coloniality of the assertion of Canadian state power by professing its compatibility with Indigenous world-views. Conversely, Indigenous peoples are depicted as potential traitors to their own ecological values (Nadasdy 2005), making the settler colonial state's efforts to protect 'the environment or endangered species' from over-zealous and exploitative exercise of Aboriginal rights ostensibly necessary.

In Canadian constitutional discourse on Aboriginal rights, settler colonialism is perpetuated through (mis)recognition of Indigenous peoples as potentially inhumane and irresponsible subjects of law, and animals as non-human objects of law — a formulation that reasserts Canadian law's sovereignty over Indigenous and animal others. The juridification of the relationship between Indigenous humans and non-human animals binds both to the settler colonial state. And the ambiguity of the status of Indigenous peoples and non-human animals from the perspective of Canadian law — the projection of both into liminal spaces at the borders of law's categories — facilitates the flexible imposition of colonial juridical power over the malleable field of the human/non-human. Indigenous peoples are (now) legal persons, but their full humanity is made suspect by virtue of their 'inhumane' practices with respect to animals; non-human animals are legal property, but like humans they are also sentient and capable of suffering from 'inhumane' treatment. Appeals to Canadian law — whether to grant humans rights over non-human animal property, or to limit the enjoyment of these rights to protect non-human animals from the threat of the inhumane — buttress the settler state's claims to a juridical monopoly.

The Colonial Zoopolis

Theoretical efforts to fundamentally re-constitute the relationship between human and non-human animals — represented as radically transformative visions of justice — may also replicate settler colonial logics, relationships,

---
[7]   *R v Sparrow,* [1990] SCJ No 49 at para 74.

and political structures. *Zoopolis: A Political Theory of Animal Rights*, by Canadian academics Sue Donaldson and Will Kymlicka (2011), serves as an illuminating example. In *Zoopolis*, Donaldson and Kymlicka imagine domestic animals as citizens of human polities, feral animals as denizens, and wild animals as fellow sovereigns. Human multicultural citizenship (of which Kymlicka is a leading theorist[8]) and Indigenous sovereignty are used as analogues for their zoopolitical theory. The limitations of liberal multiculturalism's colonial horizons (Alfred and Corntassel 2005) are reinscribed in the extension of the theory to recognize non-human animals, circumscribing its liberating potential and foreclosing possible decolonial futures.

By representing the human-animal hierarchical binary as a virtually universal problematic[9] requiring rectification through zoopolitical theorization, Kymlicka and Donaldson participate in the 'reproduc[tion of] colonial ways of knowing and being by enacting universalizing claims and, consequently, further subordinating other ontologies' (Sundberg 2014: 34). While the zoopolis is described as being compatible in many respects with Indigenous perspectives on human-animal relationships, these perspectives are not seriously engaged or drawn upon as intellectual and ethical traditions. Instead, the principal philosophical interlocutors and foundations for Donaldson and Kymlicka are Euro-American thinkers and theories.[10] Indigenous cosmologies are, in the end, subjugated to non-Indigenous interpretations of what justice for animals requires. For example, the assertion that human hunting of non-humans should be absolutely impermissible in Rawlsian 'circumstances of justice' (Donaldson and Kymlicka 2011: 41) universalizes the particular (liberal animal rights) juridico-moral framework in which hunting is inevitably a violation of the 'right' to life (ibid.: 44–45). Indigenous hunting practices are implicitly demeaned as regrettable concessions to the non-ideal 'circumstances of injustice' within which Indigenous societies have lived (ibid.: 47), rather than expressions of conceptualizations of justice built on other-than-European foundations.

---

[8] Kymlicka's extensive writings on multiculturalism include *Multicultural Citizenship: A Liberal Theory of Minority Rights* (1995), *Politics in the Vernacular: Nationalism, Multiculturalism, and Citizenship* (2001), and *Multicultural Odysseys: Navigating the New International Politics of Diversity* (2007).

[9] See, for example, Kymlicka and Donaldson (2011: 5): 'Western (and most non-Western) cultures have for centuries operated on the premise that animals are lower than humans on some cosmic moral hierarchy, and that humans therefore have the right to use animals for their purposes. This idea is found in most of the world's religions, and is embedded in many of our day-to-day rituals and practices.'

[10] The Euro-American location of these thinkers and theories is never explicitly identified, perpetuating the projection of Western philosophizing as universal and untethered to the particularities of the time and place of its articulation (Dabashi 2015).

Moreover, the particular zoopolitical model proposed by Donaldson and Kymlicka reinforces anthropocentric settler colonial state power through the incorporation of non-human animals within its political structure — just as White supremacist settler colonial state power may be reinforced through multiculturalist incorporation of non-European human others (see, Hage 2000; Lawrence and Dua 2005; Thobani 2007). The enduring anthropocentricism of the Donaldson-Kymlicka zoopolis is evident in their more concrete explanations of how such a mixed human-animal political community would function. For instance, humans are expected to retain paternalistic prerogatives to control the sex and reproduction of domesticated animals;[11] human surveillance of non-human animal citizens is recommended to prevent them from eating one another;[12] and non-human political participation is envisioned as occurring primarily, if not entirely, through human mediation and proxy representation (ibid.: 152–154, 209).

While notions of citizenship and sovereignty are *adapted* for non-human animal subjects, these concepts still privilege Eurocentric, human modes of political subjectivity and organization as normative. 'The mythology of the state is hegemonic,' Taiaiake Alfred (1999: 57–58) argues,

> and the struggle for justice would be better served by undermining the myth of state sovereignty than by carving out a small and dependent space for indigenous peoples within it. … The unquestioned acceptance of sovereignty as the framework for politics today reflects the triumph of a particular set of ideas over others — and is no more natural to the world than any other man-made object.

Kymlicka and Donaldson cite Alfred's objection to the concept of sovereignty, but peremptorily dismiss it without argument (see, Donaldson and Kymlicka 2011: 172). Instead, the territorial nation-state (with its associated array of

---

[11] See Donaldson and Kymlicka (2011: 146–147): 'Where animals do not or cannot self-regulate their reproduction … imposing some limits on their reproduction is, we believe, a reasonable element in a larger scheme of cooperation. … There are many relatively non-invasive ways in which we can control the reproductive rates of domesticated animals — birth control vaccines, temporary physical separation, non-fertilization of chicken eggs, etc.'

[12] See Donaldson and Kymlicka (2011: 149–150): 'Dog and cat members of mixed human-animal society do not have a right to food that involves the killing of other animals … Cat companions are part of our community, and this means that insofar as we are able, we need to limit their ability to inflict violence on other animals — just as we would inhibit our children from doing so. In other words, part of our responsibility as members of a mixed human-animal society is to impose regulation on members who are unable to self-regulate when it comes to respecting the basic liberties of others.'

institutions, like citizenship) is projected as the universal framework for arranging political community,[13] while non-Indigenous sovereigns are centred as the primary locus for non-human animals' — as well as non-White humans' — recognition, assimilation, and protection.

For example, state criminal law in the envisaged zoopolis is expanded to safeguard non-human animals from abuse and cruelty (see, ibid., 131–133). In settler states like Canada (where Donaldson and Kymlicka are writing from), this entails further entrenchment of colonial philosophies and institutions of criminalization (Nichols 2014). The state-centric carceral post-humanism embraced in *Zoopolis* is problematically embedded within settler colonial politico-juridical formations that remain largely un-interrogated. Another revealing example is the argument that wild animals are entitled to exercise sovereignty over their own territories assumes the power of human state governments to define the borders of non-human territories, and to accord recognition to the animal communities dwelling within them as sovereign.[14] This mode of recognition is transparently anthropocentric. It also takes for granted the state's sovereign authority to allocate land to animal populations. This is a particularly problematic assumption in settler states, where sovereignty is a colonial artifact and the state's claims to territory (including the power to dispose of it) are fundamentally contested by Indigenous nations. The coloniality of this proposal is exacerbated by the suggested criterion for distribution of territory to non-humans: 'all habitats not currently settled or developed by humans should be considered sovereign animal territory' (Donaldson and Kymlicka 2011: 193), an articulation which bears ominous echoes to the standard employed to justify Indigenous dispossession of land 'insufficiently' settled and developed.

Ultimately, Kymlicka and Donaldson's treatment of racial justice (purportedly achieved through multiculturalism and recognition of Indigenous sovereignty) as a mere *analogy* for animal justice artificially positions race and species as separate systems of hierarchy. The entanglement of racial domination and species domination in sustaining settler colonialism is obscured. The result is an analysis which advocates for animal justice through inclusion of non-human species *within* the colonial structure of the settler nation-state.[15] The

---

[13] See, for example, Donaldson and Kymlicka (2011: 13): 'According to contemporary theories of citizenship, human beings are not just persons who are owed universal human rights in virtue of their personhood; they are also citizens of distinct and self-governing societies located on particular territories. That is to say, human beings have organized themselves into nation-states, each of which forms an "ethical community" in which co-citizens have special responsibilities towards each other in virtue of their co-responsibility for governing each other and their shared territory.'

[14] For this argument, see Donaldson and Kymlicka (2011: 191–196).

[15] See, for example, Donaldson and Kymlicka (2011: 73): 'In this respect, the

explicitly 'forward-looking' orientation adopted in *Zoopolis* takes the settler colonial state as a *fait accompli*, precluding any deep critique or contestation of the political formation being zoopolized. As Donaldson and Kymlicka (2011: 192–193) write,

> [f]rom the European conquest of the Americas to the Soviet colonization of the Baltic republics, the generations originally responsible for unjust colonization/settlement have given way to subsequent generations who know no other home, and have not themselves committed unjust acts of colonial occupation and conquest ... A plausible political theory of territory has to start from the facts on the ground (where people currently live, and the boundaries of existing communities and states).

Settler colonialism is imagined as an 'event' that has already happened in the past, rather than a 'structure' that is continuously and actively reconstituted in the present. For Donaldson and Kymlicka, the main source of injustice is exclusion from the political structure, not the coloniality of the structure itself; and so recognition, not decolonization, is seen as being the remedy. Coulthard's incisive indictment of the colonial politics of recognition lays bare the limitations of this approach: 'where "recognition" is conceived as something that is ultimately "granted" or "accorded" a subaltern group or entity by a dominant group or entity [this] prefigures its failure to significantly modify, let alone transcend, the breadth of power at play in colonial relationships' (Coulthard 2014: 30–31).

In *Zoopolis,* settler colonialism is solidified through the assimilation of non-human animals, while anthropocentricism is preserved through the reconfiguration of human-animal relationships within settler colonial

---

domestication of animals is like the importation of slaves from Africa, or of indentured labourers from India or China, who were brought into countries solely to provide labour, without the expectation of membership and without any right to become citizens. ... But whatever the original intent, the only legitimate response today – the only possible basis for reorganizing relationships on a just foundation – is to replace older relations of hierarchy with new relations of co-citizenship and co-membership in a shared community.' As well, see Donaldson and Kymlicka (2011: 79): 'The original process by which Africans entered America was unjust, but the remedy to that historic injustice is not to turn back the clock to a time when there were no Africans in America. Indeed, far from remedying the original injustice, seeking the extinction or expulsion of African Americans compounds the original injustice, by denying their right to membership in the American community. ... Similarly, there is no reason to assume that the remedy to the original injustice of domestication is to extinguish domesticated species. ... The remedy, rather, is to include them as members and citizens of the community.'

governmentality. This illustrates the pitfalls and perils of de-anthropocentricizing ventures that are not also decolonizing. For neither non-human nor human colonial subjects can be 'recognized' into liberation by the settler state constituted through their subjugation.

References

Alfred, T. (1999) *Peace, Power, Righteousness*. Oxford: Oxford University Press.

Alfred, T. and Corntassel, J. (2005) Being Indigenous: Resurgences Against Contemporary Colonialism. *Government & Opposition* 40(4): 597–614.

Anderson, K. (2000) 'The Beast Within': Race, Humanity, and Animality. *Environ Plan D* 18(3): 301–320.

Anderson, V. D. (2004) *Creatures of Empire*. Oxford: Oxford University Press.

Anghie, A. (1996) Francisco De Vitoria and the Colonial Origins of International Law. *Social & Legal Studies* 5(3): 321–336.

Anghie, A. (2005) *Imperialism, Sovereignty, and the Making of International Law*. Cambridge, UK: Cambridge University Press.

Arneil, B. (1996) The Wild Indian's Venison: Locke's Theory of Property And English Colonialism In America. *Political Studies* 44(1): 60–74.

Asch, M. (1989) Wildlife: Defining the Animals the Dene Hunt and the Settlement of Aboriginal Rights Claims. *Canadian Public Policy / Analyse De Politiques* 15(2): 205–219.

Asch, M. (2002) From Terra Nullius To Affirmation: Reconciling Aboriginal Rights With The Canadian Constitution. *Canadian Journal of Law and Society* 17(2): 23–39.

Belcourt, B-R. (2014). Animal Bodies, Colonial Subjects: (Re)Locating Animality in Decolonial Thought. *Societies* 5(1): 1–11.

Bisgould, L. and Sankoff, P. (2015). The Canadian Seal Hunt As Seen In Fraser's Mirror. In: Sankoff, P., Vaughan, B. & Sykes. K. eds. *Canadian Perspectives on Animals and the Law*. Toronto: Irwin Law. pp. 105-132.

Borrows, J. (1997). Frozen Rights in Canada: Constitutional Interpretation And The Trickster. *American Indian Law Review* 22(1): 37–64.

Borrows, J. (2000). Sovereignty's Alchemy: An Analysis Of Delgamuukw V British Columia. *Osgoode Hall Law Journal* 37: 537–596.

Borrows, J. (2012). (Ab)originalism And Canada's Constitution. *Supreme Court Law Review* 58: 351–397.

Borrows, J. (2015). The Durability of Terra Nullius: Tsilhqot'in Nation V British Columbia. *University Of British Columbia Law Review* 48(3): p.701.

Brighten, A. (2011). Aboriginal Peoples and the Welfare of Animal Persons: Dissolving The Bill C-10B Conflict. *Indigenous Law Journal* 10: 39–72.

Bryan, B. (2000). Property as Ontology: On Aboriginal and English Understandings of Ownership. *The Canadian Journal of Law and Jurisprudence* 13(01): 3–31.

Chakrabarty, D. (2000). *Provincializing Europe*. Princeton, N.J.: Princeton University Press.

Coulthard, G. S. (2014). *Red Skin, White Masks*. Minneapolis: University of Minnesota Press.

Dabashi, H. (2015). *Can Non-Europeans Think?* London: Zed Books.

Deckha, M. (2007). Animal Justice, Cultural Justice: A Posthumanist Response to Cultural Rights in Animals. *Journal of Animal Law and Ethics* 2: 189–229.

Deckha, M. (2008). Intersectionality and Post-Human Visions of Equality. *Wisconsin Journal of Law, Gender and Society* 23: 249–268.

Deckha, M. (2006). The Salience of Species Difference for Feminist Theory. *Hastings Women's Law Journal* 17: 1–38.

Deckha, M. and Pritchard, E. (2016). Recasting our Wild Neighbours: Contesting Legal Otherness in Urban Human-Animal Conflicts. *University of British Columbia Law Review* 49: 161–202.

Donaldson, S. and Kymlicka, W. (2011). *Zoopolis*. Oxford: Oxford University Press.

Elder, G., Wolch, J. and Emel, J. (1998). La Pratique Sauvage: Race, Place, and the Human-Animal Divide. In: Emel, J. & Wolch, J. eds. *Animal Geographies: Place, Politics, and Identity in the Nature-Culture Borderlands*. London & New York Verso. pp. 72-90.

Esmeir, S. (2012). *Juridical Humanity*. Stanford, CA: Stanford University Press.

Gombay, N. (2014). 'Poaching' – What's in a Name? Debates About Law, Property, and Protection in the Context of Settler Colonialism. *Geoforum* 55: 1–12.

Hage, G. (2000). *White Nation*. New York, NY: Routledge.

Huggan, G. and Tiffin, H. (2010). *Postcolonial Ecocriticism*. London: Routledge.

Isin, E. F. (2012). Citizenship After Orientalism: An Unfinished Project. *Citizenship Studies* 16(5-6): 563–572.

Kim, C. J. (2015). *Dangerous Crossings: Race, Species and Nature in a Multicultural Age*. Cambridge: Cambridge University Press.

Kymlicka, W. and Donaldson, S. (2014). Animal Rights, Multiculturalism, and the Left. *Journal of Social Philosophy* 45(1): 116–135.

Kymlicka, W. and Donaldson, S. (2015). Animal Rights and Aboriginal Rights. In: Sankoff, P., Vaughan, B. & Sykes. K. eds. *Canadian Perspectives on Animals and the Law*. Toronto: Irwin Law. pp. 159-186.

Lawrence, B. and Dua, E. (2005). Decolonizing Antiracism. *Social Justice* 32(4): 120–143.

MacIntosh, C. (2015). Indigenous Rights and Relations With Animals: Seeing Beyond Canadian Law. In: Sankoff, P., Vaughan, B. & Sykes. K. eds. *Canadian Perspectives on Animals and the Law*. Toronto: Irwin Law. pp. 187-208.

Maldonado-Torres, N. (2014). AAR Centennial Roundtable: Religion, Conquest, and Race in the Foundations of the Modern/Colonial World. *Journal of the American Academy Of Religion* 82(3): 636–665.

Metallic, C. and Monture-Angus, P. (2002). Domestic Laws Versus Aboriginal Visions: An Analysis Of The Delgamuukw Decision. *Borderlands* 1 (2). Available at: http://www.borderlands.net.au/vol1no2_2002/metallic_angus. html

Miller, R. J., Ruru,J., Behrendt, L. and Lindberg, T. (2010). *Discovering Indigenous Lands*. Oxford: Oxford University Press.

Nadasdy, P. (2005). Transcending the Debate Over The Ecologically Noble Indian: Indigenous Peoples And Environmentalism. *Ethnohistory* 52(2): 291-331.

Nadasdy, P. (2011). "We Don't *Harvest* Animals We *Kill* Them": Agricultural Metaphors And The Politics Of Wildlife Management In The Yukon". In: Goldman, M.J., Nadasdy, P. & Turner M.D.. eds. *Knowing Nature: Conversations at the Intersection of Political Ecology and Science Studies*. Chicago: University of Chicago Press.

Nadasdy, P. (2007). The Gift in the Animal: The Ontology of Hunting and Human-Animal Sociality. *American Ethnologist* 34(1): 25-43.

Nichols, R. (2014). The Colonialism of Incarceration. *Radical Philosophy Review* 17(2): 435-455.

Pasternak, S. (2014). Jurisdiction and Settler Colonialism: Where Do Laws Meet? *Canadian Journal of Law and Society* 29(02): 145-161.

Plumwood, V. (1993). *Feminism and The Mastery of Nature*. London: Routledge.

Salih, S. (2007). Filling Up the Space Between Mankind and Ape: Racism, Speciesism and the Androphilic Ape. *ARIEL: A Review of International English Literature* 38(1): 95-111.

Sankoff, P., Black,V. and Sykes, K. (2015). Introduction. In: Sankoff, P., Vaughan, B. & Sykes. K. eds. *Canadian Perspectives on Animals and the Law*. Toronto: Irwin Law. pp. 1-8.

Schneider, L. (2013). "There's Something in the Water": Salmon Runs and Settler Colonialism on the Columbia River. *American Indian Culture and Research Journal* 37(2): 149-164.

Sundberg, J. (2013). Decolonizing Posthumanist Geographies. *Cultural Geographies* 21(1): 33-47.

Thobani, S. (2007). *Exalted Subjects*. Toronto, Ontario: University of Toronto Press.

Tuck, E. and Yang, K. W. (2012). Decolonization Is Not A Metaphor. *Decolonization: Indigeneity, Education & Society* 1(1): 1-40.

Willems-Braun, B. (1997). Buried Epistemologies: The Politics of Nature in (Post)Colonial British Columbia. *Annals of the Association of American Geographers* 87(1): 3-31

Wolfe, P. (2006). Settler Colonialism and the Elimination of the Native. *Journal of Genocide Research* 8(4): 387-409.

Wynter, S. (2003). Unsettling the Coloniality of Being/Power/Truth/Freedom: Towards the Human, After Man, Its Overrepresentation--An Argument. *CR: The New Centennial Review* 3 (3): 257-337.

Zahara, A. RD. and Hird, M.J. (2015). Raven, Dog, Human: Inhuman Colonialism and Unsettling Cosmologies. *Environmental Humanities* 7(1): 169-190.

Cases

Delgamuukw v British Columbia, [1997] 3 SCR 1010.

R v NTC Smokehouse LTD, [1996] SCJ No 78.

R v Sparrow, [1990] SCJ No 49 at para 74.

R v Tsilhqot'in Nation v British Columbia [2014] SCJ No 44.

R v Van der Peet, [1996] SCJ No 77.

5

A Post/Decolonial Geography beyond 'the Language of the Mouth'

AMBER MURREY

In this chapter I reflect upon what was a transformative conversation during research in Nanga-Eboko, a town in central Cameroon that is located along the pathway of the Chad-Cameroon Oil Pipeline. This brief conversation, I argue, was figurative of the on-going debates about political epistemologies and knowledge making within border-ridden fossil fuel capitalism, including the ways in which, despite a rich literature that criticises extraction, researchers and scientists continue to play significant roles in providing information and validating the socio-economic agendas of oil and gas corporations. More than this, the conversation is an avenue through which we might demystify the World Bank and oil pipeline sponsorship of primary school construction along the Chad-Cameroon pipeline.

Recent criticism of the 'epistemic murk' obscuring the social worlds of oil and gas (Appel et al. 2015) emphasizes the continued need to focus on the infrastructures, structures, networks, and border making constitutive of resource extraction. More than this, the 'epistemic murk' of the global oil and gas industry is deeply political and is situated within a global coloniality of knowledge: such 'murk' is often intentionally generated and it is an important component of the dismissal of people's everyday confrontations with violences of extraction as unsubstantiated, unmeasured (often unmeasurable) and unverified by 'experts.' Oil corporations and the International Financial Institutions that often finance oil development projects actively contribute to the corporate manufacturing of uncertainties regarding the social, ecological, and political costs associated with extraction. At the same time, cleverly crafted knowledge management and marketing ventures cast oil companies as eco-friendly corporations that operate on behalf of women, Indigenous, and 'local' people.

Working from a decolonial orientation, I explore the ways in which the Chad-Cameroon oil consortium (comprised of ExxonMobil, Petronas and, until recently, Chevron) and a major financer, engineer, and proponent of the pipeline, the World Bank, embarked upon highly publicized and celebrated projects to support 'local' education though the building of schools as a mechanism of community compensation. These endeavours cast the oil pipeline as a development project. Through a decolonial orientation, I situate my intellectual and existential consciousness *against* the geopolitics of knowledge embedded within the World Bank's policies, projects, and amnesias — what I call 'the language of the mouth' (as you will see below). Despite claims that the oil pipeline would empower 'local' people through various consortium-sponsored educational initiatives, the narratives of people in the villages near Nanga-Eboko and Kribi in Cameroon reveal key insufficiencies in such claims. I focus particularly on the claim that the oil pipeline contributed in a meaningful way to educational development along the pipeline. Without subscribing to the trope of grassroots politics or 'giving voice' to subaltern perspectives (Spivak 1988), I argue for a decolonial research consciousness that is foremost attentive to the productions, circuits, policing(s), and geopolitics of knowledge within socially, culturally, and psychologically destructive forms of imperial development and extraction.

These approaches refrain from claims to authority (see Icaza, this volume) and challenge the positivist notions of objective knowledge that are central to the operating mechanisms of neoliberal projects (see interview with Mignolo, this volume), including the multiple powerful actors of the Chad-Cameroon Oil Pipeline. This is an ethos that is questioning, humble, and grounded in the respectful turn and return to the voices and stories of people. Much like Rosalba Icaza's chapter in this volume, I am interested in seeking, thinking, and experiencing a place of conscious dwelling that unsettles the privileges that are ascribed by modernist thought to myself-as-author. Here I approach knowledge as co-created through conversation and endeavour to incorporate forms of de-privileged knowledge expression, including poetry, joke-telling, and narrative.

Nanga-Eboko, Cameroon, August 2012

Seated on a wooden bench under the raffia-thatched roof of Monsieur Tené's courtyard stall, I listened as he recounted the story of the Chad-Cameroon Oil Pipeline's construction in 2000. The construction of the pipeline dispossessed his family of their ancestral mixed cacao, banana, and avocado plantation. As he spoke, a tall woman walked along the roadside nearby. He called her over to join us.

'She is my neighbour and can tell you about the pipe,' he said by way of explanation.

The woman was on her way to sell food to a group of migrant labourers employed by a Chinese road construction company nearby. An iron pot was balanced neatly atop her vivid red hat. The woman, who I would later learn was called Nadine, walked up to where we were seated and placed the pot on the bench next to Monsieur Tené. She eyed me with a mixture of curiosity and suspicion. She did not sit down.

Monsieur Tené told her that I was there 'to ask questions about the pipe.'

She replied, 'Aiikiéééééé, encore vous?'

Her words, 'you again,' were said in reference to her previous interactions with researchers working along the pipeline: the academics, journalists, non-profit employees, oil consortium representatives, and World Bank researchers who visited Nanga to conduct studies, surveys, and interviews on-and-off for the preceding decade.

Figure 1: *'La Langue De La Bouche'*

Clapping her hands together for emphasis and then rolling them outward with a graceful flick of her fingers, Nadine said, 'Nothing ever comes of the visits from researchers to Nanga village.' She succinctly concluded, 'tout ça c'est la langue de la bouche. Moi, je m'en vais vendre ma viande.' All of that is the language of the mouth. I am going to sell my meat. She resettled the pot atop her hat and walked back down the road (see Figure 1: *La Langue de La Bouche*). As she strode briskly away, she continued talking about the 'n'importe quoi' and futility of the pipeline, her hands gesticulating on words as she looked intermittently back up at us.

Nadine's expression, 'la langue de la bouche,' distinguishes between an *inactive* language of the mouth and an *active* language of movement and of the body. Her provocative monologue was a challenge against the language of inaction: the 'empty words' of politicians, professionals and, too often, academics, from whose mouths come words — or from whose fingers come pages of words — that are 'merely speculative, merely theoretical' (Hall 1974: 151) and without material effect. Within the presence of substantial contestations of global knowledge — as diverse actors negotiate to establish evidence, fact, proof, and truth — the languages and experiences offered by Nadine and those living along the pipeline are often de-legitimized and dismissed by more powerful actors (government officials and corporate entitles) as non-factual or as unsubstantiated.

In his analysis of Frantz Fanon's existential phenomenological technique, Lewis R. Gordon (1995: 45, emphasis in original) argues, 'An existential standpoint rests upon the following thesis: that the lived body is the subject of agency ... [and that] however universal the hostile structures against black presence may be, we must ... remember that all those structures are *situationally* lived by the people of flesh and blood.' In my work along the oil pipeline in Cameroon I return again and again to the '*situationally* lived' sufferings of the compound disasters of colonial violence: social, ecological, epistemic. My time of eight months living in two communities in Cameroon along the Chad-Cameroon Oil Pipeline, Nanga-Eboko and Kribi, brought me face-to-face with tangible, lived politics of knowledge among vulnerable and resisting people who have experienced long-term systemic and colonial violence(s), including land dispossession, displacement in-place (through socio-ecological destructions, see Murrey 2015a) and consequent cognitive violence(s) (see Figure 2).

Figure 2: *'L'e Cri Vain'*

My commitment to post-/decolonial praxis is centred upon the concurrent need to (i) critique the colonial geopolitics of knowledge that sustains the 'coloniality of power' as well as to (ii) '"learn … from" those who are living in and thinking from colonial and postcolonial legacies' (Mignolo 2000: 5). Herein, I offer reflections on complexities characteristic of the pursuit of decolonial ethics while seeking knowledge on the ground, during exchanges with people.[1] A range of intellectual efforts have sought to 'decolonise knowledge' and yet many times such efforts are made with little specification of the exact processes crucial for the decolonisation of the knowledge regimes at the centre of the (post)colonial global order (Shilliam 2014). Addressing Nadine's critique, I draw from heterogeneous post-/decolonial thought to outline a holistic decolonial ethos (or, an orientation) that critiques and moves toward the creation of epistemes against la langue de la bouche. I understand my efforts as part of a larger collective energy to decolonise knowledge and think at the borders (Anzaldúa 1999), or what Walter Mignolo (2000: 5) describes as 'creating a locus of enunciation where different ways of knowing and individual and collective expressions mingle.'

I am inspired by the 'decolonial turn' as well as the burgeoning body of work

---

[1]   For a related decolonial analysis on the resistance potentials and limitations of epistemologies of witchcraft along the pipeline, see Murrey (2015b; 2016).

on Indigenous methodologies to elucidate an orientation that is grounded in storytelling, narrative, and sustained efforts to de-centre and de-privilege the scholar/author/self (without erasing my presence from the project). This is possible, I posit by echoing decolonial thinkers, through an attention to the scholar's place of conscious dwelling. This dwelling place, following Walter Mignolo (2000; also this volume), is metaphysical, geographical, and temporal; that is to say, it is sustained and committed through time. Rather than an exclusive focus on my positionality, the emphasis is placed on building and maintaining sustained (long-term) relationships with people where we work and a grounded ethical and political orientation that is attentive foremost to the voices and experiences of the people.

An Orientation That Pursues Life: Vivons Seulement

Decolonising ethics focuses on healing, dignifying, and advancing a community rather than a discipline. In order to break from the trajectory of colonialism and the 'coloniality of power' (Quijano 2000), these orientations firmly centre life (human, animal, plant) in the knowledge project. This distinguishes decolonial thought from conventional scholarship, where the transformation of the discipline and the making of a 'contribution to theory' is the central focus. 'On est déjà die ici au pays!'[2] Valery Ndongo, the Cameroonian comedian, joked in one of his political skits: We are already dead in this country! Again, in his satirical song, *Touche Pas Mon Manioc Avec le Mfian Owondo,* he establishes the tongue-in-cheek tone of the song in the beginning with a nonchalant, 'On va tous die ici au pays-ééé.' We will all die in this country. Against a seeming permanent presence of death is a celebration of life, conveyed through the popular Cameroonian expression, 'vivons seulement' (just live) — often said in dire or grim circumstances (see Figure 3).

---

[2]   Camfranglais vocabulary is a mix of French, English, and Indigenous Cameroonian patwas. .

Figure 3: *'On a falli die sans vivre!'*

Nurturing a scholarly consciousness attuned to people is an approach useful for navigating the entangled histories of colonialism and the imbalances of power in (post)colonial places. This approach refrains from claims to absolute authority and challenges the positivist notions of objective knowledge that are central to the operating mechanisms of neoliberal projects, such as the Chad-Cameroon Oil Pipeline. This is an orientation that is questioning, humble, and grounded in the respectful turn and return to the voices and stories of people (Chi'XapKaid 2005; Chilisa 2012; Tuhiwai Smith 2012).

The decolonising orientations articulated here are not a neatly synthesisable or formulaic set of rules intended to determine or authorise certain knowledges.[3] Instead, they arise within a contextualisation of the geopolitics of knowledge in Nanga-Eboko and Kribi. Geopolitics of knowledge refers to the ways in which knowledge and knowing are embedded in and reproduce global structures of political economy, in this case an intellectual project juxtaposed with (neo)colonial epistemic dispossession.[4] The epistemic possibilities of established social sciences are limited by their foundation within the rigid rules and regulations of 'the methodology.'[5] Inflexible and pre-

---

[3]   See Sholock (2012) on the significance of 'epistemic uncertainty.'

[4]   See Murrey (2015a; 2015b; 2015c).

[5]   For a critique of 'disciplinary decadence' in which 'becoming "right" is simply a

set methodologies preserve boundary-making and border-making within academia, wherein the delineations between academic and non-academic knowing are mapped, regulated, and policed. Particular 'methodologies' are endorsed as 'effective' means of 'producing' valid, scientific knowledge. Historically the 'methodology' has been rooted in an obscuring of the 'knower' or the researcher's subjectivities and personal engagements. Santiago Castro-Gómez (2005) calls this 'la hybris del pinto cero': the hubris of the zero-point. This hubris has been essential to academic border-making, in which an 'unbiased,' non-corporeal, scholar is presumed to be capable of universal, fact-based abstractions for scientific 'truth.' More than this, la hybris del pinto cero is a mechanism for the de-legitimisation of other ways of knowing; it functions by relegating Other knowledges (embodied, subjected, and emotional) to the margins (as lacking measurability, calculability). Along the pipeline, it is precisely this hierarchisation of knowledge that created the contexts within which complaints about the pipeline's social, economic, ecological, and other consequences were dismissed as 'lacking substance.'

Rather than a methodology, I outline an ethical and political ethos that is established on the ground, in meeting with people. This ethos is constantly and uniquely negotiated through the organic maturing of relationships within the course of knowledge-creation (not 'knowledge production') over time.

Post-/decolonial Orientations

A post-/decolonial orientation arises in response to a discomfort with the limitations of reflexive social science. The 1980s and 1990s witnessed a reflexive turn in research methodologies, as the researcher's position *vis-à-vis* the people involved in the research became a central focus of criticism. This moment produced an important body of literature identifying and critiquing notable weaknesses and biases in the scientific production of knowledge, including the racisms, sexisms, and inadequacies of such observations (hooks 1984; Minh-ha 1989; Collins 1990; Haraway 1991, 1992; Behar 1996; Rose 1997; Mountz 2010).

The reflexive turn failed, however, to bring about a wholesale transformation of *how* knowledge is co/created, made, gathered, and assessed. In some cases, the move gave rise to what Richa Nagar and Susan Geiger (2007) characterize as a 'paralyzing' reflexivity as the centrality of the author prompts self-centred reflections that lead to political inertia (see also Maxey 1999; Horner 2002; Moser 2008). This re-centring of the author reinforces the power hierarchy between 'the scholar' and 'the subject.' Furthermore, the focus on positionality is limited, I note, in the tendency to compartmentalise the

matter of applying the method correctly,' see Gordon (2011).

researcher's self-reflexivity within the methodological section of the write-up, after which there is a sort-of return to business-as-usual, as Eurocentric and/ or Western ontologies, epistemologies, and theories remain dominant frameworks and reference points (this is particularly reflected in postgraduate student training and requirements). Mignolo (2000; 2011) argues instead that scholars make explicit the conscious place from which knowledge emerges as a means to decolonise the fictitious hybris del pinto cero without (re) centring the author. This consciousness within the geopolitics of knowledge is existentially, geographically, politically, and ethically committed to decolonisation. This conscious place where we think is a geopolitical and metaphysical space.

Against La Langue de la Bouche along the Chad-Cameroon Oil Pipeline

For me, this consciousness within the geopolitics of knowledge requires first and foremost an engagement with la langue de la bouche in Cameroon, including the epistemological dispossessions effected first through missionary education and subsequently through the International Financial Institute-endorsed neo-liberalisation (taken to mean the withdrawal and minimization of the state) of education since the 1980s. La langue de la bouche — not only inactive but also repressive knowledge — in Cameroon has been enacted at multiple levels: the service of colonial knowledge to socio-political and economic control, which was intimately tied with missionary activity and the development of the sciences, including agronomy, anthropology, geography, medical, and pharmaceutical science (Leslie 2013).

In the 1700s, British Baptist missionaries settled permanently in Limbe (at the time the town was named 'Victoria') on the coast of Cameroon. By the early 1870s, American Presbyterian missionaries had established settlements at Grand Batanga, where today the Chad-Cameroon Oil Pipeline extends eleven kilometres beneath the Atlantic Ocean (in a marine pipeline) to the floating storage offloading vessel (see Figure 4).

Figure 4: *'Map of Chad-Cameroon Oil Pipeline'*

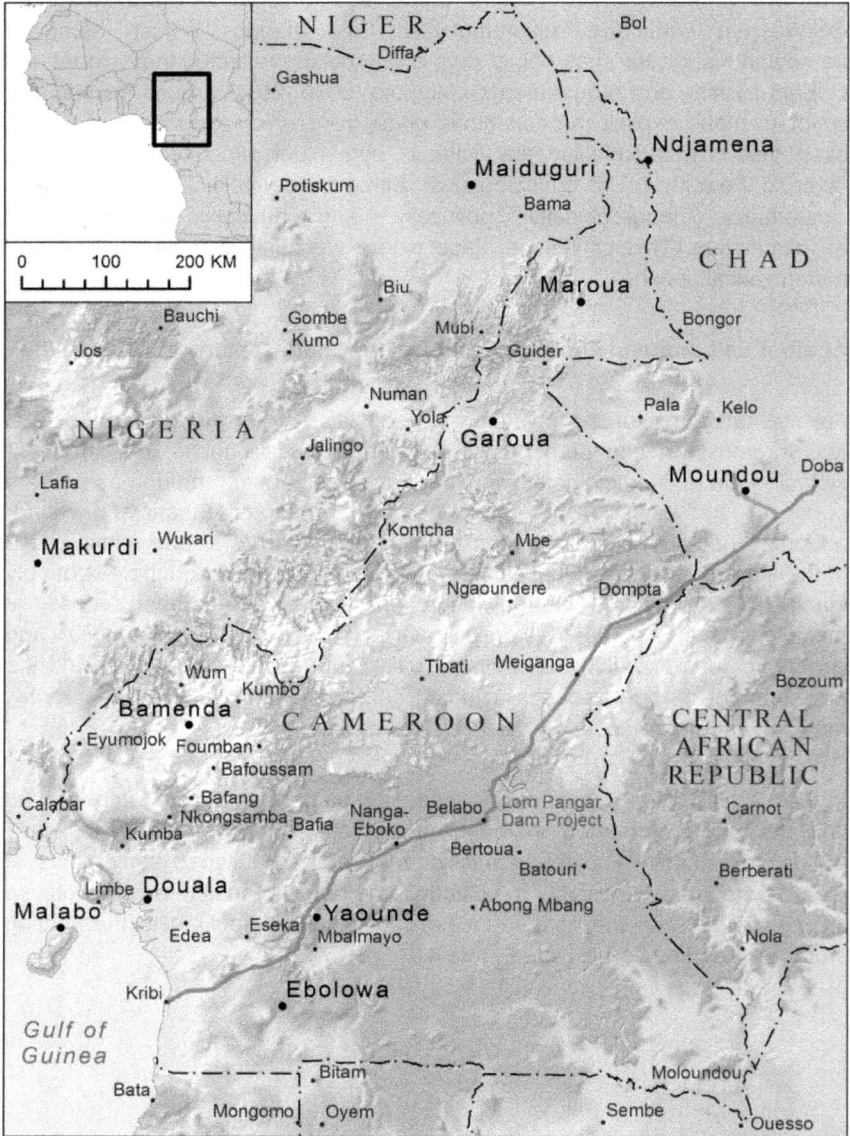

Early missionaries and charter company employees prepared the landscape (sometimes directly, other times indirectly) for colonialism. They set up permanent trading posts with guns and cannons that would facilitate the violent appropriation of resources. They also established the missionary schools that educated people in European languages and socialised pupils as human capital for brutal and often forced colonial labour (Kanu 2006). This implementation of Eurocentric, Christian-oriented, fixed-classroom instruction was unlike previous oral-based and practice-based educational styles, which focused on holistic wellness — physical, moral, emotional, spiritual — of the community and self (Diang 2013).[6] Pre-colonial educational practices centred upon family- and community-engaged learning, with mothers responsible for a child's education until age eight, after which the mother and female relatives continued teaching girl children and the father and male relatives would teach boy children. Through storytelling, legends, proverbs, riddles, and arithmetic, education consisted of fostering an awareness of the community through social engagement, respect for elders through interaction, observance of custom through practice, and respect for nature through living on the land — so that the centre of knowledge encompasses the ethical, intellectual, and physical simultaneously (Che 2008). The implementation of Christian values in missionary education — including 'forgiveness, submissiveness… patience [and the belief] that life on earth was temporary and should be a preparation for eternal life' (Diang 2013: 10) — alongside a condemnation of Indigenous world views, supplanted previous conceptualisations of community and self, effecting epistemic dispossessions on a grand scale (see Figure 5).

---

[6]   Here the focus is on the role of Christian missionaries as they were more common in the central, southern, and western regions of Cameroon and not Islamic schooling, which was more common in the northern regions. For an analysis of Islamic schooling in Cameroon, see Diang (2013).

Figure 5: *'Close your eyes to really believe'*

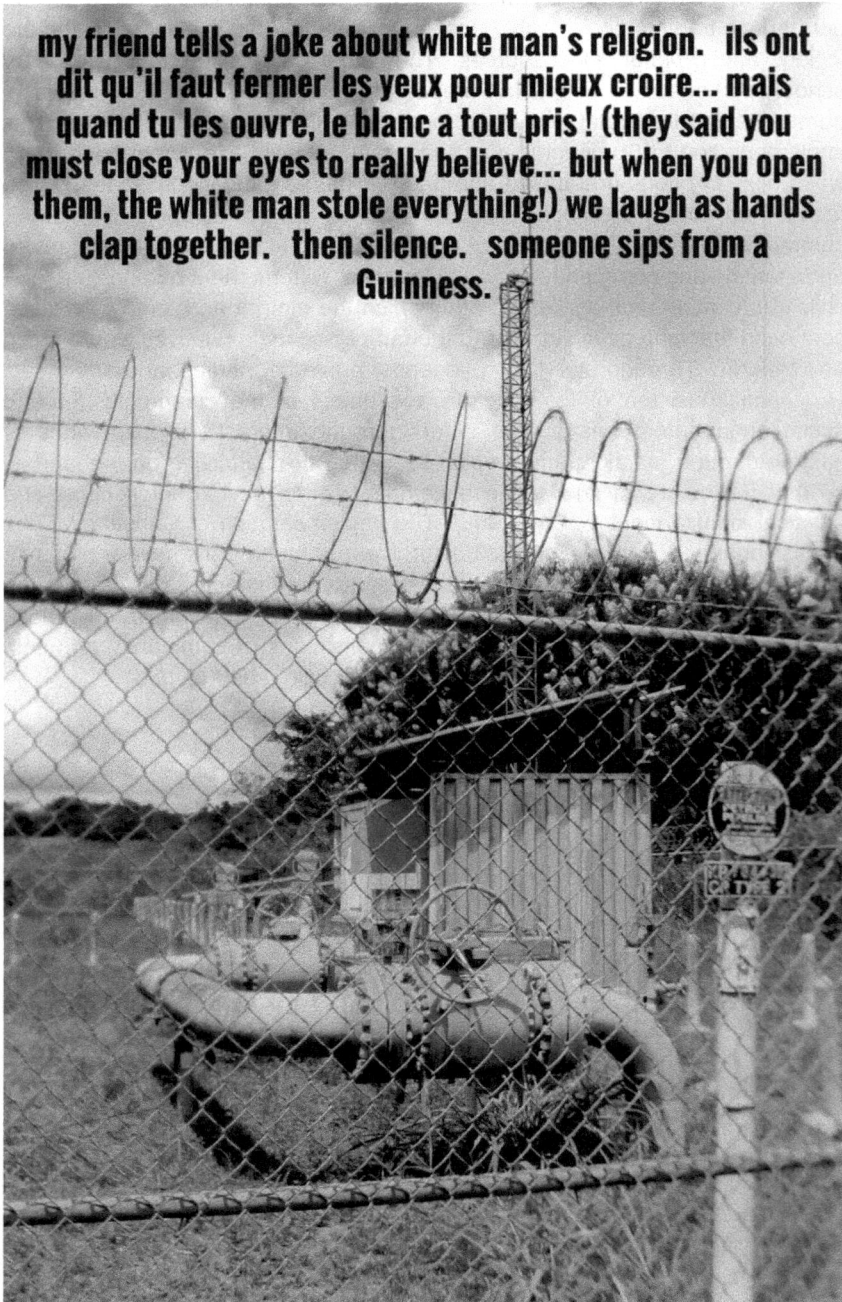

my friend tells a joke about white man's religion. ils ont dit qu'il faut fermer les yeux pour mieux croire... mais quand tu les ouvre, le blanc a tout pris ! (they said you must close your eyes to really believe... but when you open them, the white man stole everything!) we laugh as hands clap together. then silence. someone sips from a Guinness.

Nearly one hundred years later, the engineers of the Chad-Cameroon Oil Pipeline drew upon the framework of missionary ideology in positing the pipeline project as another venture in 'African development.' The multinational-corporation-as-development-instrument echoes the ways in which early European charter companies and missionaries were rhetorically presented as a continuation of 'la mission civilisatrice' (Césaire 1955). There are uncanny similarities between these charter companies, cast as quasi-humanitarian bodies in an Enlightenment epistemology of human evolution that naturalises the domination of one people over another (Mudimbe 1985) and the ethos of social corporate responsibility in today's multinationals.[7] Elizabeth Ocampo and Dean Neu (2008: 9), in *Doing Missionary Work: The World Bank and the Diffusion of Financial Practices,* argue that 'The powerful church of the colonial era has been replaced by a cadre of institutions that are equally, if not more, powerful than the church ever was.' In this newer missionary paradigm, 'the field of dissemination is not religious but economical. And the main objective is corporate globalization. These central institutions, uniquely positioned within the web of the world's major economic players, be they countries or corporations, are the World Bank, the International Monetary Fund (IMF) and the Organization for Economic Cooperation and Development (OECD)' (ibid.).

La langue de la bouche along the pipeline can be conceived of as the techno-scientific vocabulary embedded within and supporting the ideological paradigm of economic growth based on the primordiality of the market — a language that facilitates material violence and has enormously destructive consequences for the peoples, ecologies, and epistemologies subsumed within their schematic worlds. Indeed, la langue de la bouche was fundamental to the World Bank's framing of the pipeline project. In this case, the 'civilising' agenda was a 'civil-society agenda.' Central components of the consortium's developmental approach to oil exploitation in the Chad-Cameroon Oil Pipeline were its educational initiatives and apparent efforts to support educational infrastructure, almost exclusively through the construction of schoolrooms. In Chad, the World Bank's Petroleum Revenue Management Law (PRML) earmarked eighty per cent of oil revenue for public health and poverty alleviation measures, including education. In Cameroon, the consortium constructed schoolrooms as a mode of community compensation (at the individual, communal, and regional levels) and held educational campaigns on oil and pipeline safety.

In Etog-Nang village near Nanga, two brothers explained to me that the local schoolroom built by the Cameroon Oil Transportation Company (COTCO) as

---

[7]   See Ottaway (2001) for a compelling examination of such 'reluctant missionaries' in the oil industry.

a part of community reimbursement for the passage of the pipeline was never filled with benches or a chalkboard. The brothers, Elie and Joseph, explained that one of the exterior walls of the schoolroom partially collapsed during a rainstorm while the children were inside attending class. 'Fortunately,' Joseph said, 'the wall fell *out* instead of *in*.' COTCO declined to pay for building repairs and the parents collected money over a period of several months to replace the wall. During this time, children continued to attend school, as Joseph said sarcastically, 'en plein air': in the open air (see *Figure 6*).

Figure 6: *'In Kamer, they say primary school is "free"…'*

In another case, in Mpango village near Kribi, the parents, who were already working together to collect funds, initiated construction for a school building and 'then COTCO,' Sewa, the son of the chief of Mpango village outside Kribi, explained, 'came in and completed the funds.' Sewa and I had many such conversations during my time in Kribi. He earned his Bachelor's degree at the Université de Douala and returned to Kribi after graduation. With a young son to care for, he was the only young man in a group of sixteen (during a later discussion) from Mpango who was employed. In 2013, he was working as a negotiator and real estate agent.

The schoolrooms built by COTCO as community compensation were not staffed with teachers nor filled with desks, benches, chairs, chalkboards, nor books. With 'école' painted on the doors and the signs outside, these are little more than rectangular rooms: four walls and a roof. Sultan Oshimin, an artist who popularised 'le reggae Kamer,' powerfully critiques the tendency of a minimalist educational infrastructure in Cameroon, from primary school through to university. In his song, Quelle École (What School?), Oshimin sings,

Ils disent l'école primaire au Kamer c'est 'gratuit'
Les frais de l'APE sont toujours exigés
Des parents n'ont pas d'argent pour acheter des livres
...Les jeunes ont compris, ils sont tous au centre ville
Ils vendent des bonbons, ils vendent des arachides
...Babylone rigole, rigole, rigole
...Amphi 500 pour trois mille étudiants
'Université'—il y'a pas des toilettes
...Viens faire un tour du coté de SOA
Ya pas d'eau potable, pas de campus étudiants
Le premier ministère a construit ça...
Mais on dit 'école', 'école'
Mais on dit, on dit 'université'

(translated) In Kamer, they say primary school is 'free'
[Yet] PTA [Parent Teacher Association] fees are still required
Parents do not have money to buy books
...The youth understand: they're all in the city centre
They're selling candy, they're selling peanuts
  ...Babylon [i.e., the West] laughs, laughs, laughs
  ...Amphitheatre [#]500 seats 3,000 students
  'University' [they say, but] there are no toilets
  ...Come take a tour of [the University of Yaoundé] SOA
There is no drinking water, there is no student campus
The prime minister 'built' that...
But we say 'school', 'school'
But we say, we say 'university'

The song provides a critique of the hollow language or naming of 'school' and 'university,' demanding that we look beyond empty buildings at the human infrastructure of education.

More than the lack of infrastructure — books, instructors, benches, chalkboards, notebooks, writing utensils, drinking water, toilets — people's conversations revealed that there is a lack of 'real teaching' or 'relevant knowledge.' For example, in Mpango along the pipeline, Jean said, 'nearly every village between Kribi and Douala has a primary school, so why do they keep building more schoolrooms? We need technical training! We need jobs... We do not need more training in le bon français [speaking proper French].' Jean echoes Oshimin's assertion that a material classroom does not translate into education. Likewise, education does not translate into wisdom or knowledge. Nor does education translate to employment, for that matter.

I have recounted this exchange as a means of demonstrating a disconnect between a neoliberal promise of education and concrete pervasive joblessness and epistemic violence in (post)colonial Cameroon. The schoolrooms constructed by the Chad-Cameroon Oil Pipeline were quite literally empty. As I explore more elsewhere, the impetus for schoolroom construction along the oil pipeline is particularly hollowed when situated within the longer and on-going paradigm of 'knowledge management' by the World Bank in Cameroon, beginning with its shifting educational paradigms in the 1970s (Murrey 2015c). This is, in résumé, la langue de la bouche that Nadine linked my research and writing with. In this paradigm, border thinking — or creating a 'condition of possibility for constructing new loci of enunciation' (Mignolo 2000: 5) that is attentive to 'knowledge from a subaltern perspective [that is] conceived from the exterior borders of the modern/colonial world system' (ibid.: 11) — is empowering as a set of tools to advance those 'undisciplined forms of knowledge [that have been] reduced to subaltern knowledge' (ibid.: 10). But how do we ensure that this knowledge moves beyond yet another form of language of the mouth?

By Way of Conclusion

In Cameroon we tell each other that, 'on est ensemble.' 'We are together,' I say, even as we close our convivial exchange. Relationships are a basic edifice to our senses of being in the world. A relational, sustainable conception of the world is one in which, 'I am because you are.' In a decolonial orientation, relationships are central to life, research, cosmology, and ontology. Wilson (2008: 39, 80) argues that an, 'axiology of relational accountability' is central — so central that, 'we are the relationships that we hold.' A researcher's relationship(s) with the community informs the knowledge that emerges from the project. How we speak to others and are spoken to as well as how we are embraced or pushed away shape the politics, the practices, and the form(s) of our knowledge.

In the current moment of neoliberal capitalist global expansion and its concurrent manifestations of the commercialisation of land, landlessness, land grabs, displacement, displacement in-place, and place-based struggles, an ethos that returns to the ground and is grounded by human dialogue and human voice is immanently urgent (Escobar 2008). At the same time, the historic centres of global knowledge production are being continuously ruptured and displaced: 'Knowledge, like capitalism, no longer comes from one centre; it is geographically distributed' (Mignolo 2013: para. 1). The ground that we walk on, the buildings that we inhabit, the air that we breathe, the food that we eat, the people that we engage with, and the language that we speak are all ingredients that shape knowledge in particular ways. Who we are with on the ground and how we consciously politically and ethically orient our intellectual projects are all decisive in shaping social worlds, politics, and imagination.

Nurturing a political and ethical consciousness attuned to people and relationships is an approach useful for navigating the entangled histories of colonialism and the imbalances of power within the creation of knowledge. The place where we think is a geopolitical and metaphysical space; it is a place 'that has been configured by the colonial matrix of power' (Mignolo 2011: xvi). *Where* we *consciously* locate ourselves is a deliberate and mindful place-making process. Our place of dwelling is our political and ethical ethos or consciousness. It is an approach that is forever mindful of the language of the mouth.

References

Ake, C. (1979) *Social science as imperialism: the theory of political development.* Ibadan, Nigeria: Ibadan University Press.

Anzaldúa, G. (1999) *Borderlands/la frontera: the new mestiza.* San Francisco: Aunt Lute Books.

Behar, R. (1996) *The vulnerable observer: Anthropology that breaks your heart.* Boston: Beacon Press.

Castro-Gómez, S. (2005) *La hybris del punto cero: Ciencia, raza e ilustración en la Nueva Granda (1750-1816).* Bogatá: Universidad Pontificia Javeriana.

Che, Megan. (2008). Domestic and international power relations in a Cameroonian mission school system. *International Journal of Educational Development* 28(6): 640-655.

Chi'XapKaid or Pavel, M. (2005). Decolonizing through storytelling. In: Waziyatawin, A.W. and Yellow Bird, M. eds. *For indigenous eyes only: a decolonization handbook.* Santa Fe, NM: School of American Research. pp. 109-126

Chilisa, B. (2011). *Indigenous research methodologies.* London: Sage Publications, Inc.

Césaire, A. (1955). *Discourse on colonialism.* New York: Monthly Review.

Diang, M. C. (2013). Colonialism, neoliberalism, education and culture in Cameroon. *College of Education, DePaul University.* Paper 52. Available at: http://via.library.depaul.edu/soe_etd/52

Escobar, A. (2008). *Territories of difference: place, movements, life,* redes. Durham, NC: Duke University Press.

Gordon, L. R. (1995). *Fanon and the crisis of European man: an essay on philosophy and the human sciences.* London: Routledge.

Gordon, L. R. (2011). "Shifting the geography of reason in an age of disciplinary decadence." *Transmodernity* 1(2): 95-103.

Haraway, D. J. (1991). *Simians, cyborgs, and women.* London: Routledge.

Haraway, D. J. (1992). *Primate visions: gender, race, and nature in the world of modern science.* London: Verso.

Hooks, b. (1984). *Feminist theory: from margin to center.* Cambridge, MA: South End Press.

Horner, B. (2002). Critical ethnography, ethics, and work: rearticulating labor. *Journal of Advanced Composition* 22(3): 561-584.

Jackson, J. L. Jr. (2004). An ethnographic flimflam: giving gifts, doing research, and videotaping the native subject/object. *American Anthropologist* 106(1): 32-42.

Juris, J. S. and Alex Khasnabish, eds. (2013). *Insurgent encounters: transnational activism, ethnography, and the political.* Durham and London: Duke University Press.

Lassiter, L. E. and Campbell, E. (2010). What will we have ethnography do? *Qualitative Inquiry* 16(9): 757-767.

Low, S. M. and Merry, S. E.. (2010). Engaged Anthropology: Diversity and Dilemmas. *Current Anthropology* 51(2): 203-226.

Madison, S. (2012). *Critical Ethnography: Method, Ethics, and Performance.* 2nd Edition. London: Sage Publications, Inc.

Magnat, V. (2011). Conducting embodied research at the intersection of performance studies, experimental ethnography and Indigenous methodologies. *Anthropologica* 53(2): 213-227.

Maxey, I. (1999). Beyond boundaries? Activism, academia, reflexivity and research. *Area* 31(3): 199-208.

Moser, S. (2008). "Personality: a new positionality?" *Area* 40(3): 383-392.

Mountz, A. (2010). Feminist politics, immigration, and academic identities. *Gender, Place & Culture: A Journal of Feminist Geography* 9(2): 187-194.

Mignolo, W. D. (2000). *Local histories/global designs: coloniality, subaltern knowledges and border thinking*. Princeton: Princeton University Press.

Mignolo, W. D. (2011). *The darker side of Western modernity: global futures, decolonial options.* Durham and London: Duke University Press.

Minh-ha, T. T. (1989). *Woman native other*. Bloomington and Indianapolis: Indiana University Press.

Murrey, Amber. (2015a). Narratives of life and violence along the Chad-Cameroon Oil Pipeline. *Human Geography—A New Radical Journal,* 8(1): 15-39.

Murrey, A. (2015b). Invisible power, visible dispossession: the witchcraft of a subterranean pipeline. *Political Geography* 47: 64-76.

Murrey, Amber. (2015c). *Lifescapes of a pipedream: a decolonial mixtape of structural violence and resistance in two towns along the Chad-Cameroon Oil Pipeline*. PhD dissertation in Geography and the Environment, University of Oxford.

Murrey, A. (2016). Slow Dissent and the Emotional Geographies of Resistance. *The Singapore Journal of Tropical Geography* 37(2): 224-248.

Mudimbe, V.-Y. (1988). *The invention of Africa: gnosis, philosophy, and the order of knowledge*. Bloomington and Indianapolis: Indiana University Press.

Nagar, R. and Geiger, G. (2007). Reflexivity, positionality and identity in feminist fieldwork revisited. In: Tickell,A., Sheppard, E., Peck, J. & Barnes, T. eds. *Politics and practice in economic geography.* London: Sage. pp. 267-278

Rose, G. (1997). Situating knowledges: positionality, reflexivities and other tactics. *Progress in Human Geography,* 21: 305–320.

Robben, A. C. G. and Nordstrom, C. (1995). The anthropology and ethnography of violence and socio-political conflict. In: Robben, A. C. G. and Nordstrom, C. eds. *Fieldwork under fire: contemporary studies of violence and survival.* Berkeley: University of California Press. pp.1-24.

Sholock, A. (2012). Methodology of the privileged: white anti-racist feminist, systematic ignorance, and epistemic uncertainty. *Hypatia* 27(4): 701-714.

Thomas, J. (1993). *Doing critical ethnography.* Newbury Park, London and New Delhi: Sage Publications.

Tuhiwai Smith, L. (2012). *Decolonizing methodologies: research and Indigenous peoples.* 2nd Edition. London: Zed Books, Ltd.

Wilson, S. (2009). *Research is ceremony: Indigenous research methods.* Manitoba, Canada: Fernwood Publishing Co., Ltd.

Zilberg, E. (2004). Fools banished from the kingdom: remapping geographies of gang violence between America and El Salvador. *American Quarterly* 56(3): 759-779.

6

Ontologicidal Violence: Modernity/Coloniality and the Muslim Subject in International Law

PIERRE-ALEXANDRE CARDINAL

The white man wants the world; he wants it for himself alone. He finds himself predestined master of this world. He enslaves it. An acquisitive relation is established between the world and him. But there exist other values that fit only my forms.

– Frantz Fanon, *Black Skin, White Masks* (1986: 97, author's translation).

Frantz Fanon, in correspondence with Ali Shari'ati, commented on the Iranian sociologist's theology of liberation and affirmed that 'Islam has, more than all other social forces and alternative ideologies, an anticolonial capacity and anti-western character' (Fanon 2015: 543, author's translation). For both the Martinican and the Iranian, recovery from the alienation and denial of agency caused by the 'colonial matrix of power' (Quijano 1992) was through the affirmation of one's identity (Fanon 1965; 1982; Shari'ati 1979; 1981; 2011; Chatterjee 2011). Most importantly, 'identity' required, for the existentialist thinkers, a 'Self' to assert, a capacity for one to understand the world that remained, at its core, immanent, embodied, and unmoved by the alienation caused by the modernity/coloniality project. The alienation caused by this Eurocentric project sought to obliterate ontologies that did not reflect that of the Cartesian Ego (or the Heideggerian Dasein for that matter), and was given effect through the normative power of European sciences. I will argue in this inquiry that the 'ontologicidal' push of this project was given effect through the technologies and modes of operation of international law, a Eurocentric normative pattern of social/inter-social relations. The underlying claim I put forward is the ethical failure of the Eurocentric world-system.

Indeed, the 'inter-national' is only so in as much as it is through the shared and embodied experience of European colonization, and the imperial geographies through which international law was circulated in the late nineteenth century. This alienating project, Schmitt's *Nomos der Erde* (2003), imposed a singular hermeneutical scheme of reference from which to make sense of the whole world (Mignolo 2016). What international law provided was a very specific set of references from which the world could be made sense of, a singular monistic vision from which to cognate perceptions external to the subject. The problem here lies with the fact that the *Nomos der Erde* was Eurocentric; it gave meaning to the world from the perspective of the conquering, colonial European Ego (Dussel 1993; 2008). The *Nomos der Erde* is constituted when Europe constitutes itself as a more or less homogenous Ego, against an Other or Others that, in the words of Enrique Dussel is not 'dis-covered,' but rather 'covered-up' according to what Europe assumed it to be (Dussel 1993: 66). The Other(s) are then covered-up as what they are not, as what the European perceives them to be from their own scheme of reference, edified into the monolithic normative project of the *Nomos der Erde*. The project of international law, then, is rooted in a foundational *misrecognition* of the Other(s); a view that their ways of Being, of making sense of the world, are not coeval to those of the West. This project does away with the way of making sense of the world of the Other(s), emphasizing that it stands *beyond the border*, as an irrational worldview, an irrational Being because it does not follow the standards of the European episteme.

What I wish to submit is that the medium of legal Orientalism, through various international legal modes of operation and mechanisms such as the subject of this inquiry, imperial *capitulations*, has served to repress non-European forms of social organization and their superposed normative networks. Through such modes of operation, Eurocentric international law could further absorb 'savages,' the 'periphery,' the 'underdeveloped,' and the newly organized Third World states in imperial geographies. In other words, I wish to substantiate my claim that the colonial mode of operation of international law is what allowed this normative view of the world and its views as to who is and who is not a subject (and thus what is legal and illegal) to be disseminated in a way that created and reinforced the imperial geographies that gave meaning to the 'inter-national.' There would be no 'inter-national' without a normative standard, the *Nomos der Erde*, that disciplined the Other(s) into the imperial geographies of Europe, articulated around the concept of the 'state.' The way out of the geographies of Empire, I argue, was (and arguably still is) through the resurgent corpo-realities of the wretched of the earth, opposing the *nomos* of the earth, as we will see in this short essay in the case of Iran.

Firstly, I will argue that the concept of sovereignty had, in the context of the rise of the Islamicate nation-states, a modular and relative *value*, or a set of premises, that were based on Eurocentric premises. My proposition is that this specific conception of sovereign power and its afferent principles (such as, for example, the principles of secularism and later that of permanent sovereignty over natural resources, which I will not have time to explore in this piece) furthered the European modern/colonial project. This project then instituted an international legal 'common sense,' a 'hubris of point zero' (Castro-Gómez 2005), that presented the European experience as the only possible grounds for the establishment of 'equal' relations between polities, or quite literally a standard of civilization. I will finally propose that legal orientalism, the medium of this misrecognition of the Other(s), can be destabilized through the resurgence of a Muslim subjectivity.

The Exclusive Club of States

The legal field unsurprisingly reproduces the biases that stem from the epistemic privilege of modernity (Cardinal 2016). This paradigm gives effect to a 'universalization' of a Eurocentric conception of the world (Chakrabarty 2000) and, most notably in international law, the statist bias or what international relations theory has called 'methodological nationalism' (Giddens 1984; Beck 2007; Chernilo 2010; 2011; Dumitru 2014). International law thus suffers from the very specific bias that ties it to the European experience, where the conceptual apparatus of the state is etiologically located as a foundational moment of Europe (Anghie 1996; 2005; Koskenniemi 2002; Bowden 2005). This bias originates in the myth of Westphalia (Michaels 2013; De La Rasilla Del Moral 2015), which inaugurated the state as the central legal actor of modernity, the medium through which this project becomes articulated (Ruskola 2013). The primary function of international law has since been to identify 'as the supreme normative principle of the political organisation of mankind, the idea of a society of sovereign states ... by stating and elaborating this principle and by excluding alternative principles' (Bull 2002: 140). This section will flesh out how this project was given effect in the Islamicate world through specific technologies and modes of operation. My inquiry will focus on Persia in the nineteenth and twentieth centuries.

As already briefly proposed, 'international' law was a European creation that gave European authorities the epistemic privilege to decide which people stood on what side of the border of international legality. Its purpose was to define who was a subject, and who was not (the legal and the ill/legal) using epistemic criteria, or the standards, of the European Ego. The epistemic standard of modernity, the Cartesian Ego, gave a substantive blueprint of the 'rational subject' with the state becoming the extension of this ego in terms of inter-social legal subjectivity. To this effect, Judge Bedjaoui introduces his treatise on international law, by noting that,

> [b]efore the First World War there was an "exclusive club" of States which created what has been called a "European International law" or a "European public law", which broadly speaking, governed relations not only among members of the "club" but also between them and the rest of the world. If the scope of this law, which was geographically specific, had a universal character, it had nevertheless been conceived simply for the use and benefit of its founders, the states that were called "civilized" (Bedjaoui 1991: 5).

As Anghie (1996) argues, what interested the early thinkers of the discipline was not so much the issue of order among a group of states but rather that of order amongst culturally different societies, an objective of inter-cultural regulations. In other words, what Vitoria and later thinkers were interested in is the *border* that separates culturally different societies, and the rules that regulate this border. As proposed by Bedjaoui, international law imposes itself as a relational structure between the 'club,' the civilized, and its Other(s). The lands of the Islamicate world, those organized independent polities informed by, but not reducible to Islam (The Ottoman Empire and Persia) (Hodgson 1974), remained on the periphery of this select club of European nations. Their interactions with the imperial powers, however, were still informed by the European conceptions of international law.

I contend that it was the shared experience with Eurocentric 'legality,' articulated around the principle of equality amongst sovereigns, that was one of the determinants of the discipline's internationalization — the relational claim that instituted a dividing border. Equality amongst sovereigns was then not a substantively neutral ethical principle. Sovereigns had to follow a certain pattern that replicated the European experience to attain this status. This is what I claim is the Orientalist mode of operation of international law, the translation of Orientalist biases in legal variations that misrecognize and thus *create* the Orient, inscribing international law into the project of modernity/coloniality. The cannons of eighteenth and nineteenth century European sciences articulated such a bias, notably found in anthropology in the opposition between the modern and the traditional. This dichotomy opposed Western democracy and Oriental despotism, and enshrined the underlying essential opposition of the West and Islam, making the latter's 'backwardness' determined by the former. Montesquieu's *Lettres Persanes*, amongst others, substantiated claims that the despotic kingdoms of the East were in fact lands of lawlessness, creating the East as such, and thus justifying their subtraction from the privileges of a European community and therefore from sovereign equality. This binary denotes the idea that modernity, defining itself as a more advanced historical phase, happens;

> when one sheds the substantive limitation imposed by traditional values and ways of life. Substantive values limit one's access to a wider field of possibilities; the widest field of possibilities is correlated to an "empty" self, defined by its formal role of maximizing chosen satisfactions or attaining its goals with greatest efficiency (Kolb 1986: xii).

The modern/colonial project and its modes of operation are then means of creating a Self, opposed to an Other or Others that are created through the same process.

My proposition is that the Orientalist mode of operation of international law was furthered by specific legal technologies that were used specifically to discipline what Europe perceived as its lawless periphery, to make into a reality the Other(s) it created. European legal imperialism, I claim, was grounded in the usage of certain international legal documents to foment particular changes in the Islamicate world — changes that were geared to the particular experience of Europe. In this short development, I will focus primarily on the very specific legal effects produced by the *capitulations* system implemented in the lands of Persia by Russia and Great Britain. This usage of specific legal terms and forms transposed the modern/colonial project in international law, as a means to regulate relations with those polities that were not directly colonized and thus could not be directly manipulated into imperial geographies, such as Persia or the Ottoman Empire. What I am also interested in is the effect of such technologies not merely on the 'international' or external sphere, but also and most importantly the internal dimensions of the affected societies. My hypothesis is that the feeling of self-loathing of the colonized described by Fanon (1965) — what Maldonado-Torres further theorized as the 'coloniality of Being' (Maldonado-Torres 2007) as the lived experience of encounter with the imperial power — was the effect of the apparatus of legal Orientalism. Ill/legality forced on the Persian subject the full force of this feeling of self-loathing. Ill/legality is then a socio-political construction of wretchedness that could only be 'cured' by resorting to the means and methods of modernity made available by international law.

Westphalia and Secularism

Due to the importance of Islam in the East, the modern/colonial project then required the means of instituting a relationship with this reality. International law had to propose a way of *creating* the backwardness of the Eastern Others' reliance on religious knowledge, which the Westphalian birth of secularism allowed. Equating the conception of the state with the Treaty of Westphalia and its enshrinement of the principle of religious tolerance further led to an equation of state and secularism. The state and its institutions could not, after the violent religious wars that devastated Europe, be derived from religious legitimacy, nor be affiliated to any particular sectarian identity. Proto-international law shifted from a secular transcendent naturalist jurisprudence before Westphalia, to a secular positivist legal theory with thinkers such as Zouch and Gentili affirming that international legal principles were a *jus voluntarium* deriving from the consent and reason of sovereigns. Scholars from the Islamicate world have also proposed, following the Orientalist claims of Westerners, that the positivist mindset of international law originating in the post-Westphalian order distinguished it and gave it a 'universal' standing above the particular, and more traditional iterations of inter-social norms that were based in sacred narratives (Khadduri 1956; Bahar 1992). While the pre-Westphalian system theorized by Vitoria and Grotius was Eurocentric, post-Westphalia positivism would have changed the biased premises of the system to make it stem from a 'universal science.' However, the methodological frame of both jurisprudential methods, the proto-modern and Westphalian, remain the same. Both systems of jurisprudence establish a clear divide, an epistemic barrier between the two separated poles — a 'dynamic of difference' (Anghie 2005). The two poles at play in this essay are the modern European and Islamic poles; the first mode of Vitorian/Grotian jurisprudence situated the sources of natural law in the customary practices of the civilized societies of Europe, while the second Westphalian positivist jurisprudence found the norms of international law in the 'raison d'état' of states based on a secular European model. In other words, the roots of international law are, all the way down, Eurocentric in that they propose the radical otherization of the religious.

Beaulac claimed that after Westphalia the concept of sovereignty, whether an actual reality or not, became the keystone of the discipline and the means by which the organizing structural elements of Empire imposed themselves on the world. It became the central signifier according to which relations between

(European) nations were given meaning (Beaulac 2004). The national sovereign then maintains a vantage point in the translation of the project of modernity/coloniality in international law as the normative core that establishes the norms and authorities, the metanarrative structure that defines its own epistemic privilege. The state becomes the cognizing Ego from which international law is made. It is the central pole that produces meaning about the world, giving it an ethereal appearance outside of its Eurocentric geo-epistemic origin (Castro-Gómez 2005; 2007; Mignolo 2009). Westphalia and modern European sovereignty thus *created* a reality whose meaning made sense only in a world of 'sovereign equals' — that of European states. Outside of it, beyond the 'border,' was lawlessness, which needed to be disciplined into the cannons of the statist paradigm. Sovereign equality was then not an ethical premise but rather a substantive set of criteria that replicated the European experience, whose actual existence was to be 'observed.' The parameters of Westphalia then define how a particular colonial experience can be scientifically or positively observed as having attained the status of a 'universal' modernity.

This epistemic barrier, while establishing the backwardness of the Islamic ways of understanding the world and regulating it through norms, also hints at the idea that Muslims in themselves, because of their religion and their legal system, are a backward people that cannot comprehend the principles of modern international law. A French foreign agent in Istanbul wrote to the International Committee of the Red Cross in 1868, concerning the Ottoman adhesion to the 1864 Geneva Convention, that

> [o]n a, dans toute affaire, à lutter à Constantinople contre une force d'inertie dont rien ne peut donner l'idée; et il faudrait des efforts inouis pour obtenir la formation sur le papier d'un comité qui ne fonctionnerait jamais et dont les Turcs ne comprendront jamais l'utilité, eux qui ramènent tout à la Providence et n'admettent pas qu'on cherche à se soustraire à ses décrets (Boissier et al. 1978: 288).[1]

The underlying rationale of the encounter between the modern and its Islamic Other(s) is that secularism is the driving force of normative progress, of the legal possibility of civilization as the 'inertia' created by religion. The Ottoman

---

[1]   "We have, in all affairs in Constantinople, to struggle against a force of inertia that no words could accurately reflect; it would require incredible efforts to obtain, on paper, the formation of a committee that would never function, and of which the Turks would in any case never understand the utility thereof, as they refer everything back to Providence, and cannot admit that anything could be subtracted from its ordinances" (author's translation).

reliance on 'la Providence' is what holds back the people of the Islamicate world. Societies that lack secularism are contrasted with its presence in the West, and the presence of religion in the face of modern secularism is equated with the backwardness of a society.

The underlying claim of this rationale is thus that sacred narratives cannot sanction ontological claims, or a claim to legal subjectivity (for an ontological possibility in law), for they lack the epistemic criteria required by positivist jurisprudence, namely the reliance on the observation and apprehension of 'natural phenomena.' In other words, sacred narratives lie on the *wrong side of the border*. The state is the European direction of a society's existence through its ownership of land and organization of a population under a political authority derived from mankind. Religion, and more specifically Islam, cannot rely on its principle of divine vice-regency to attain a claim to sovereignty as legal subjectivity. Secularism then asserts that law and legal subjectivity cannot be derived from religious sources, for they would lack the objectivity required by science for the voicing of a claim. The Ottoman Empire and Persia, because of their reliance on an Islamic signifier and their lack of the universal civilizing value of secularism, could not be part of the 'exclusive club of states' that Bedjaoui identifies. The pernicious element of this argumentative structure is that it proposes that the only way to attain legal subjectivity is by imitation and replication of the historical experience of Europe.

Capitulations in Service of Empire

Starting with Persia's defeat to Russia in 1828, and the ensuing treaty of Peace and Commerce of Turkmanchay that sealed relations between the two nations, Persia granted Russian diplomatic representatives, in the peace dispositions, the rights of extraterritorial jurisdiction over Russian nationals in Persia (Hurewitz 1956: sec. 10). Moreover, the commercial treaty, in article II, established that contracts, bills of exchange, and bonds between Russian and Persian subjects were to be registered before both a Russian consul and a Persian *hakem* (governor). Those further legal measures also granted special courts and various commercial privileges to Russians in pursuit of legal matters, going as far as conferring Russian officials jurisdiction over Persian individuals in criminal cases in which they were incriminated (ibid.: sec. 8). Consequently, sovereign Persian authorities had no power over Russian-*protected* subjects, except in cases provided for under an agreement. The Turkmenchay model was then extended to other foreign nations — most importantly Great Britain in 1841 (ibid.) and then Belgium, Germany and France — so much so that capitulations were signed with most European powers by the end of the nineteenth century. Now, while the fairly similar capitulation texts did not provide for the establishment of mixed courts, British and Russians dignitaries forced Persia under political pressure to establish such tribunals at its own costs. At the turn of the century, the submission of Persian jurisdiction under capitulations — with legal protections accorded to foreigners and their protected individuals[2] — amounted to relegating Persia to a sort of semi-colonial status (Hershlag 1964).

Underlying this dispensation from jurisdiction is the idea that the laws of Persia were inappropriate for Europeans who lacked knowledge of them and were not Muslim. Interestingly, Western thinking limits the traction of Islamic norms and knowledge to that of a socially constructed and thus relative 'culture' or 'tradition' against the universal possibility of modern law. The famous English legal scholar John Westlake explained the logic of capitulations on the basis that the societies of Turkey and Persia were differing from those of Europe, and that 'Europeans or Americans in them form classes apart, and would not feel safe under the local administration of justice which, even were they assured of its integrity, could not have the machinery necessary for giving adequate protection' (Westlake 1894: 102). From this, the feeling of foreigners towards the laws of the Islamicate world is self-explanatory; not only are its substantive norms lacking, but the system in itself lacks in integrity and form. The lacking Islamic legal systems of the Ottoman Empire and Persia required a replication of European norms and guarantees and the establishment of a model of European governance in order to ensure the rights *of Europeans* when they lived and traded in those lands (Anghie 2006). Capitulations and the logic of extra-territoriality were then the legal technologies that allowed Europeans to legally *create* the invalidity of religious norms through legal orientalism and also rectify it. Modern law, by being interested mostly in the rights of Europeans in the lands of the Other, established in parallel a logic of colonial obliteration of the ontological legal possibility of Muslims. Indeed, because an Islamic legal subjectivity was denied the status of an ontological possibility, Muslims could only attain an equal status by accepting the standards of the Eurocentric law.

As a matter of fact, the *Mashruteh* (Constitutional) Revolution provides a case in point in the development of the ensuing variance of self-Orientalism in Persia. The land of the Qajar Shahs was the first in the Islamicate world to change its governmental system to a parliamentary democracy founded on a constitution based on the Belgian model. The adoption of a Western legal form of this importance, as a foundation of society in the last years of the Qajar era, unavoidably led to the adoption of a Western legal system to supplement it. Necessarily, this process led to the consequent eviction of

---

2   This often included Persian political actors and, in the early twentieth century, Mohammad Ali Shah Qajar himself after his ouster by the *Majlis* the Iranian parliament.

Islamic law from the fields of public law at the national and international levels. Inevitably, this new system relegated Islam, like in many other states in the region, to mere private and doctrinal concerns (Bedjaoui 1992). This new constitution then institutionalized Persia's total submission to the legal imperatives of the modern West, consecrating the lesser status of Islamic law. The *Supplementary Laws* clearly stated that the 'Supreme Ministry of Justice and the judicial tribunals are the places officially destined for the redress of public matters,' as opposed to the religious tribunal that have jurisdiction only under ecclesiastical matters (Pirnia et al. n.d.: sec. 71). It is clearly stated that political and civil matters are to be judged under the rules and tribunals provided by the Ministry of Justice (ibid.: secs. 72–73). Moreover, while it must be stated in all due fairness that articles 1 and 2 of the *Supplementary Laws* did recognize that Islam was the religion of Persia, and that all laws were to be approved by a committee of Shi'i clerics, those measures only reproduced legal Orientalist imperatives highlighted earlier. Indeed, the *Supplementary Laws* clearly established that the Islamic legal framework was to remain secondary to the new modern imports; laws adopted by the legislature did not have to be *Islamic*, but rather only had to be 'conformable' to Islam (ibid., sec. 2). The original normative framework of the legislature was then not derived from Islam, but from a purely secular vision of the state. In other words, laws could be un-Islamic, while not being *against* or *contrary* to Islamic law.

Indeed, the achievement of what was perceived as a certain level of sovereign equality required polities to accept the epistemic categories and criteria of the West, and thus to perceive their own episteme and their own Being as flawed. The Islamic 'Self' of Persia was then undermined and negated through the effects of capitulations, a legal technology that sought to replicate the legal episteme of European modernity in order to serve the interests of Empire. Extra-territorial jurisdiction explicitly enforces a system of exception as it provides for an externally imposed exception to the local legal system, and thus to its normative core, the principle of sovereign authority. It would appear from this that non-European polities were sovereign only insofar as they replicated the model of the European sovereign and only insofar as they submitted to the Eurocentric canons of modernity. Indeed, 'through the western gaze, oriental laws became essentialised, homogenised, exoticised, distanced, contrasted and made to look primitive and backward by the standards of European laws' (Tan 2013: 5–6).

Conclusion

As proposed earlier, the conception of the 'border' maintains a very symbolic role in international law, both in the sense of its 'real' field (i.e., its *conception* of reality), and in the sense of its disciplinary boundaries. Modern international law is that structure which institutes this border between the legal and the ill/legal. The epistemic privilege that modernity confers to it allows international law to define its own borders, its field of application. In other words, it determines what constitutes a subject or an object of international law, and what does not as well as which situations fall within its application and which situations do not. Modern international law, by its inception with Westphalia has, as I have argued, instituted one such border between the secular and the religious, a criteria based on an Orientalist mode of operation — i.e., a set of biased premises that *create* the wretchedness of the Other(s). This criterion then institutes a set of premises on which the norms of international law and its technologies articulate the relational structure that interacts with the border. International law then creates the border from its epistemic privilege and by doing so reproduces the Eurocentric biases at its roots in its relational structure.

As a conclusion, I would like to propose, however, that this Eurocentric international legal project is fundamentally and critically unstable (Fitzpatrick and Tuitt 2004; Pahuja 2011).Indeed, because of its reliance on a 'dynamic of difference,' a relational structure articulated around the *border* epistemic divide, it is a *critical threat* to itself (in the sense of critique), pointing to its own illogical claim to universality and rejection of the Other(s). It is also fundamentally a *critical constitutive element* of itself, in that its creation of its own borders and rejection of the Other(s) is fundamental to its reproduction. The denial of ontology and the epistemic violence that results from international law's dynamic instability is a specific character of the project of modernity/coloniality transposed in the West's incapacity and, to an extent, refusal to acknowledge or account for the specificities of the East and its normative ways of understanding the world and its agency. I claim that the instability of international law then is fundamentally based on its modern roots, and its refusal of the possible 'coevalness' (Rosa 2014: 857; see, also, Mignolo 2012) of other social existences, forms, and knowledges — a process that underlies modernity.

In short, international law is premised on a hierarchical organizing of cultures based on the centrality of the experience of Europe as the epistemic and ontological arm of the imperial project. International law is then critically unstable at its core because its own biases undermine its claims to universality (especially the democratic claims of liberal institutional international law centred on the United Nations system), a dichotomy that is however central to the reproduction and constitution of the field. Moreover, as I have proposed, this critical instability is a threat to the structure itself, pointing to its inherent deficiency, and thus how claims to 'equality in difference,' or pluriversalism, could be destructive to the inherent contradictions of the international law. As a question for further inquiry, an analysis of resurgent claims to this 'equality in difference,' such as that which my other research endeavours have found in the Islamic Revolution of Iran, could provide avenues for dismantling and rearranging the contradictions of international law. A hypothesis I would like to frame on that matter would be that the wretchedness created by modernity cannot be cured by relying on the premises of the structure that create it (international law and sovereignty), but only by not accepting (but not necessarily wholly rejecting) the Master's frame of thought. This entails a reappropriation of this modernity, an epistemic disobedience that rejects the epistemic claims of modern international law, and subverts them by enriching one's own being, an 'identité-relation' (Glissant 2009), and not in rejection, which is the frame of thought of imperial modernity. I would conclude then on the necessity for a resurgence of the Muslim Being in international law with a short quote from Sayyid Qutb's *Milestones*, which speaks to the necessity of a self-referential nature of this resurgence to avoid the ontologicidal urges of international law: 'There is no nationality for a Muslim except his creed which makes him a member of the Islamic Ummah in the abode of Islam' (Qutb 2006: 103).

References

Anghie, A. (1996) Francisco De Vitoria and the Colonial Origins of International Law. *Social & Legal Studies* 5(3) : 321–36.

Anghie, A. (2005). *Imperialism, Sovereignty, and the Making of International Law*. Cambridge: Cambridge University Press.

Anghie, A. (2006, July 1.). The Evolution of International Law: Colonial and Postcolonial Realities. *Third World Quarterly* 27(5): 739–53.

Bahar, S. (1992). Khomeinism, the Islamic Republic of Iran, and International Law: The Relevance of Islamic Political Ideology. *Harvard International Law Journal* 33 (1): 145–90.

Beaulac, S. (2004). *The Power of Language in the Making of International Law: The Word Sovereignty in Bodin and Vattel and the Myth of Westphalia*. Leiden: Martinus Nijhoff Publishers.

Becker L. A. (2014). *Mestizo International Law: A Global Intellectual History 1842-1933*. Cambridge: Cambridge University Press.

Beck, U. (2007). The Cosmopolitan Condition: Why Methodological Nationalism Fails. *Theory, Culture & Society* 24(7-8): 286–90.

Bedjaoui, M. (1991). *International Law: Achievements and Prospects*. Leiden: Martinus Nijhoff Publishers.

Bedjaoui, M. (1992). The Gulf War of 1980-1988 and the Islamic Conception of International Law. In : Dekker, I.F., Post, H.H.G. & Nederlands Instituut voor Sociaal en Economisch Recht eds..*The Gulf War of 1980-1988: The Iran-Iraq War in International Legal Perspective*. Leiden: Martinus Nijhoff Publishers. 277-300.

Boissier, P., Dursnd, A., Rey-Schyrr,C., Perret, F. and Bugnion, F. (1978). *Histoire du Comité International de la Croix-Rouge*. Genève: Institut Henry-Dunant.

Bowden, B. (2005). The Colonial Origins of International Law. European Expansion and the Classical Standard of Civilization. *Journal of the History of International Law* 7(1) : 1–24.

Bull, H. (2002). *The Anarchical Society: A Study of Order in World Politics*. New York: Columbia University Press.

Cardinal, P.-A. (2016, *forthcoming*). Resistance and International Law; De-Coloniality and Pluritopic Hermeneutics. *Inter Gentes: McGill Journal of International Law & Legal Pluralism* 1 1)

Castro-Gómez, S. (2005). *La hybris del punto cero: ciencia, raza e ilustración en la Nueva Granada (1750-1816)*. Pontificia Universidad Javeriana.

Castro-Gómez, S. (2007, March 1). The Missing Chapter of Empire. *Cultural Studies* 21(2–3): 428–48.

Chakrabarty, D. (2000). *Provincializing Europe: Postcolonial Thought and Historical Difference*. Princeton: Princeton University Press.

Chatterjee, K. (2011). *Ali Shari'ati and the Shaping of Political Islam in Iran*. New York: Palgrave Macmillan.

Chernilo, D. (2010). Methodological Nationalism and the Domestic Analogy: Classical Resources for Their Critique. *Cambridge Review of International Affairs* 23(1): 87–106.

Chernilo, D. (2011, August 1.). The Critique of Methodological Nationalism: Theory and History. *Thesis Eleven* 106(1): 98–117.

De La Rasilla Del Moral, I. (2015). The Shifting Origins of International Law. *Leiden Journal of International Law* 28(3): 419–40.

Dumitru, S. (2014). Qu'est-ce que le nationalisme méthodologique ? Essai de typologie. *Raisons politiques* (2): 9–22.

Dussel, E. D. (1993). Eurocentrism and Modernity (Introduction to the Frankfurt Lectures). *Boundary 2* 20(3): 65–76.

Dussel, E. D. (2008). Meditaciones Anti-Cartesianas: Sobre el origen del anti-discurso filosófico de la modernidad.*Tabula Rasa : Revista de Humanidades* (9): 153.

Fanon, F. (1952) *Peau noire, masques blancs.* Paris: Editions du Seuil.

Fanon, F. (1982) *Les damnés de la terre*. Paris: F. Maspero.

Fanon, F. (2015). *Écrits sur l'aliénation et la liberté*. Khalfa, J. & and Young, R. J. C. eds.. Paris: La Découverte.

Fitzpatrick, P. and Tuitt, P. (2004). *Critical Beings: Law, Nation, and the Global Subject*. Burlington: Ashgate.

Giddens, A. (1984). *The Constitution of Society: Outline of the Theory of Structuration*. Berkeley: University of California Press.

Glissant, E. (2009). *Philosophie de la relation: poésie en étendue*. Paris: Gallimard.

Hershlag, Zvi Yehuda(1964). *Introduction to the Modern Economic History of the Middle East.* Leiden: E.J. Brill.

Hodgson, M. G. S. (1974). *The Venture of Islam: Conscience and History in a World Civilization*. Vol. 1. Chicago: University of Chicago Press,.

Hurewitz, J. C. ed. (1956). *Diplomacy in the Near and Middle East : A Documentary Record.*, Vol. I. Princeton: Van Nostrand. pp. 96-102.

Khadduri, M. (1956). Islam and the Modern Law of Nations. *The American Journal of International Law* 50(2): 358–72.

Kolb, D. (1986). *The Critique of Pure Modernity: Hegel, Heidegger, and After*. Chicago: University of Chicago Press.

Koskenniemi, M. (2002). *The Gentle Civilizer of Nations: The Rise and Fall of International Law, 1870-1960*. Cambridge: Cambridge University Press.

Maldonado-Torres, N. (2007, March 1.). On the Coloniality of Being. *Cultural Studies* 21(2–3): 240–70.

Marcelo C. R. (2014). Theories of the South: Limits and Perspectives of an Emergent Movement in Social Sciences. *Current Sociology* 62(6): 851–67.

Michaels, R. (2013). Globalization and Law: Law Beyond the State. In: Banakar, R. & Travers, T. eds. *Law and Social Theory*. Oxford: Hart Publishing. pp. 311-328.

Mignolo, W. (2009). "Epistemic Disobedience, Independent Thought and Decolonial Freedom." *Theory, Culture & Society* 26(7–8): 159–81.

Mignolo, W. (2012). *Local Histories/Global Designs: Coloniality, Subaltern Knowledges, and Border Thinking*. Princeton: Princeton University Press, 2012.

Mignolo, W. (2016). The Making and Closing of Eurocentric International Law. *Comparative Studies of South Asia, Africa and the Middle East Comparative Studies of South Asia, Africa and the Middle East* 36(1): 182–95.

Pahuja, S. (2011). *Decolonising International Law: Development, Economic Growth, and the Politics of Universality*. Cambridge: Cambridge University Press.

Pirnia, H., Pirnia, H., and Mumtaz, I. (n.d.) The Supplementary Fundamental Laws of October 7th 1907. *Foundation for Iranian Studies*. Available at : http://fis-iran.org/en/resources/legaldoc/iranconstitution.

Quijano, A. (1992). Colonialidad Y Modernidad/racionalidad. *Perú Indígena* 13(29): 11–20.

Qutb, S. (2006). *Milestones*. al-Mehri, A.B. ed.. Birmingham: Maktabah Booksellers and Publishers.

Ruskola, T. (2013). *Legal Orientalism: China, the United States, and Modern Law*. Cambridge: Harvard University Press.

Schmitt, C. (2003). *The Nomos of the Earth in the International Law of the Jus Publicum Europaeum*. Translated by G. L Ulmen. New York: Telos Press.

Shari'ati, 'A. (1979). *On the Sociology of Islam: Lectures*. Berkeley: Mizan Press.

Shari'ati, 'A. (1981). *Man and Islam*. Houston: Free Islamic Literature.

Shari'ati, 'A. (2011). *Retour a soi*. Beirut: Albouraq.

Tan, C. G.S. (2013). On Law and Orientalism. *Journal of Comparative Law* 7(2): 5–17.

Westlake, J. (1894). *Chapters on the Principles of International Law*. Cambridge: Cambridge University Press.

7

Multiculturalism at the Crossroads: Learning Beyond the West

MARC WOONS

In the Western world — i.e., Western European states and those it established through settler colonialism like Canada, the United States, Australia, and New Zealand[1] — the standard claim is that we only need to go back about forty-five years to discover multiculturalism's founding moment (Wayland 1997; Wong & Guo 2011; Bevelander and Taras 2012). Facing the growing threat of secession on the part of the French-speaking population concentrated in Québec, Canadian Prime Minister Pierre Trudeau stood in Parliament to announce official multiculturalism on 8 October 1971. He said that 'the government will support and encourage the various cultures and ethnic groups that give structure and vitality to our society. They will be encouraged to share their cultural expression and values with other Canadians and so contribute to a richer life for us all' (Trudeau 1971: 8545–8546).

Today, multicultural policies exist in nearly every Western state. While Canada continues to lead the pack in terms of greater public recognition, tolerance, and support for religious and cultural diversity among immigrants, national minorities, and Indigenous peoples,[2] only a few examples, like the treatment of immigrants and religious minorities in Denmark and Switzerland

---

[1]   Lorenzo Veracini (2011) explains the differences between standard colonialism as it took place primarily in Africa and southeast Asia and *settler* colonialism as it took place primarily in the Americas, Australia, and New Zealand.

[2]   This view of Western multiculturalism mirrors the more prominent Western definition as found, for example, in works by Will Kymlicka (1995) and Tariq Modood (2007).

or national minorities in Greece, are considered non-multicultural.[3] And while leaders like German Chancellor Angela Merkel and former British Prime Minister David Cameron have recently spoken of multiculturalism's failure (Malik 2015), multicultural policy experts argue that only a few states like the Netherlands have backtracked as others have changed little or even promoted greater multiculturalism despite the claims of various heads of government (Banting & Kymlicka 2012; Taras 2012). Populist rhetoric clearly receives more attention than the daily grind of policy development and implementation, though some signs do suggest that multiculturalist policies are not always delivering on their promises of peace, tolerance, and shared feelings of belonging. From the burning of holy sites in places like the United Kingdom, the Netherlands, and Sweden to popular gains being made by xenophobic political parties, conflict and intolerance by a growing minority persists regardless of whether one believes the solution is more multiculturalism (faulting the government or majority population) or less multiculturalism (faulting 'minorities') — or, as I will try to explore, a somewhat different multicultural approach that draws on the positive lessons that can be gained from experiences beyond the West understood as both a place and as an epistemic position (as others in this volume more explicitly discuss).

This is done with a focus on Azerbaijan, a highly diverse state with a rich, complex, and difficult history located — according to notable historian Tadeusz Świętochowski (1994) — at the 'crossroads' or (to use the predominant term found in this volume) in the borderland between Europe and Asia. In contrast to Europe's emerging scepticism, Azerbaijan is enthusiastically embracing multiculturalism and highlighting its support for religious and cultural diversity, directly and indirectly challenging Westerners to (re)consider its nature and importance. From the 2008 launch of the 'Baku Process' to declaring 2016 'The Year of Multiculturalism,' Azerbaijan's President Ilham Aliyev regularly shares his belief that Azerbaijan is 'not only a geographic bridge between East and West, but also a cultural bridge. For centuries, representatives of religions, cultures lived in peace and dignity in Azerbaijan ... Religious tolerance, multiculturalism were always present here. There was no word multiculturalism, but the ideas were always present' (Aliyev 2016). Azerbaijan, he contends, is one of the world's great centres of multiculturalism.[4]

---

[3]   For a detailed overview of how various Western states score in terms of their multicultural policies, at least according to prominent Western understandings, see Will Kymlicka's Multicultural Policy Index at http://www.queensu.ca/mcp/ (last accessed 30 August 2016).

[4]   I realize that many, particularly from the West, will argue that little should or could be learned from countries like Azerbaijan that have developed a strong reputation for corruption, control of the media, etc. Without getting mired in this difficult quandary, my simple response to this, which I later repeat to some extent, is two-fold: 1) these are

Despite having a generally negative image in the West, at least according to various Western-centric indices rating economic liberalism, corruption, democracy, and so on, Azerbaijan's foray into the wider conversation should be welcomed for two reasons, both hinted at by President Aliyev. The first is *historical*, and focuses on the ways in which a shared community's history, for better or worse, must inform a multicultural present and future. Though Western states are certainly not alone in this regard, their particularly troublesome history of imperialism and colonialism suggests they have had less than stellar records in terms of their treatment of religious-spiritual difference, national minorities, and Indigenous peoples, which goes some way in explaining why they selectively emphasize recent history as if it could be abstracted from the much longer timeline. It will be argued that failing to give history its due — i.e., recognizing even the tumultuous and divisive aspects of a collective past and taking the difficult yet crucial steps towards addressing it — explains many of Western multiculturalism's contemporary challenges. For President Aliyev's claim that 'there was no word multiculturalism, but the ideas were always present' to have meaning and force, history and the treatment of history must be closely examined for the lessons they might provide us today.

The second reason could be described as *geographical*. Though not simply tied to the more commonly associated notion of place, but drawing in some of the 'border thinking' elaborated upon by many of this volume's contributors, it suggests that much can be learned from recognizing that multiculturalism is not simply an idea from the West to be improved in the West and exported to the East; rather, we might be better served by, again echoing President Aliyev, building a 'bridge between East and West' or, to paraphrase Walter Mignolo, dwelling in the borderland between the two.

Both dimensions are important parts of any fulsome investigation covering the mutual lessons to be learned at 'the crossroads.' Though the two aspects cannot and should not be separated, this chapter's relatively short foray into the subject focuses more on the former aspect by comparing how Canada and Azerbaijan approach their histories related to their respective multicultural projects of today. The underlying aim is to challenge the perception that multiculturalism is a universal or singular set of ideas to be exported from West to East, as leading Western scholars over-emphasize.[5] Instead, I

Western standards and not universal standards so we should not be surprised that Western states/nations score dramatically higher. Second, adopting such an attitude will cause blind spots in terms of any good work that is happening in areas like multiculturalism *despite* the unique circumstances and challenges being faced by such states/nations owing to contingent factors like global history and geography.

[5]   One need not look much further than Will Kymlicka's work since he developed his prominent and widely-accepted theory of liberal multiculturalism (Kymlicka 1989; 1995).

explore the possibility that we should not simply try to promote and strengthen multiculturalism in the East or in the West, but between East and West by building bridges of tolerance and inclusion between places as well as ideas, values, cultures, and religions through learning rather than dismissive judgement.[6] In this spirit, the conclusion focuses on what Canada can learn from Azerbaijan on the relationship between multiculturalism and history despite the popular view that Canada comes across as offering more to learn in this and other areas. Indeed, it seems to me that this possibility still exists *because of* this popular view and the blind spot it creates.

Canadian Multiculturalism: Rejections of the Past

Western multiculturalism — more commonly referred to in more neutral, universal, and even authoritative terms as 'liberal multiculturalism' or simply 'multiculturalism' — tends to entrench itself by making claims *against* the past. Like many political-philosophical creeds deeply associated with modernity and the Enlightenment, it strives to free modern (European) subjects from the imperialist and colonialist sins of their forefathers by demarcating clear historical and conceptual breaks between assimilation and tolerance; genocide and inclusion; tyranny and democracy; ignorance and reason. On such an understanding, multiculturalism represents one of the

---

For instance, he has co-edited numerous books on promoting Western multiculturalism in Eastern Europe (Kymlicka & Opalski 2001), Asia (Kymlicka & He 2005), and the Middle East (Kymlicka & Pföstl 2014). This is not to suggest that Kymlicka is unaware of the challenges this presents, writing that 'Western models ... may not suit the specific historical, cultural, demographic, and geopolitical circumstances of the region. Moreover, many Asian societies have their own traditions of peaceful coexistence amongst linguistic and religious groups, often dating to precolonial times' (Kymlicka & He 2005: 1) It is, however, one thing to recognize these facts and another to give them normative weight in the wider conversations and power struggles between multicultural models.

[6]   Though I lack the space to delve into this here, I would be concerned that Western multiculturalists are not as open to non-Western ideas and models as they could and perhaps should be, choosing instead to invest their energies in supporting *liberal* multicultural models rather than promoting greater tolerance of the sort being proposed here and by others. For more on Kymlicka's limited ambivalence on this, see Ivison, Patton, and Sanders (2000: 11) who flag the danger of 'assumptions elaborated within various western anthropological, political or legal doctrines.' At some pains to distinguish himself from Kymlicka, Tariq Modood (2007: 7) highlights well the opening I wish to highlight here when he says that while 'multiculturalism presupposes the matrix of principles, institutions and political norms that are central to contemporary liberal democracies ... [it is] also a challenge to some of these norms, institutions and principles. In my view, multiculturalism could not get off the ground if one totally repudiated liberalism; but neither could it do so if liberalism marked the limits of one's politics.'

more recent developments that tries to close the curtains on the Middle Ages and realize ever-improving universal Enlightenment values of liberty, equality, and tolerance. At the same time, it also tries to cope with notable excesses of the Enlightenment that led to religious persecution to defend science, the murdering of Indigenous peoples in the name of racial superiority, and the assimilation of national minorities as part of building modern, unified nation-states. To the extent that Western multiculturalism has played a role in discrediting such acts, it should be praised as an improvement over the unprecedented bloodshed of the last two hundred years. On the other hand, all this bloodshed and its lasting legacies cannot now simply be swept under the rug as if it never happened, as if it does not have serious lingering impacts.

When Canada acts on a difficult past, it typically aims to bury it rather than express it. Consider the first of two official state apologies by Prime Minister Stephen Harper about a decade ago. In 2008, he apologized for atrocities committed in Indigenous residential schools run by the state typically in partnership with Christian organisations from the nineteenth century until the last one closed in 1996. Serious problems plagued the apology stemming from what Matt James (2013: 37) calls 'neoliberal heritage redress' whereby the state

> seek[s] actively to construct popular understandings of injustice in ways congenial to the neoliberal project of remaking the public sphere devoid of critical dissent ... singular past government acts [are] abstracted from any deeper consideration of the long-term structural and attitudinal racism that tends to give rise to historical wrongs in the first place.

Through such abstraction — the disconnection between the unjust acts and the bulk of the long-lasting consequences — the state makes things worse by trying to establish a general perception that the matter has been resolved even when the opposite is closer to the truth, particularly from the perspective of those most affected.

With this in mind, it becomes easier to understand the general conclusion, reached within Indigenous and academic communities, that the apology falls far short of atoning for the ways residential schools irreversibly disrupted, harmed, and weakened Indigenous individuals, families, and communities by forcibly separating generations of children from their parents *and* subjecting them to inhumane conditions. According to Jennifer Henderson and Pauline Wakeham (2013: 12-13), the apology occluded broader consideration of the long history of colonial genocide and its other constitutive components such as the establishment of reservations, the expropriation of land and resources, the deliberate suppression and distortion of Indigenous languages, beliefs, and cultural practices, and the disruption of kinship networks. Not to mention the present conditions of poverty, incarceration, and compromised health lived by many Aboriginal people.

Eva Mackey (2013: 54) adds, in a piece appropriately called 'The Apologizers' Apology,' that the state's apology completely overlooked 'Canada's calculated expropriation of resources and the use of cultural genocide practices as a means to hold on to those resources.' Even more shocking, Prime Minister Harper proclaimed, less than a year later at a G20 meeting in 2009, that Canada has 'no history of colonialism' (Wherry 2009). For the apology to achieve meaningful reconciliation and healing it would have to address the concerns raised by Henderson, Wakeham, and Mackey; above all it would require recognizing important aspects like Indigenous sovereignty over traditional lands. This does not necessarily or even primarily entail territorial independence, but equal partnerships among, in this case, nations sharing sovereignty over territories they inextricably co-exist upon. Unfortunately, all signs suggest that the act of apology has been used to promote not meaningful and lasting redress, but duplicity; remembering *and forgetting*, action *and inaction*. It should therefore come as no surprise that the apology has not mended the rift between Indigenous peoples and the state (see, e.g., Gray 2008). The apology has instead exposed multiculturalism's paradoxical nature in that its noble claims of unity only strive to mask or simply avoid powerful societal divisions. By refusing to accept apologies that deny aspects of historical and ongoing suffering, Indigenous peoples can only but fight to keep the possibility for meaningful redress alive against a resistant state that wants to believe that it has settled the matter once and for all.

The second example is one of partial success though it highlights similar challenges. Two years earlier, in 2006, Prime Minister Harper apologized for the discriminatory Chinese immigration head tax instituted from 1885 to 1923, which exclusively kept Chinese families from reuniting and forced many into poor working and living conditions given burdensome debts. Despite the apology, many Chinese-Canadians feel that the state resists their 'long-standing struggle to keep alive a recognition of the problematic and deeply uneasy nature of Canadian citizenship ... [that must return] again and again to difficulties in its foundations' (Cho 2013: 96). In Lili Cho's account, the apology and symbolic financial compensation, while achieving some measure of redress, are not currency to be traded for closure and moving on. The apology is instead the *beginning* of ensuring such issues remain ever-present with their full implications yet to be revealed as part of ever-changing ideas concerning shared and inclusive citizenship. As both examples show, the multicultural state instead tries to mark an *ending*[7] without recognizing that redress as rupture between the past and the present cannot occur without jeopardizing the inclusivity gained by the apology in the first place.[8] To abandon the idea of returning 'again and again,' as counterintuitive as it might seem, risks reopening wounds that have only begun healing, at least from the perspective of the wounded. To follow the analogy, returning to the trauma in an educational, respectful, and compassionate way is like continuously applying a healing balm (even if it cannot help but leave a scar), whereas doing nothing is like providing no medicine and only allows the wound to worsen.

A multicultural state that allows itself to even partially forget or intentionally misremember its racist, ethnocentric, and generally exclusive past therefore maintains or risks repeating the associated problems, i.e., leaving unchallenged the structures and perspectives that necessitated redress in the first place. Though the two apologies are not easily compared given the different circumstances and stakes involved, in large part explaining their varying (lack of) impact, both highlight the fact that victimized groups disproportionately carry the burden of fighting for inclusivity and understanding against a state that prefers to apologize, push history aside, and then quickly move on while fundamentally changing very little. Advocating what he calls 'critical' or radical' multiculturalism, Richard Day (2000: 222) seems to agree, worrying that Canadians *must* be reminded that 'Canada is in fact an Empire formed through violent conquest — though this has been kept very quiet, supported first by a fantasy of voluntary 'confederation,' and now by one of voluntary 'multiculturalism." Yet, he does not reject the idea or term of multiculturalism outright, suggesting that allowing for greater diversity — particularly in line with an openness to new and different (re)interpretations of 'those aspects of this history that have been most vigorously excluded and repressed' — will work if Canada actively 'allow[s] itself to discover that the history of Canadian diversity in fact *does* contain what is necessary for its own overcoming' (Day 2000: 223, emphasis in original). Although promoting historical sensitivity and inclusivity can be time-consuming, even perhaps risking short-term instability and uncertainty (or perhaps not), it can also

---

[7]   In 2013, Jason Kenney, who was at that time the Minister of Citizenship, Immigration, and Multiculturalism, said that redress efforts 'don't go on in perpetuity, they have an end date' (Friesen 2013).

[8]   In more concrete terms, the children of head tax victims have not received any formal recognition or compensation because they did not pay the tax themselves. This fails to recognize the fact that the tax had tremendous inter-generational impacts as many families could not easily reunify due to the hardship imposed on the immigrating parent.

promote longer-term feelings of trust, stability, and inclusion. Anything else simply sacrifices multiculturalism to meet other demands as Canada has arguably done to ensure its own nation-state-building agenda continues with minimal interference from deeper, more 'radical' multicultural claims. In this sense, one could argue that even though Canadian multiculturalism has many strengths, it is not multicultural to the extent that it rejects history, or at least the contested view of history, and the possible implications this would have on promoting greater inclusion and the sharing of power within society.

Azerbaijani Multiculturalism: Reflections of the Past?

So what can Canada and other Western states possibly learn by looking into President Aliyev's assertion that Azerbaijan indeed does positively link its multicultural present to the past? And how well does this promote multiculturalism in Azerbaijan? Azerbaijan's history can be divided into four general periods: pre-Tsarist rule (pre-1828), the Tsarist period (1828–1920), the Soviet period (1920–1991), and independence (post-1991). Also noteworthy, the short-lived independent Azerbaijan Democratic Republic from 1918 to 1920 came to represent the culmination of Azerbaijani multiculturalism's deeper historical linkages as developed particularly during the second half of the Tsarist period. Given that this chapter is neither explicitly historical nor comprehensive in nature, but examines the role of history in promoting contemporary multiculturalism, the investigation only goes back to the nineteenth century. It is during this period that most experts believe the region's identities formed largely in relation to Iran (Persia), Russia (Soviet Union), Turkey (Ottoman Empire), and increasingly the West (see Souleimanov 2012; Ismayilov 2015). Going farther back, while useful and important, is not entirely necessary for understanding history's role as the historical identities and tensions in the region — such as, but certainly not only, the conflicts between Azerbaijan and Armenia[9] — tend to reflect rather than defy this much longer history. Of greater interest is how each state in the region, and Azerbaijan in particular, deals with such conflicting ideas and identity claims. This section will suggest that Azerbaijan does particularly well *in light of* the unique and challenging circumstances it faces in terms of not just honouring its past history of inclusion, tolerance, and peace, but also in the face of difficult contemporary challenges beyond multiculturalism that certainly make matters more difficult. This allows for a more meaningful reflection in the conclusion on how this relates to the Canadian experience and what lessons can or cannot be drawn from the Azerbaijani experience. To put it more plainly, the idea is not to measure performance, especially against some set of general or universal standards however considered they may be,

---

[9]   For a concise account of the Azerbaijan-Armenia conflict's historical roots and how they relate to today, see Rasizade (2011).

but to emphasize context for the purposes of social learning rather than abstract comparison.

After a century of repeatedly trying to annex Transcaucasia, Tsarist Russia finally secured control over the region in 1828 with the Treaty of Turkmenchay demarcating the Aras River as the border with the Persian Empire — a legacy still reflected along part of Azerbaijan's southern border with Iran. With Russian imperialism came relative peace between Azerbaijan and its neighbours as many of them similarly fell under Moscow's central authority. New ideas began entering the country as Russian settlers moved to the region and economic ties with Europe increased as Azerbaijan became an early global leader in oil production during the late-nineteenth century (Najafizadeh 2012). Despite the strong presence of both Shia and Sunni Muslim populations in the country, some of whom would have preferred their political vision of Islam to prevail, Azerbaijani intellectuals (drawing in part on new ideas coming from Europe) promoted a vision for the nation-state that was more 'modernist' and secular (Özcelik 2013).

The real evidence of the power of these new ideas and how they combined with old ones came when chaos in Russia during the 1917 October Revolution provided the people of Azerbaijan with the opportunity to achieve independence (Rasizade 2011). In 1918, the Azerbaijan Democratic Republic (ADR) became the first secular democracy in the Muslim world (Alieva 2006), embodying the culmination of growing support for the 'Azerbaijani Enlightenment Movement' (Najafizadeh 2012: 83) among secular nationalists and the 'Jadid Movement' among Muslims who 'believed that the Muslim faith must respond to the cataclysmic changes brought on by the Industrial Revolution' (Karagiannis 2010: 48). The risk of violence along the Sunni-Shia divide was therefore mitigated as shared values of tolerance bound the Azerbaijani people along ethnic lines. All of this led the people of Azerbaijan to pursue numerous fundamental political decisions that promoted peace, tolerance, and inclusion not just among the ethnic Azerbaijani or Muslim majority, but many other minorities. The short-lived ADR gave voting rights to women, another first in the Muslim world and notably earlier than most Western countries (Cornell 2011; Najafizadeh 2012); promoted socio-economic equality through a market economy with a strong middle class (Alieva 2006); and, introduced a multi-party system led by the Musavat ('Equality') party with coalitions through proportional representation (Karagiannis 2010). Foreshadowing Western multiculturalism even more, the ADR ensured prominent ethno-cultural and religious groups would have guaranteed representation by providing them with parliamentary seats. Of the 120 total seats, twenty-one were allocated to Armenians, ten to Russians, and one each for ethnic Germans and Jewish populations (Cornell 2011).[10] Most notable here in terms of reflecting a history of intermingling is that the majority saw fit to give a significant number of seats to the Armenians and Russians, groups with whom they share a difficult past. Thus, we can say that Azerbaijani multiculturalism took official shape at least as far back as 1918 using ideas that likely would have risen to the surface decades earlier had it not been for Russian imperialism. Moreover, the ADR did not simply import Western ideas, but represented a unique multicultural balance between 'democratic liberal knowledge and modernity on one hand and Islam and traditionalism on the other in the country's cultural profile' (Ismayilov 2015: 12). Unfortunately for (proto-)multiculturalists, the ADR came to an end in 1920 as the Red Army marched on Baku, assuring that Azerbaijan would again experience external domination albeit this time within the Soviet Union as the Azerbaijan Soviet Socialist Republic (ASSR).

While I skim over the ensuing Soviet period, it is important to note that it shared some traits with the ADR and departed from it in other ways. The Soviets shared a desire to keep the peace between Sunnis and Shias by promoting state secularism, which was very much in line with the wider Soviet ideology. Yet, the Soviets did this by cracking down on religion, closing almost all mosques (Keller 2001). Unlike in the ADR, the Soviets discouraged minority languages, even promoting Russian over Azerbaijani, which formally persisted until 1978 when the ASSR constitution was amended to give Azerbaijani official status (Garibova 2009). Though Azerbaijan managed to gain more control as time went on, particularly as the Soviet Union's demise seemed inevitable, multicultural policies were not a significant priority for the Soviets, nor could the people of Azerbaijan do more than make incremental victories in an effort to painstakingly bring back aspects of the ADR.

The Soviet Union's collapse allowed Azerbaijan to reestablish its independence in 1991. Leila Alieva (2006: 148) puts it best when she writes that 'the [ADR's] national idea ... was powerful enough to live on as an inspiration for many despite more than seven decades of brutal Soviet tyranny.' In the same spirit as the ADR, the new Constitution, in article 1, states that 'the Republic of Azerbaijan proclaims itself a democratic, secular, legal and social state whose highest values are an individual, his life, rights and freedoms.' This is no small commitment in a society made up of tremendous internal diversity with different Turkic, Iranian, Caucasian, Semitic, and Slavic groups speaking many different languages and following at least three major world religions (not to mention prominent denominational differences and secular beliefs). Moreover, there is an increased need for

---

[10]   This is not to say there are no examples in the West. For instance, a small number of guaranteed Māori seats have existed in New Zealand's Parliament since 1867.

stability against external claims to Azerbaijan's state sovereignty, notably from Armenia. Today, Azerbaijan, like Canada and many other states, maintains a delicate balance between the need to promote stability with developing an open society that promotes diversity. This seems to be working. For the most part, Azerbaijani identity has found a way to express itself as an inclusive civic identity that unites diverse peoples by both offering public support to different groups where needed and taking a hands-off approach where possible to allow historical communities to flourish unimpeded (see Ismayilov 2015). Azerbaijan's promotion of peaceful relations amid incredible diversity by organically respecting more than forcibly supplanting historical differences is most evident in three areas: (1) religious diversity, (2) linguistic diversity, and (3) ethno-cultural diversity with a focus on Armenians generally and Nagorno-Karabakh specifically. As will be shown, in some cases tolerance and respect for difference is even extended to those with whom Azerbaijanis have (had) strained relationships with like ethnic Armenians and Russians.

Starting with religious diversity, consider first their relationship to the Jewish population. Jewish people have been able to preserve their unique identity in Azerbaijan, living in places like Krasnaya Sloboda (near Quba) since the thirteenth century in what is believed to be the only all-Jewish city outside Israel. Many Jews are now returning from Israel to take advantage of economic opportunities and the general peace secured by the Azerbaijani government (Cornell 2011). Within the Muslim majority, and despite some who fear that political Islam is challenging national secularism, there are many more who previously identified with minority Muslim ethnic groups — like the Lezgins, Talysh, and Kurds — now voluntarily sharing in the wider Azerbaijani identity (ibid.). While the state tolerates all religions, it only supports those that are compatible with the state's wider secular ideology of tolerance (Grant 2011; De Cordier 2014).[11] Azerbaijan has effectively, to paraphrase Hikmet Hajizade (2011: 11–12), made all religions minorities by honouring them to the extent that they promote peaceful co-operation.

In the area of language, the state has found a delicate balance between actively promoting second languages alongside Azerbaijani and allowing different linguistic communities to decide for themselves how best to sustain them, with smaller languages doing much better than in many places around the world (Garibova 2009). Even Russian — the former occupier's language — receives significant respect and attention as something of 'a first among minority languages' (Fierman 2009: 92). The overall effect is widespread multilingualism, even to the point of keeping alive many languages that would

---

[11]   On the success of such efforts, Bruce Grant (2011: 655) writes that 'As with shrines across the region, one could often find Sunni and Shi'i or even Muslim and Christian under a single roof, united in the belief that belief itself could evoke other worlds.'

otherwise be at (greater) risk (Clifton 2009; Garibova & Zuercher 2009; Mammadov 2009). Finally, drawing on the challenging Armenian example to highlight ethno-national differences, and even if not entirely for altruistic reasons, Azerbaijan has pursued a plan of peace, tolerance, and acceptance despite the real possibility that military conflict could work given the internationally recognized illegal occupation of Nagorno-Karabakh. Such tolerance and a desire for peace even exists despite the fact that some believe Azerbaijan has gained the military and economic upper hand over Armenia and could return its control over its whole territory should it wish to do so unilaterally.[12] Azerbaijan even seems willing to grant the Armenian people of Nagorno-Karabakh significant autonomy within a fully restored Azerbaijan should such an eventuality arise (Rasizade 2011). Although the conflict has reached an impasse, it is not for a lack of trying on the part of an Azerbaijani state that has turned towards its multicultural roots for answers on how to live together. Many aspects are of course beyond any one state's control, but the ideas and values being espoused by Azerbaijan certainly promote solutions based in large measure on tolerance and recognition of the peoples involved.

Conclusion: Multicultural Lessons at the Crossroads

It seems that all too often and all too quickly Westerners find reasons to not engage with multiculturalism beyond the West, arguing that what they see is not multiculturalism at all. Yet, the people of Azerbaijan could similarly look at Canada and argue that nothing can be learned from a country that steals land from Indigenous peoples, commits barbaric acts of genocide, and refuses to make amends. But this is not a way to start a conversation, but to stop one before it even begins. Nor is such an approach in line with multicultural values, as in most cases we are not dealing with unreasonable tyrants, but more often than not 'Others' who simply live differently than us and grapple with unique challenges given complex local factors as well as global political dynamics linked to power differentials.

What might Canada and the West learn from Azerbaijan's experience with multiculturalism and its understanding of history? By now, it should come as no surprise that I believe much can be learned from Azerbaijan — a state that promotes multiculturalism *despite* many unique external and internal challenges respectively related to hostile neighbours and an emerging economy. In a sense, Azerbaijan is arguably doing much more to exceed expectations than Canada, where more can and should be done especially

---

[12] Of course, the external involvement of the international community arguably plays an even bigger role, though this should not overshadow Azerbaijan's support for peaceful solutions in line with respecting the people of the region and international law.

given the fact that Canadians enjoy tremendous stability and economic security while still allowing serious injustices to persist. With this in mind, two lessons from Azerbaijan that stand out are briefly considered.

The first lesson that comes through seems to be the way Azerbaijan gives linguistic, cultural, and religious minorities the physical, political, and/or social space to self-govern without always resorting to some sort of government mechanism or presence. In this way, historical communities can carry on as they see fit with minimal external interference. We saw this in the way linguistic communities are simply left to promote their languages in an organic way alongside those of the larger community. While some languages are under threat, this seems less dramatic than in Canada where languages have already been dying off *because of* past state wrongs such as residential schools, and with the state doing too little to ensure their public survival and resurgence stemming from such wrongs. Other examples exist for religious or ethnic communities as we saw with the Jewish people and even Armenians now illegally occupying territories. While it is true that in Canada ethnic minorities receive self-government and other minority rights, they are always determined by the state in a very explicit way that acts like a cage, arguably with little flexibility when it comes to Indigenous peoples (see, e.g., Kanji in this volume) or the people of Quebec (see, e.g., Laforest 2014). Moreover, many self-government agreements fail to provide enough to ensure that organic development in line with history can occur, particularly in the face of the overwhelming presence of the state. While it is true that Indigenous nations in Canada are much smaller than most communities in Azerbaijan, we should, once again, expect more from Canada given its wealth and stability. Instead, we see Azerbaijan doing as well, if not better in a number of crucial areas.

While this first lesson should be given its due, the second lesson seems to be the more important one. Azerbaijan may offer lessons on why it is important to emphasize those elements of a shared past that promote multicultural values. Despite years of occupation and ongoing conflicts, many people in Azerbaijan seem to be making a conscious decision to focus on those values that have brought them peace and happiness, rejecting those who might want to impose their own ideas or intolerant views according to some religious, ethnic, or cultural difference. The 1995 Constitution is a testament to the durability of multicultural ideas that can be traced back at least seven decades to the ADR, sustained and even developed in the face of Tsarist and Soviet rulers. Independence did not simply result in a replication of the same system of domination with different masters, but a rejection of many aspects of the model itself. This is no small feat. Azerbaijanis had a constitutional moment and looked to the past — both good and bad — and chose to promote its multicultural legacy. Canadians, on the other hand, do not always make such a choice, and often feel little can be learned from heeding Richard Day's words that the tools for a multicultural future can be — indeed, must be — found by also looking to the past. This is exactly what some leading scholars in Canada have argued, pointing to early treaty relationships between settlers and Indigenous peoples (and even between early Anglophone and Francophone communities), suggesting that we restore the civic virtues of peace, tolerance, respect, and shared sovereignty that informed such nation-to-nation agreements (see, e.g., Tully 1995; Asch 2014). Instead, the Canadian government has turned its back on the early treaty relationship, attempting to mask its domination over Indigenous peoples and claiming that peace prevails when in fact most Indigenous peoples continue to suffer in relatively poor conditions and with little power to change their predicament.

All of this is not to deny that both Azerbaijan and Canada are global multicultural centres. Though necessarily very different in their approaches, given that they must each tackle different circumstances, both countries seem committed to pursuing multiculturalism in one way or another, with unique challenges internal and external to the process of doing so. While I have emphasized — and perhaps sometimes overemphasized — some of the differences between the two countries, there is a lot of ground that can be built upon to benefit the diverse peoples of both countries and firmly establish learnings between East and West — even blur the distinction between East and West given an increasingly complex interconnected world. The more general lesson that I hope readers take away is that we learn more *not* by comparing approaches to knock others down, but by putting such judgements aside if only to find ways to build one another up. It is not important to win the competition of who is more multicultural or who has better multicultural policies, as if some externally applied set of criteria could easily be applied to the complexity of each case. Rather, the goal is to improve on peace, tolerance, and respect across differences whether small or great no matter where one begins and where one might be going.

References

Alieva, L. (2006). Azerbaijan's Frustrating Elections. *Journal of Democracy* 17(2): 147–160.

Aliyev, S. (2016). Multiculturalism — A State Policy in Azerbaijan. *Trend News Agency*. Available at: http://en.trend.az/azerbaijan/politics/2524987.html.

Asch, M. (2014). *On Being Here to Stay: Treaties and Aboriginal Rights in Canada*. Toronto: University of Toronto Press.

Banting, K. and Kymlicka, W. (2012). *Is There Really a Backlash Against Multiculturalism Policies? New Evidence from the Multiculturalism Policy Index*. Barcelona: GRITIM Working Paper no. 14.

Bevelander, P. and Taras, R. (2012). The Twilight of Multiculturalism? Findings from Across Europe. In Taras, R. ed. *Challenging Multiculturalism: European Models of Diversity*. Edinburgh: Edinburgh University Press.

Blaser, M. (2014). Ontology and Indigeneity: On the Political Ontology of Heterogeneous Assemblages. *Cultural Geographies* 21(1): 49–58.

Cho, L. (2013). Redress Revisited: Citizenship and the Chinese Canadian Head Tax. In Henderson, J. and Wakeham, P. eds. *Reconciling Canada: Critical Perspectives on the Culture of Redress*. Toronto: University of Toronto Press.

Clifton, J. M. (2009). The Future of the Shahdagh Languages. *International Journal of the Sociology of Language* 198: 33–45.

Cornell, S. E. (2011). *Azerbaijan Since Independence*. London: M. E. Sharpe.

Day, R. J. F. (2000). *Multiculturalism and the History of Canadian Diversity*. Toronto: University of Toronto Press.

De Cordier, B. (2014). Islamic Social Activism, Globalization and Social Change. *Journal of Muslim Minority Affairs* 34(2): 134–151.

Fierman, W. (2009). Language Vitality and Paths to Revival: Contrasting Cases of Azerbaijani and Kazakh. *International Journal of the Sociology of Language* 198: 75–104.

Friesen, J. (2013, February 27). Chinese head-tax redress funds clawed back. *The Globe and Mail*. Available at: http://www.theglobeandmail.com/news/politics/chinese-head-tax-redress-funds-clawed-back/article9101632/.

Garibova, J. (2009). Language Policy in Post-Soviet Azerbaijan: Political Aspects. *International Journal of the Sociology of Language* 198: 7–32.

Gabriova, J. and Zuercher, K. (2009). Ön Söz: An Overview of Sociolinguistic issues in Azerbaijan. *International Journal of the Sociology of Language* 198: 1–5.

Grant, B. (2011). Shrines and Sovereigns: Life, Death, and Religion in Rural Azerbaijan. *Comparative Studies in Society and History* 53(3): 654–681.

Gray, L. (2008, June 12). Why silence greeted Stephen Harper's residential-school apology. *The Georgia Straight*. Available at: http://www.straight.com/article-150021/unyas-lynda-gray-responds-prime-ministers-apology.

Hajizade, H. (2011). *Islam and Religious Freedom in Independent Azerbaijan*. Saarbrücken: Lambert.

Henderson, J. and Wakeham, P. (2013). Introduction. In Henderson, J. and Wakeham, P. eds. *Reconciling Canada: Critical Perspectives on the Culture of Redress*. Toronto: University of Toronto Press.

Ismayilov, M. (2015). Postcolonial Hybridity, Contingency, and the Mutual Embeddedness of Identity and Politics in Post-Soviet Azerbaijan: Some Initial Thoughts. *Caucasus Analytical Digest* 77: 7–13.

Ivison, D., Patton, P., and Sanders, W. (2000). Introduction. In: Ivison, D., Patton, P., and Sanders, W. eds. *Political Theory and the Rights of Indigenous Peoples*. Cambridge: Cambridge University Press.

James, M. (2013). Neoliberal Heritage Redress. In Henderson, J. and Wakeham, P. eds. *Reconciling Canada: Critical Perspectives on the Culture of Redress*. Toronto: University of Toronto Press.

Karagiannis, E. (2010). Political Island in the Former Soviet Union: Uzbekistan and Azerbaijan Compared. *Dynamics of Asymmetric Conflict* 3(1): 46–61.

Keller, S. (2001). *To Moscow, Not Mecca: The Soviet Campaign Against Island in Central Asia, 1917–1941*. London: Praeger.

Kymlicka, W. (1995). *Multicultural Citizenship: A Liberal Theory of Minority Rights*. Oxford: Oxford University Press.

Kymlicka, W. and Opalski, M. eds. (2001). *Can Liberal Pluralism be Exported? Western Political Theory and Ethnic Relations in Eastern Europe*. Oxford: Oxford University Press.

Kymlicka, W. and He, B. (2005). eds. *Multiculturalism in Asia*. Oxford: Oxford University Press.

Kymlicka, W. and Pföstl, E. (2014). *Multiculturalism and Minority Rights in the Arab World* Oxford: Oxford University Press.

Laforest, G. (2014). *Interpreting Quebec's Exile Within the Federation: Selected Political Essays.* Frankfurt: Peter Lang.

Mackay, E. (2013). The Apologizers' Apology. In Henderson, J. and Wakeham, P. eds. *Reconciling Canada: Critical Perspectives on the Culture of Redress.* Toronto: University of Toronto Press.

Malik, K. (2015). The Failure of Multiculturalism: Community versus Society in Europe. *Foreign Affairs* 94(2): 21–32.

Mammadov, A. (2009). The issue of Plurilingualism and Language Policy in Azerbaijan. *International Journal of the Sociology of Language* 198: 65–73.

Mann, J. (2012). The Introduction of Multiculturalism in Canada and Australia, 1960s–1970s. *Nations and Nationalism* 18(3): 483–503.

Mignolo, W. D. (2000). *Local Histories/Global Designs: Coloniality, Subaltern Knowledges, and Border Thinking.* Princeton: Princeton University Press.

Modood, T. (2007). *Multiculturalism.* Cambridge: Polity Press.

Najafizadeh, M. (2012). Gender and Ideology: Social Change and Islam in Post-Soviet Azerbaijan. *Journal of Third World Studies* 29(1): 81–101.

Özcelik, Y. (2013). The Development and Establishment of Political Identity in the Republic of Azerbaijan. *Euxeinos* 9: 27–33.

Rasizade, A. (2011). Azerbaijan's Prospects in Nagorno-Karabakh. *Mediterranean Quarterly* 22(3): 72–94.

Souleimanov, E. (2012). Between Turkey, Russia, and Persia: Perceptions of National Identity in Azerbaijan and Armenia at the Turn of the Nineteenth and Twentieth Centuries. *Middle East Review of International Affairs* 16(1): 74–85.

Świętochowski, T. (1994). Azerbaijan: A Borderland at the Crossroads of History. In Starr, F. ed. *The Legacy of History in Russia and the New States of Eurasia.* New York: M. E. Sharpe.

Taras, R. (2012). *Challenging Multiculturalism: European Models of Diversity*. Edinburgh: Edinburgh University Press.

Trudeau, P. E. (1971, October 8). Announcement of Implementation of Policy of Multiculturalism within Bilingual Framework. *Library and Archives Canada. Canada,* Parliament. House of Commons. Debates, 28th *Parliament, 3rd Session, Volume 8: 8545–8548.*

Tully, J. (1995). *Strange Multiplicity: Constitutionalism in an Age of Diversity*. Cambridge: Cambridge University Press.

Veracini, L. (2011). *Settler Colonialism: A Theoretical Overview*. London: Palgrave Macmillan.

Wayland, S. V. (1997). Immigration, Multiculturalism and National Identity in Canada. *International Journal on Group Rights* 5: 33–58.

Wherry, A. (2009, October 1). What he was talking about when he talked about colonialism. *Maclean's*. Available at: http://www.macleans.ca/politics/ottawa/what-he-was-talking-about-when-he-talked-about-colonialism/.

Wong, L. and Guo, S. (2011). Multiculturalism Turns 40: Reflections on the Canadian Policy. *Canadian Ethnic Studies* 43(1–2): 1–4.

8

De-EUropeanising European Borders: EU-Morocco Negotiations on Migrations and the Decentring Agenda in EU Studies

NORA EL QADIM

Recent media attention devoted to the so-called 'migrant' or 'refugee crisis' — in other words the revelation of difficulties in the functioning of European asylum systems —once again exposed Eurocentric perceptions of migrations and human mobility. Although some academic analyses of the recent 'crisis' (as well as previous ones) have unpacked and countered such perceptions (see, e.g., Pallister-Wilkins 2015; Zaragoza Cristiani 2016; Bilgin 2016), this form of Eurocentrism continues to be reflected in a large part of the research on European migration policy.

This chapter builds on the existing critique of International Relations (IR) and security studies as being Western- or Eurocentric, contributing to a decentring research agenda on European Union (EU) migration policy and on the EU's external policy more generally by looking at EU-Morocco negotiations on migration. The purpose is to identify specific ways through which this agenda can be implemented. This chapter also tries to further this agenda by examining how the ideas and suggestions this agenda proposes can converge with research on migration policies and border control, which are precisely concerned with the varying definitions of borders and unequal, asymmetric mobilities. First, I will examine how the decentring agenda intersects with the study of EU migration policies, including its implications for developing research strategies. Second, I will show how these strategies can be helpful in examining EU negotiations with a neighbouring country, in this case Morocco, and how the study of migration policies offers a particularly useful case for decentring the study of the EU's external policy.

Decentring the EU's External Migration Policy: EU Studies Meets Postcolonial Approaches

Since the 1990s, EU studies has been subjected to numerous criticisms that aim to deconstruct the mythologies of European integration, a linear progress towards federalism, or an 'ever-closer union.' Several authors have recently underlined the Eurocentrism of EU studies, especially in analysing the EU's external action, calling for a decentring of EU studies, along with a decentring of the study of the foreign policies of Western countries and IR more generally. These criticisms unpack the different components of the Eurocentrism of EU studies, such as 'civilizational' mythologies and ideologies (Bilgin 2004; Fisher Onar and Nicolaïdis 2013), various dynamics of othering (Diez 2004; 2005), and the role of Europe's self-image (Nicolaïdis and Howse 2002; Cebeci 2012; Patel 2013). They converge with the emergence of greater reflections on Western- and Eurocentric biases within IR and international studies (Hobson 2012). Indeed, some IR scholars aim to decentre the discipline (Acharya 1995; Doty 1996; Tickner 2003; Acharya and Buzan 2010; Bilgin 2010). They have pursued Chakrabarty's injunction to 'provincialise Europe' (2000), and some have thus advocated a postcolonial or non-Western approach to IR (Tickner and Waever 2007; Tickner and Blaney 2012; Tickner 2013) and security studies (Barkawi and Laffey 2006; Bilgin 2010). In a sense, this is comparable to decolonial thinking and Mignolo's (2000) call for border thinking as a way of critically reflecting on knowledge production from the outside.

From Eurocentric Bias to Questioning Asymmetry in EU Migration Policies

Migration is a central policy for tackling Eurocentrism in EU studies. Migration policies are typically marred by the singular histories different European Member States have with their former empires. Moreover, as argued by Catarina Kinnvall, migration, European integration, and the colonial discourse are tightly intertwined. She writes that, 'Europe and European integration must be read within the context of colonial and postcolonial globalization, migration and ethnicity. Hence the discourse of European unity and integration cannot be automatically discharged from the core elements of a colonial discourse' (Kinnvall 2016: 155). Interestingly, migration policy has also been central to the construction of external competences for EU institutions, particularly in the field of Home Affairs; the Directorate General in charge of Home Affairs, officially created in 1999 on the basis of a pre-existing small task force,[1] has used the idea of an 'external dimension' of migration policies and home affairs to gain competences (at the expense of the directorates in charge of development or of external relations), as well as funding and personnel over the years. Within the EU narrative, migration policy is central to the construction of 'external borders,' exemplifying the historicity and specificity of the borders/migration nexus which is, as Walters (2015) underlines, far from being universal.

It is not surprising then that the literature on European external migration policy is particularly representative of Eurocentric tendencies within EU studies. It has long tended to focus on European actors, be they from EU institutions or from Member States. For example, the notion of 'external governance' has been central in explaining migration policies. It has helped show how the EU has tried to export its endogenous security model to neighbouring countries in order to enlarge the scope of its influence without opening its 'institutional borders.' The notion of external governance questions the idea of European external policy as the sum of the national foreign policies of Member States (Lavenex 2004). Part of the literature in this field focuses on readmission agreements, which organise the administrative process of deportation by obtaining and regulating the collaboration of origin countries to make it easier to deport undocumented migrants to a third country. Readmission agreements are seen as one of the main tools of the EU's external action in migration matters. When it comes to analysing negotiations on readmission, a common hypothesis is that the EU's negotiating ability is limited by how competencies are delegated. However, although analyses through this lens underline the role of internal compromise in defining European external policy, they tend to overlook resistances to EU external policy *outside* the EU. Such resistance is mainly described as the end result of internal European conflict between Member States and the EU Commission for negotiations with third countries (Lavenex 2006; Coleman 2009). State actors of these countries are only taken into account indirectly, as recipients of the uncertainties of negotiated intra-European decision-making, be it in the field of democratization (Schimmelfennig and Sedelmeier 2004) or migration policies (Wunderlich 2010; 2012).

This bias is the consequence of most studies concentrating on official texts produced by European institutions, which typically produce more documentation than institutions from third countries. Interviews are another important source for research. However, the extent in which these interviews are representative of official discourse is rarely clarified. Despite the

---

[1]   This was created in 1995 within the Secretariat of the EU Commission.

insistence of the first studies of external governance on sociological reflection (Lavenex and Uçarer 2002), it is often difficult to distinguish between the analysis and the discourses of EU actors (Lavenex and Wichmann 2009). Moreover, the asymmetry in the accessible sources and actors is rarely questioned by those who research EU relations with neighbouring countries.

This relates to one of the main limits when viewing EU external policies through the lens of external governance; the asymmetry of EU relations with surrounding countries is not taken into account as such, although these 'neighbours' are mostly less powerful both militarily and economically. Asymmetry is only slightly more prominent in more recent work, inspired by the notion of 'complex interdependence' developed in International Relations (Keohane and Nye 1977) and applied to the analysis of migrations through the idea of 'global governance' (Betts 2009; 2011) or 'multi-layered governance' of migration (Kunz, Lavenex, and Panizzon 2011). Even those that mention asymmetry rarely unpack its meaning, especially the impact of the EU's domination on surrounding countries. From the domination of economically dependent countries, some former colonies of various Member States, to the complex relationship with Russia, the modalities of the relations with the EU's 'neighbours' are not always the same. Yet domination is most of the time usually implicitly assumed rather than examined.

Asymmetry is also more prominent in studies that underline the externalisation of migration controls and its effects in third countries. Huysmans (2000) has demonstrated how externalisation and securitization go hand in hand. The representation of migrants as potential threats has led to the strengthening of border controls in order to prevent the arrival of undocumented migrants and to the organization of deportations for those who do manage to enter European countries. The term externalisation highlights the domination of European countries and the EU over surrounding countries, which have been pressured into adopting similar securitised norms of migration control (Guiraudon and Lahav 2000; Boswell 2003; Geddes 2005; Guild, Carrera, and Balzacq 2008; Bigo and Guild 2010). Readmission agreements, dealing with deportation procedures, have thus also been frequently described as a case of externalisation (Gabrielli 2008; Coleman 2009). Morocco is an example of this (Elmadmad 2004; Belguendouz 2005). While the analysis of externalisation takes asymmetry seriously, such interpretations also leave little room for the perspective of actors from countries surrounding the EU. They are implicitly understood as submitting to, and carrying out, European demands. In that sense, this literature also remains rather Eurocentric, and cannot fully explain the evolution of EU policies. By overlooking the agency of actors in dominated countries, it neglects their possible influence on negotiations and ultimately on EU policies.

Possible Strategies For Decentring the Study of EU Migration Policies

Migration policies lend themselves well to questioning the asymmetry of IR, which can be a starting point for decentring the study of the EU's external policies. Several authors have questioned the asymmetry of international relations, and highlighted the agency of so-called 'origin countries.' Some have underlined that the governments of emigration states can have their own objectives (e.g., economic), negotiating with destination countries without necessarily taking the lives of migrants into account (Sayad 2004). In the case of Morocco, several studies have shown how the Moroccan State tried to organise the emigration of some of its citizens (Brand 2006; Iskander 2010). Moreover, other studies have shown how emigration countries could pressure destination countries by using migration as a threat in foreign policy negotiations (Teitelbaum 1984). Kelly Greenhill (2000), for instance, analyses the diplomatic use of migration in the world and talks about 'weapons of mass migration.' The case of South-North migrations in the Mediterranean has also been analysed from this perspective. Several case studies have considered the positions of third countries, showing how they can sometimes use negotiations to their advantage (Cassarino 2007; El Qadim 2010; Içduyglu and Aksel 2014; Wolff 2014). Jean-Pierre Cassarino (2010), for instance, describes a relative 'empowerment' of origin countries when confronted with the EU on the issue of readmission and its manipulation, while Emanuela Paoletti (2010) talks of a 'migration of power.' These studies all underline that asymmetrical relations are not fixed, and that sectoral negotiations can question the domination of one party by the other. However, these studies mostly concentrate on high-level negotiations and official discourses. They also present a conception of sending states as unitary and homogeneous, mostly focusing on the 'interest' of origin countries without unpacking this concept or opening up the black box of the state.

The decentring of the study of migration policies could be furthered. In this respect, the postcolonial critique of IR, security studies, or EU studies all underline the need for useful research strategies in developing a different, renewed, and less Euro- or Western-centric research agenda. Meera Sabaratnam (2011) has, for example, identified six possible 'decolonising strategies for the study of world politics.' They range from historical and historiographic analysis, often favoured in postcolonial studies, to questioning the presumed psychology of IR subjects, which usually tends towards a rationalist subjectivity, implicitly understanding states as reified identities. Similarly, studies of EU external policy also point to the steps necessary for pursuing a decentring agenda. In order to 'provincialise' Europe (Chakrabarty 2000), we are told we must truly engage with others (Fisher Onar and Nicolaïdis 2013). Moreover, they underline the entanglement of this research agenda with normative and ethical concerns (Bilgin 2010;

Rutazibwa 2010). These calls have laid out an agenda for research that would 'envisag[e] other countries and regions as centres of their own geostrategic and geopolitical concerns, while recognizing that legacies of a more Eurocentric era may inflect, for better or for worse, upon actors' perceptions and preferences to this day' (Fisher Onar and Nicolaïdis 2013: 296). Nevertheless, this agenda remains, for the time being, largely programmatic. Case studies that explore EU policies in neighbouring countries, including through fieldwork with non-EU actors, rarely dwell upon the meaning of doing so. This is either because the main question they ask concerns the implementation of EU policies (as is the case in the literature on external governance, for example) or because they are mainly interested in deconstructing the labels used by the EU in these external policies.

Here I want to review and explore the strategies that proved useful in my own research on decentring the study of EU-Morocco negotiations on migrations. While it is clear that migrants and their role in shaping these policies should also be taken into account (Mezzadra 2004), my main concern here is with the dynamics of state-to-state relations when these relations are asymmetric. First, I use a strategy closely related to what Sabaratnam (2011: 789) calls 'pluralising the various potential subjects of social inquiry and analysing world politics from alternative subaltern perspectives.' This is also what Fisher Onar and Nicolaïdis (2013) call for when they speak of engagement with others. While this is a corollary to another strategy Sabaratnam (2011: 787) identifies, which consists in 'deconstruct[ing] ... the West as the primary subject of world history,' it involves concentrating on different actors, namely non-Western ones. In practice, this involves pluralising sources, be they written, oral, or of other types, as well as a strong commitment to interpreting and understanding a variety of ways of thinking. It also involves an effort to understand other viewpoints as well as values and subjectivities — and, in some cases, also language skills. This allows for a deeper questioning on the functioning of asymmetric relations, since engagement with these 'others' gives the possibility of envisaging agency and dynamics of resistance that would otherwise not necessarily be visible. Ethnographic approaches and the study of practices can be particularly useful in this endeavour (Côté-Boucher, Infantino, and Salter 2013).

Second, as Sabaratnam (2011: 793) notes, decolonising IR requires trying to displace 'the rationalist, masculinist subjectivity/psyche attributed implicitly to states' relations with each other ... with one that is more complex, situated, affective and particular.' This anthropomorphic idea of the interests of states is also very prominent in the study of migration policies and negotiations. These interests are often defined relative to political and economic stakes, which usually underlie explanations of migration and border policies in the North. However, concentrating on the discourses and practices of state actors in the South reveals different considerations, where more complex, affective, and moral considerations are put forward. While this does not mean that such considerations are not part of political decisions on migrations in so-called 'destination countries' (Fassin 2005), they are more readily put forward as parts of the legitimate rationale of migration policies in so-called 'origin countries.' In the same way border thinking encourages us to accept a broader understanding of what knowledge means (Mignolo 2000), decentring the analysis of migration and border policies forces us to envisage different, contending rationales for apprehending human mobility.

What We Can Learn from Decentring the Study of the EU's External Policy: The Case of EU-Morocco Negotiations on Migrations

EU-Morocco negotiations on migration are particularly interesting in terms of decentring the study of EU external policy. Although a specific agreement has yet to be reached, negotiations have been ongoing since 1999, the year that the European Commission obtained the mandate from EU Member States to deal with the external dimension of migrations. Such a protracted process is puzzling if the analysis centres largely on the EU and its Member States. In fact, it can only be understood by looking closely at Moroccan actors in the negotiations.

These negotiations have overwhelmingly centred on the theme of readmission, a persistent issue in EU-Morocco relations since 2003. Readmission agreements, as described above, focus particularly on organising and promoting a speedy delivery of consular *laissez-passers* by the authorities of origin countries for undocumented individuals who do not present any identification proving their citizenship. Another important objective of EU negotiations on readmission has been collaboration on the deportation of so-called 'transit migrants' — i.e., undocumented individuals who are not citizens of the signatory state but have 'transited' through its territory before reaching an EU country. The collaboration of origin countries in this field is often difficult to obtain, mostly because it does not benefit them in any way (Ellermann 2008). These negotiations appear to be a good case for the study of two important dimensions that have been overlooked in the study of international relations on migrations: (1) the agency of 'third countries' in the South, which is often underestimated; and, (2) the importance of symbolic dimension in international relations, which are often minimised in accounts highlighting a rationalist logic of international actors.

Locating Agency in Asymmetric International Relations

Despite more than ten years of negotiations on an EU-wide readmission agreement, the Moroccan state has so far managed to avoid signing such an agreement. These negotiations originally began because Member States found it difficult, in the 1990s, to ensure collaboration from Morocco on deportation. Even where bilateral, more or less official readmission agreements existed, origin countries did not — and still do not — always implement them (Cassarino 2007; El Qadim 2014). After initial discussions within the Council, especially the High-Level Working Group on Migration and Asylum, the competence to negotiate readmission agreements was given to the Commission in 2000. The idea was that the EU could exercise more leverage in negotiations than individual Member States (Coleman 2009; Cassarino 2010). Negotiations with Morocco specifically started in April 2003. Despite numerous negotiation rounds, the European Commission has found it difficult to convince Moroccan negotiators to agree to the terms of the agreement, especially on the deportation of 'third country nationals.' Moroccan actors have thus used these negotiations to their benefit. This argument brings to light two important lessons. First, it reminds us of the existence of an autonomous agenda in 'origin' or 'transit countries.' Second, it highlights the existence of avoidance practices and resistance by governmental actors of countries usually considered as mere executors of policies formulated in 'destination countries.'

As an initial point, when researching EU external policy, it is easy to forget that neighbouring countries have their own agenda, both in the international arena and on national matters. It is important to unpack the 'interests' of 'origin' or 'transit countries' to distinguish between the aggregated interest of a country, domestic costs for the government, and administrative capacities and rivalries (Reslow 2012). Moroccan officials can be concerned with various matters of domestic policy, ranging from managing emigration, unemployment, and unrest (Brand 2006; Iskander 2010) to fighting terrorism or dealing with immigration to Morocco (Natter 2013). As important as it might be to understand the 'two-level game' (Putnam 1980) of the foreign policy of so-called 'origin countries,' it is also essential to comprehend this foreign policy as not only oriented towards the EU, as it sometimes seems to be understood in analyses of its external policy. For example, one can highlight the importance of Moroccan policy in Africa and the ties of the Kingdom with West African countries (Messari and Willis 2003). These ties matter in discussing migration control with European countries, and partly explain why Moroccan officials refuse to portray their country as 'Europe's policeman' (Belguendouz 2003) or to institute visa requirements for the entry of West Africans. It is also necessary to underline the fact that Moroccan officials are not only involved in discussions on migration with European countries. They also tackle these issues in international forums such as the framework put in place by the Global Forum on Migration and Development. Finally, EU Member States sometimes overshadow the EU in Moroccan foreign policy.

Indeed, Member States also have their own foreign policies, and if they cannot obtain cooperation on deportation through the EU, they seek to obtain it directly, through bilateral relations.

This leads to my second point, which deals more directly with the agency of 'origin' and 'transit countries.' Indeed, the co-existence of EU-wide international relations and bilateral relations, by providing multiple arenas to third countries, can provide more opportunities for avoidance or resistance. It also gives rise to the possibility of seeking support from one partner in negotiations with another. This might explain why we can observe what Cassarino (2011) dubbed 'resilient bilateralism' where EU Member States continue to pursue negotiations on issues linked to readmission despite the exclusive mandate given to the EU Commission. Instead of negotiating a 'readmission agreement,' they negotiate, for example, on police cooperation, which in its implementation entails cooperation on deportation. Elsewhere, I have also shown how bilateral bargaining happens in the implementation of pre-existing agreements or with the sending of specialised liaison officers (El Qadim 2014). A widely publicised recent case of bilateralism in this field was that of collective deportations organised in early 2016 between Germany and Morocco after discussions at the highest level between Angela Merkel and King Mohammed VI (*Le 360* 2016).

In practice, this resilient bilateralism means that Moroccan diplomats and civil servants are engaged in discussions with European Member States as well as EU officials. These discussions at various levels and in various arenas provide multiple opportunities for resistance. In the case of EU-Morocco negotiations, interviewing an equal number of EU, Member State, and Moroccan actors shows how Moroccan negotiators have used the multiplicity of their interlocutors to continue avoiding the signature of a very visible EU-wide readmission agreement. This is accomplished primarily by obtaining the support of specific Member States in EU arenas, or by making an EU-wide agreement unnecessary for them through the pursuit of a more intensive, less visible cooperation on deportation in bilateral relations. Interviews also reveal how negotiation and bargaining happen at every level of international relations. In the case of deportation policies, mid-level bureaucrats in charge of organising cooperation between police services are central to understanding the ways in which agreements on the circulation (including deportation) of persons are implemented. These bureaucrats use such opportunities to challenge the ways in which 'destination' countries (in this case, France) envisage cooperation by challenging the statistics they used to evaluate this cooperation (El Qadim 2014). Looking below the usual level of negotiations between states reveals the dynamics of resistance and brokering that are otherwise not visible. Examining these dynamics allows us to nuance the image of unilateral domination and point to the agency of state actors from third countries. It highlights in particular their leeway and the interstices in international relations of domination.

Symbols in the Decentring Agenda

Arguments based on symbols, emotions, or different moral stands have often been rejected as futile or meaningless. As Doty (1996: 8) argues, the *a priori* givenness of certain categories of analysis 'both presumes the relevance of particular categories (and the irrelevance of others) and at the same time mystifies the discursive construction of the categories themselves.' This has also been the case, to a certain extent, for discourses of governmental and administrative actors from 'origin countries' on migration policies and negotiations, which have not extensively been analysed, and are often dismissed as purely tactical. However, careful attention to discourses and arguments in 'origin' or 'transit countries' provides a story that also needs to be reported. In the case of EU-Morocco negotiations, it is important to understand that the promotion by Moroccan officials of an alternative to a purely security-oriented framework in migration policies was motivated by more than just economic and political interests as defined by European actors (economic interests, fighting against unemployment and limiting political unrest, or even international relations with countries in the region).

One interesting example in this respect is that of Moroccan officials often mentioning dignity and (self-)respect as important motivations for their country's policy in matters of migration and border control. European officials overwhelmingly interpret these arguments as purely tactical, downplaying their importance, while researchers pay little attention to them.[2] I argue that the discourses of Moroccan officials should be taken as seriously as the discourses promoted by EU and Member State officials. This does not mean that they should be immune to critical analysis, but that the logic of these motives should also be examined. Dignity and respect are mentioned mostly in relation to the EU's visa policy, and the difficulty (some) Moroccans experience in obtaining visas, as well as the humiliations they encounter in the process. Although 'visa facilitation,' a relatively new bargaining chip offered by the EU after the Arab revolutions, would not really change the situation for most Moroccans in relation to the possibility of obtaining a visa, Moroccan officials insisted on negotiating such an agreement. They insisted particularly on the need to negotiate a visa facilitation agreement without making it conditional to the signature of a readmission agreement, with conditionality being interpreted as paternalistic, unfair, and contemptuous.

---

[2]   There was only one exception out of forty interviews conducted with EU and French officials.

Following this line of argumentation, the dignity of the Moroccan people was repeatedly asserted, and often equated with, or used as a symbol for, the dignity of the State. Denouncing the disrespect of EU and European Member State officials is very close to the denunciation of European visas as a type of '*hogra*.' Indeed, a study showed that visas were perceived as such by the Moroccan citizens, especially the youth (Chattou, Aït Ben Lmadani, and Diopyaye 2012). This Arabic term usually refers to the humiliation imposed by the State — i.e., the contempt of the government for its citizens. It has been widely used in the context of the revolutions in North Africa beginning in 2011, and it is frequently used to qualify the treatment of the unemployed by the government. Both the Moroccan population and officials thus tend to equate the requirements of the EU and its Member States in migration matters with a form of international contempt, a negative sign for Moroccan nationals — and by extension in this context, the international standing or status of the Moroccan state. This points to two important dimensions concerning the attempt to decentre the study of European borders and more generally of migration and border policies. The first relates to the issue of autonomy in the reflection on thinking about international relations, while the second concerns the issue of language in studying international relations and as part of 'border thinking.'

Indeed, the importance and recurrence of 'dignity' and the parallel between a domestic situation and international relations highlight the importance of autonomy as a political concept. As Tickner (2003: 319) shows,

> in many third world contexts, autonomy … occupies a more predominant place in thinking about IR … from the national borders outwards, autonomy is considered fundamental to the practice of third world IR. Rather than being rooted in juridical notions of sovereignty, it is markedly a political concept, and is viewed as an instrumental tool for safeguarding against the most noxious effects of the international system … autonomy acquires meaning in and of itself when viewed from the perspective of weak actors, given its symbolic association with factors historically denied to the third world.

These factors include dignity. The insistence of Moroccan actors on dignity thus appears to be more than a tactical claim, but rather part of a broader argument that holds it up as a symbol of the state's autonomy and its status in the international system. In addition, the use of a term usually referring to domestic politics, *hogra*, to describe an international phenomenon underlines the articulation, also noted by Tickner, of both contexts as asserting representations of autonomy.

Additionally, the case of Moroccan reactions to European offers in migration negotiations, and in particular the insistence of negotiators on visa facilitation, is also an interesting reminder of the importance of language and 'thinking in between languages' (Mignolo 2000: part 3). Indeed, it is useful to re-think the motivations of the Moroccan negotiators. Contextualising the arguments of Moroccan officials in a broader discourse on *hogra*, rather than insisting on an undefined 'culture,' is part of analysing representations. These arguments relating to dignity and respect matter as such — and not only because of the economic consequences of migration control. The use of the term *hogra* in relation to arguments on dignity in this matter goes to show that the Moroccan population and officials interpret freedom of circulation as a symbol of (international) economic and social privilege. This is no doubt the reason why the EU and EU Member State officials, as beneficiaries of this privilege, dismiss relatively easily the idea of 'respect' in relation to Morocco. Nevertheless, paying attention to the language used is helpful here in order to capture the symbolic dimension of migration control that the differentiated possibilities for free circulation also carry. The issue of language, of thinking 'in between languages' is thus closely connected here to a better consideration of the symbolic dimension and the role of representations in IR.

Conclusion

Building on the existing post- and decolonial critique of IR, security studies, and more recently EU studies, I have tried to identify tools and strategies for decentring the study of the EU's external policies. Through the study of EU-Morocco negotiations on migration, I have shown that implementing a decentring agenda requires engaging with non-Western actors. This means not only making efforts to access different sources and actors, but examining their discourses. Here the displacement of the rationalist psyche usually attributed to states in the analysis of foreign policy can help by, first, deconstructing the assumed linearity and rationality of the actions of European officials and, second, understanding the rationale of non-European officials and how they interact with the ambitions of EU migration policies.

This paper also contends that negotiations on migration, including international negotiations on migration and border control more generally, are a particularly interesting case for the decentring agenda because migration policies concern the very definition and redefinition of borders between states, between 'destination countries' or 'origin'/'transit countries.' As such, they are the locus of asymmetrical contestation between people and their free movement. This asymmetry in the freedom of circulation is indeed constantly questioned, re-asserted, and/or redefined in these negotiations.

References

Acharya, A. (1995). The Periphery as the Core: The Third World and Security Studies. *Mars*. Available at : http://yorkspace.library.yorku.ca/xmlui/handle/10315/1412

Acharya, A. and Buzan,B. ed. (2010). *Non-Western International Relations Theory. Perspectives on and beyond Asia*. Abingdon ; New York: Routledge.

Barkawi, T. and Laffey, M. (2006). The postcolonial moment in security studies. *Review of International Studies* 32(2): 32952.

Belguendouz, A. (2003). *Le Maroc non africain, gendarme de l'Europe? Alerte au projet de loi 02-03 relative à l'entrée et au séjour des étrangers au Maroc, à l'émigration et à l'immigration irrégulières!* Rabat.

Belguendouz, A. (2005). Expansion et sous-traitance des logiques d'enfermement de l'Union européenne: l'exemple du Maroc. *Cultures et Conflits*, n° 57.

Betts, A. (2009). *Protection by Persuasion: International Cooperation in the Refugee Regime*. Ithaca, NY: Cornell University Press.

Betts, A. (2011). *Global Migration Governance*. Oxford : Oxford University Press, USA.

Bigo, D. and Guild, E. (2010). The Transformation of European Border Controls. In: Ryan, B. & Mitsilegas, V. eds. *Extraterritorial Immigration Control. Legal Challenges*. Leiden, Boston: Martinus Nijhoff Publishers.pp. 257279.

Bilgin, P. (2004). A Return to "Civilisational Geopolitics" in the Mediterranean? Changing Geopolitical Images of the European Union and Turkey in the Post-Cold War Era. *Geopolitics* 9(2): 26991.

Bilgin, P. (2010). The "Western-Centrism" of Security Studies: "Blind Spot" or Constitutive Practice? *Security Dialogue* 41(6): 61522.

Bilgin, P. (2016). *How not to think about the Mediterranean "refugee crisis"*. Syddansk Universitet: Center for Mellemøststudier.

Boswell, C. (2003). The "External Dimension" of EU Immigration and Asylum Policy. *International Affairs (Royal Institute of International Affairs 1944-)* 79(3): 61938.

Brand, L. A. (2006). *Citizens abroad: emigration and the state in the Middle East and North Africa*. Cambridge : Cambridge University Press.

Cassarino, J.-P. (2007). Informalising Readmission Agreements in the EU Neighbourhood. *The International Spectator* 42(2): 17996.

Cassarino, J.-P. (2010). Dealing with Unbalanced Reciprocities: Cooperation on Readmission and Implications. In : Cassarino, J.-P. ed. *Unbalanced Reciprocities: Cooperation on Readmission in the Euro-Mediterranean Area*. Special edition. Middle East Institute Viewpoints. Washington DC.

Cassarino, J.-P. (2011). Resilient bilateralism in the cooperation on readmission' In : Cremona, M., Monar, J. & Poli, S. eds. *The External Dimension of the European Union's Area of Freedom, Security and Justice*. College of Europe Studies. Bruxelles, Bern, Berlin, Frankfurt am Main, New York, Oxford, Wien: Peter Lang Verlag. pp. 191208

Cebeci, M. (2012). European Foreign Policy Research Reconsidered: Constructing an 'Ideal Power Europe' through Theory? *Millennium - Journal of International Studies* 40(3): 56383.

Chakrabarty, D. (2000). *Provincializing Europe: Postcolonial Thought and Historical Difference*. Princeton: Princeton University Press.

Chattou, Z., Lmadani, F.A.B. and Diopyaye, T. (2012). *Printemps Arabe et Migrations Internationales : Evolution des Opinions et des Politiques au Maroc. 8.* San Domenico di Fiesole (FI): RSCAS-Migration Policy Centre.

Coleman, N. (2009). *European Readmission Policy: Third Country Interests and Refugee Rights*. BRILL.

Côté-Boucher, K., Infantino, F. and Salter, M. B. (2014). Border Security as Practice: An Agenda for Research. *Security Dialogue* 45(3): 195208.

Diez, T. (2004). Europe's others and the return of geopolitics. *Cambridge Review of International Affairs* 17(2): 31935.

Diez, T. (2005). Constructing the Self and Changing Others: Reconsidering `Normative Power Europe'. *Millennium - Journal of International Studies* 33(3): 61336.

Doty, R. L. (1996). *Imperial Encounters: The Politics of Representation in North-South Relations*. Minneapolis : U of Minnesota Press.

El Qadim, N. (2010). La politique migratoire européenne vue du Maroc: contraintes et opportunités. *Politique européenne*, n° 31: 91118.

El Qadim, N. (2014). Postcolonial challenges to migration control: French–Moroccan cooperation practices on forced returns. *Security Dialogue* 45 (3): 24261.

Ellermann, A. (2008). The limits of unilateral migration control: Deportation and inter-state cooperation. *Government and Opposition* 43(2): 16889.

Elmadmad, K. (2004). *La nouvelle loi marocaine du 11 novembre 2003 relative à l'entrée et au séjour des étrangers au Maroc, et à l'émigration et l'immigration irrégulières.* San Domenico di Fiesole (FI): EUI/CARIM-RSCAS.

Fassin, D. (2005). Compassion and Repression: The Moral Economy of Immigration Policies in France. *Cultural Anthropology* 20 (3): 36287.

Fisher Onar, N. and Nicolaïdis, K. (2013). The Decentring Agenda: Europe as a post-colonial power. *Cooperation and Conflict* 48(2): 283303.

Gabrielli, L. (2008). Flux et contre-flux entre l'Espagne et le Sénégal. L'externalisation du contrôle des dynamiques migratoires vers l'Afrique de l'Ouest. *Asylon(s)*, n° 3(mars). Available at : http://www.reseau-terra.eu/article716.html

Geddes, A. (2005). Europe's Border Relationships and International Migration Relations. *Journal of Common Market Studies* 43(4): 787806.

Greenhill, K. M. (2010). *Weapons of Mass Migration: Forced Displacement, Coercion, and Foreign Policy*. Cornell Studies in Security Affairs. Ithaca, NY: Cornell University Press.

Guild, E., Carrera, S. and Balzacq, T. (2008). *The changing dynamics of security in an enlarged European Union*. Brussels: CEPS.

Guiraudon, V. and Lahav, G. (2000). A Reappraisal of the State Sovereignty Debate. *Comparative Political Studies* 33 (2): 16395.

Hobson, J. M. (2012). *The Eurocentric Conception of World Politics: Western International Theory, 1760-2010*. New York: Cambridge University Press.

Huysmans, J. (2000). The European Union and the Securitization of Migration. *JCMS: Journal of Common Market Studies* 38(5): 75177.

İçduygu, A. and Aksel, D.B. (2014). Two-to-Tango in Migration Diplomacy: Negotiating Readmission Agreement between the eu and Turkey. *European Journal of Migration and Law* 16(3): 33763.

Iskander, N. (2010). *Creative State: Forty Years of Migration and Development Policy in Morocco and Mexico*. Ithaca, NY: Cornell University Press.

Keohane, R. O. and Nye, J.S. (1977). *Power and Interdependence: World Politics in Transition*. Boston: Little Brown and Company.

Kinnvall, C. (2016). The Postcolonial Has Moved into Europe: Bordering, Security and Ethno-Cultural Belonging. *JCMS: Journal of Common Market Studies* 54(1): 15268.

Kunz, R. Lavenex,S. and Panizzon, M. (2011). *Multilayered Migration Governance. The promise of partnership*. Abingdon: Routledge.

Lavenex, S. (2004). EU external governance in "wider Europe". *Journal of European Public Policy* 11(4): 680700.

Lavenex, S. (2006). Shifting up and out: the foreign policy of European immigration control. *West European Politics* 29(2): 32950.

Lavenex, S. and Uçarer, E.M. eds. (2002). *Migration and the externalities of European integration*. Lanham, Boulder, New York, Oxford: Lexington Books.

Lavenex, S. and Wichmann, N. (2009). The external governance of EU internal security. *Journal of European Integration* 31(1): 83102.

Messari, N. and Willis, M. (2003). Analyzing Moroccan Foreign Policy and Relations with Europe. *The Review of International Affairs* 3(2): 15272.

Mezzadra, S. (2004). The right to escape. *Ephemera. Theory and politics in organization* 4(3): 26775.

Mignolo, W. D. (2000). *Local histories / Global designs. Coloniality, subaltern knowledges and border thinking.* Princeton: Princeton University Press.

Natter, K. (2013). The Formation of Morocco's Policy Towards Irregular Migration (2000–2007): Political Rationale and Policy Processes. *International Migration*, n/a–n/a.

Nicolaïdis, K. and Howse, R. (2002). 'This Is My EUtopia ...': Narrative as Power'. *JCMS: Journal of Common Market Studies* 40(4): 76792.

Pallister-Wilkins, P. (2015, Dec. 09). There's A Focus On The Boats Because The Sea Is Sexier Than The Land: A Reflection on the Centrality of the Boats in the Recent 'Migration Crisis'. *The Disorder Of Things*. Available at : http://thedisorderofthings.com/2015/12/09/theres-a-focus-on-the-boats-because-the-sea-is-sexier-than-the-land-a-reflection-on-the-centrality-of-the-boats-in-the-recent-migration-crisis/

Paoletti, E. (2010). *The Migration of Power and North-South Inequalities: The Case of Italy and Libya.* New York : Palgrave Macmillan.

Patel, K. K. (2013). Provincialising European Union: co-operation and integration in Europe in a historical perspective. *Contemporary European History* 22(4): 64973.

Putnam, R. D. (1988). 'Diplomacy and domestic politics: the logic of two-level games'. *International Organization* 42(3): 42760.

Reslow, N. (2012). The Role of Third Countries in EU Migration Policy: The Mobility Partnerships. *European Journal of Migration and Law* 14(4): 393415.

Rutazibwa, O. U. (2010). The Problematics of the EU's Ethical (Self)Image in Africa: The EU as an 'Ethical Intervener' and the 2007 Joint Africa–EU Strategy. *Journal of Contemporary European Studies* 18(2): 20928.

Sabaratnam, M. (2011). IR in dialogue... but can we change the subjects? A typology of decolonising strategies for the study of world politics. *Millenium* 39(3): 781803.

Sayad, A. (2004). *The Suffering of the Immigrant.* Cambridge and Malden: Polity Press.

Schimmelfennig, F. and Sedelmeier, U. (2004). Governance by conditionality: EU rule transfer to the candidate countries of Central and Eastern Europe. *Journal of European Public Policy* 11(4): 66179.

Teitelbaum, M. S. (1984). Immigration, Refugees, and Foreign Policy. *International Organization* 38(3): 42950.

Tickner, A. B. (2003). Seeing IR Differently: Notes from the Third World. *Millennium - Journal of International Studies* 32(2): 295324.

Tickner, A. B. (2013). Core, Periphery and (Neo)imperialist International Relations. *European Journal of International Relations* 19(3): 62746.

Tickner, A. B. and Blaney, D.L. eds. (2012). *Thinking International Relations Differently.* New York: Routledge.

Tickner, A. B. and Wæver, O. eds. (2007). *International Relations Scholarship Around the World.* New York: Routledge.

Wolff, S. (2014). The Politics of Negotiating EU Readmission Agreements: Insights from Morocco and Turkey. *European Journal of Migration and Law* 16(1): 6995.

Wunderlich, D. (2010). Differentiation and Policy Convergence against Long Odds: Lessons from Implementing EU - Migration Policy in Morocco. *Mediterranean Politics* 15(2): 24972.

Wunderlich, D. (2012). The limits of external governance: implementing EU external migration policy. *Journal of European Public Policy* 19(9): 141433.

Le360.ma. (2016, Feb. 27). Migrants clandestins: Mohammed VI s'entretient au téléphone avec Angela Merkel. Available at : http://www.le360.ma/fr/politique/migrants-clandestins-mohammed-vi-sentretient-au-telephone-avec-angela-merkel-62234

Zaragoza C. (2016, Feb. 10). Fortress Europe? Porous Borders and EU Dependence on Neighbour Countries. *E-IR.* http://www.e-ir.info/2016/01/02/fortress-europe-porous-borders-and-eu-dependence-on-neighbour-countries/

9

'Ungoverned Spaces?' The Islamic State's Challenge to (Post-)Westphalian 'Order'

MATT GORDNER

The primary lesson that we need to learn has to do with this large, in fact global problem that we have of an ungoverned space. Those are the places that are used by international terrorists as safe havens. And those are the spaces that need to be filled one way or another. And those are not spaces that can be permanently filled by the Unites States or the West writ large. That's something that can only be done by Muslims. And so I think if there's a lesson that is reinforced by our experience in Afghanistan it's that this global struggle is really not between the West and a group of radical Islamists. This is a struggle within the Islamic world for the heart and the soul of the Islamic world. And ultimately it's Muslims who are going to determine the victor in all of this.
— Robert Grenier, former CIA Station Chief in Afghanistan and Pakistan.

Introduction: The Salafi-Jihadist Challenge

The existence of 'rogue,' 'weak,' or 'failed' states generates frequent academic debate over the ubiquity and success of an international Westphalian 'order.' To what extent can we maintain that this order is stable and lasting given the recurring evidence of its breach? Following 9/11, the 'War on Terror' called into question the coherence of the Westphalian system's most salient feature — state sovereignty — on two fronts. First, for al-Qaeda's means and ambitions to found a global caliphate, and second, for the rationale that then United States President George H. W. Bush proffered over 'selective sovereignty' in justifying the rupture of the sovereignty of certain states suspected of harbouring terrorists in order to secure the sovereignty of the so-called 'well-ordered' states (Acharya 2015).

The Islamic State's declaration of a caliphate in June 2014 reinvigorated this debate and a newfound sense of urgency. As Mark Lynch argues, 'The Islamic state has indisputably reshaped the region's strategic and intellectual agenda ... [posing] an intriguing ideational challenge to the norms of state sovereignty that underlie international society' (Lynch 2015: 2). This chapter contributes to the debate over the challenge that the Islamic State poses to Westphalian and post-Westphalian international order. The first section draws on Ikenberry's (2014) work on order as power, legitimacy, and functionality to chart the relevant intellectual terrain. The second section examines the Islamic State in terms of establishing and imposing the 'Caliphate' on local populations (power), support for its normative project (legitimacy), and its ability to provide an alternative order (functionality). In the third section, I argue that the Islamic State's ability to project an alternative 'order' derives in part from the uneven, inconsistent, and incoherent application of the tenets of global democracy and international liberalism — the same tenets that are purportedly threatened by the Islamic State's advance.

(Post-)Westphalian 'Order' and Its Discontents

Assessing the kinds of challenges that the Islamic State poses to Westphalian and post-Westphalian norms of international order requires a brief discussion of what constitutes an international order in the first place. According to Ikenberry (2014: 85), international order refers to 'the settled arrangements that define and guide relations between states.' Lasting and pervasive international orders exhibit three defining characteristics: power, legitimacy, and functionality. States can only create and enforce international order where they are materially capable of coercion and enticement (power); the institutions and the 'rules of the game' they prescribe must garner 'normative approbation' (legitimacy); and participating states must find within the order some benefit, whether the provision of services or the ability to overcome collective problems insufficiently or unsatisfactorily resolved by the previous order (functionality). New orders therefore 'need only exist relative to alternative orders that might be on offer. Orders may be more or less built around a dominant power, more or less based on a normative consensus, and more or less able to provide functional benefits and services' (ibid.: 84).

Signed in 1648, The Treaties of Westphalia (or Peace of Westphalia) brought about an end to the Thirty Years' War (1618–1648) fought between Protestant and Catholic powers in Europe. The commonly held understanding of 'Westphalia' today is that it is an international order marked by 'sovereign, equal, territorial states in which non-intervention into the internal affairs of another state is the rule' (Schmidt 2011: 602). As Falk reminds us, however, '"Westphalia" contains an inevitable degree of incoherence by combining the territorial/juridical logic of equality with the geopolitical/hegemonic logic of inequality' (Falk 2002: 312). Rival states, great powers, and domestic elites frequently breach and circumvent sovereignty and equality when and where it serves their interests to do so (Krasner 1999). Colonialism and post-colonialism both reified and weakened — at different times and in different places — the establishment of borders (Keene 2002). The idea that Westphalia is the harbinger of world 'order' leaves us with the mistaken understanding that it solved a problem of 'anarchy' elsewhere, namely, outside of Europe. For its Eurocentrism and anachronisms many scholars have thus committed to calling 'Westphalia' a myth or narrative that does more to obfuscate the realities of international relations than it does to elucidate them (Kayaoglu 2010). Students of Middle Eastern and North African (MENA) politics have long noted the differential identity politics that communities of this region subscribe to, both pre- and post-Ottoman times — many of which prioritize the family or tribe far above that of the nation (Tibi 1990). This not only complicates the Euro-centric understanding of nationalism, but it also affirms more recent studies that demonstrates how scholarship tends to consider the concept of sovereignty among MENA states and peoples as somehow deficient or lacking compared to the ideal-type assumed by the Western, European trajectory (Allinson 2016). Indeed, not all sovereignties are constructed, let alone conceived, alike. Falk argues that there are four possible 'Westphalias': the event, the idea, the process, and the 'normative score sheet'.

> As event, Westphalia refers to the peace settlement negotiated at the end of the Thirty Years War (1618–1648), which has also served as establishing the structural frame for world order that has endured, with modifications from time to time, until present. As idea, Westphalia refers to the state-centric character of world order premised on full participatory membership being accorded exclusively to territorially based sovereign states. As process, Westphalia refers to the changing character of the state and statecraft as it has evolved during more than 250 years since the treaties were negotiated, with crucial developments as both colonialism and decolonization, the advent of weaponry of mass destruction, the establishment of international institutions, the rise of global market forces, and the emergence of global civil society. As

> normative score sheet, Westphalia refers to the strengths and
> weaknesses, as conditioned by historical circumstances, of
> such a sovereignty based system, shielding oppressive states
> from accountability and exposing weak and economically
> disadvantaged states to intervention and severe forms of
> material deprivation (Falk 2002: 312).

According to Ikenberry, liberal internationalism exists uneasily alongside Westphalia. This liberal project 'has entailed a commitment to international order that is open and at least loosely rule based... most of which are complimentary but some of which conflict' (Ikenberry 2014: 93–94). Democratic rule of law at home and abroad, secured by regional and international institutions, the full-scale promotion of open markets and free trade, and shared concerns for global security and human rights all suggest liberal internationalism was at its height following the cold war (Hoffmann 1995). Yet liberal internationalism is being forced to undergo a substantial revision following from its first (Wilsonian) and second (post-cold war) iterations, both of which took place during eras of American hegemony. Proponents of liberal internationalism '3.0' face a number of obstacles: the scope and hierarchy of the previously United States-dominated versions are at odds with the more inclusive and universalized vision sought out by an increasing share of states (and regions), indicating not only the need for more robust capacity and legitimacy for international institutions, but for a consensus on the norms of intervention in the post-Westphalian system (Ikenberry 2010).

The contours and contents of post-Westphalia differ markedly within the literature along a utopian-dystopian axis. Falk imagines post-Westphalia as a turn towards cosmopolitan democracy (global citizenship) alongside economic and political regionalism. Within the economic camp lies the 'image of a borderless world dominated by markets and global corporations and banks' that are at the same time 'reinforced by the rise of cyber-consciousness with its affinities for "self-organizing systems" and libertarian critiques of government', indicating the potential formation of both supranational institutions as well as those emerging respectively 'from within and below'. The political camp aims to consolidate a 'unified world order' of global peace and security through international institutions (Falk 2002: 326). Sarkar's evaluation of the political elements of post-Westphalia is based on four facets of international relations: (1) the increasing 'agency' (read: power) of transnational corporations based particularly on 'trading states'; (2) the uptick in non-governmental organizations corresponding to the inability or unwillingness of governments to adequately address the fast paces of economic, social, and political change brought on by rapid technological advances, political fragmentation, and economic interdependence; (3) the need for a more comprehensive military policy at the international level especially given the failed United States-led military initiatives of the past decade and a half; and, (4) the tensions between humanitarian intervention — or the threat of intervention — in order to promote human rights, and the principle of sovereignty enshrined in the Westphalian order (Sarkar 2015).

Falk also raises a dystopian variant of post-Westphalia based on 'intensifying trends toward religious and ethnic exclusivism as the claimed basis for fulfilling a right of self-determination and an array of chauvinistic backlashes that seek to hijack government to carry out an anti-immigrant agenda' (Falk 2002: 332). In light of recent national and international trends, Falk's dystopian variant applies equally to democratic and non-democratic institutions and governance structures. The success of the 'leave' vote in the 'Brexit' referendum, and the ascendance of Donald Trump in the United States, all speak to the confluence of demagoguery and populism driven by political and economic pressures whose safety valves rely on exclusivist, racist, anti-immigrant, and xenophobic discourses as solutions to the problems of legitimacy and confidence in the existing structures of finance and governance. So, too, however, is the rise of the Islamic State a portent of the dystopian post- and decidedly anti-Wesphalian (dis)order, one based on a radical project to re-imagine international relations and a sharp bifurcation between 'us' and 'them' in the form of *dar-al-harb* and *dar-al-Islam* — the abode of war and the abode of peace, respectively.

The Islamic State: The Proto-State 'Caliphate'

The Islamic State's organizational roots date back to al-Tawhid wal Jihad, founded in 1998 by Abu Musab al-Zarqawi. In 2004, Zarqawi (d. 2006) pledged allegiance to Osama Bin Laden (d. 2011), and his organization was renamed al-Qaeda in the Land of the Two Rivers. Two years later, that organization morphed into al-Qaeda in Iraq (AQI) under the leadership of Abu Omar al-Baghdadi (d. 2010). Upon the death of Abu Omar al-Baghdadi, Abu Bakr al-Baghdadi was elected the new leader of AQI.

In 2011, Baghdadi sent one of his high-ranking officials, Abu Mohammad al-Jolani, to establish an al-Qaeda affiliate, Jahbat al-Nusra, in Syria, with the blessing of al-Qaeda's current leader, Ayman al-Zawahiri. Baghdadi then unilaterally declared Nusra and AQI as one under The Islamic State of Iraq and al-Sham (ISIS). When Zawahiri condemned the move and ordered ISIS to return to Iraq, Baghdadi paid no heed, and a chasm emerged that ended in waves of Nusra fighters defecting to ISIS. On 1 July 2014, The Islamic State was officially declared the 'Caliphate,' with Baghdadi the purported 'Caliph' of all Muslims worldwide.

The shortening of the Islamic State's appellation is significant for several reasons. Here, let us recall Ikenberry's three qualifications for establishing a world order: power, legitimacy, and functionality. First, it marked a point of transition from terrorist group to proto-state, including a government, central administration, and military capable of 'lasting,' and to some extent, 'expanding' (power). For another, it was a titular representation of the successful takeover of territories straddling the borders of eastern Syria and western Iraq. For many in the Arab and Muslim world, the symbolic (or not so symbolic) erasure of the border is both a political and religious goal that transcends Salafi-Jihadists' minoritarian interpretations of Islamic order.

Not even the most powerful Arab leaders like Egypt's Gamal Abdel Nasser could wipe away the colonial borders established by the secretive Sykes-Picot agreement between the British and French in 1916, and not since the Ottoman Empire has any Muslim group or leadership claimed the mantle to uphold 'true' Islam, let alone to usher in the apocalypse through the establishment of a caliphate. The Islamic State therefore positioned itself as *the* focal point for Salafi-Jihadist organizations and some Muslims who, though abhorring violence, share some affinity with the project of (re) establishing a transnational Islamic polity (legitimacy). Finally, the Islamic State is in a position to provide a model and, to a lesser extent, a means of establishing an alternative to Westphalia; an 'Islamic' order that brings religion back into the fold as a guiding and authoritative principle in politics (functionality).

The Power of the Islamic State: 'Lasting and Expanding'?

The Islamic State capitalized upon the destruction of Iraq following the 2003 United States invasion and the 2011 breakout of civil war in Syria in order to carve out vast territory over a population estimated to be six to ten million inhabitants, including most notably Raqqa in Syria and Mosul in Iraq. Although the Islamic State faces obstacles in expanding its revenue streams and normalizing its ideology (Revkin and McCants 2015), its motto — 'lasting and expanding' — will hold true in the short term:

> the more the Islamic State actually resembles a state, with its security provision and regulatory institutions, the less international actors will be able to "degrade" or "destroy" the group without also degrading or destroying the fundamental functions of the state. Attempts to degrade and destroy these emergent state institutions will likely lead to anarchy, which often comes with profoundly negative consequences (Mecham 2015: 21).

Mecham compares the Islamic State to a 'normal' state, measuring its performance along six functions, and 'grading' each of them accordingly:

1. Tax and labour acquisition   (7/10)
2. Citizenship   (4/10)
3. International security and foreign relations   (2/10)
4. Domestic security   (6/10)
5. Social services   (5/10)
6. Economic growth   (3/10)

In addition to the Islamic State's passing grades in taxation and labour acquisition, domestic security, and social service provision, a pragmatic relationship with the Syrian regime, creative use of online propaganda, enlisting foreign fighters and controlling local populations, and the maintenance and building of a centralized military apparatus are further indications that 'degrading and destroying' the Islamic State will require concerted international cooperation (Khatib 2015: 2). United States Department of Treasury estimates from 2015 show that the Islamic State benefited from more than a half a billion dollars in oil trade with Syria, and to a lesser extent Turkey (Faulconbridge and Saul 2015). At a United Nations council meeting in November 2015 Russian U.N. Ambassador Vitaly Churkin estimated that the group took in $250 million dollars from phosphate sales, $200 million from barley and rye, and an additional $100 million from cement, with $30 million allocated monthly for the purchase of weapons through Eastern European shell companies (Nichols and Irish 2015).

While popular media continues to label the Islamic State as a 'terrorist organization,' its tactics and capabilities more closely approximate an insurgency (Moghadam, Berger, and Beliakova 2014). Its shift from armed attacks and targeted killings to house demolitions and the establishment of checkpoints to control cities 'resembles the "Clear, Hold, Build" strategy of classic insurgency literature' (Bilger 2014: 11). The Islamic State operates an organized security service that includes military intelligence (*amn al-askari*), foreign intelligence (*amn al-kharji*), state security (*amn al-dawla*), and an interior ministry (*amn al-dakhili*). Estimates on the number of fighters the Islamic state had across Syria and Iraq in 2015 vary wildly, from 20,000 to 200,000 (Gerstein-Ross 2015). U.S. estimates place the figure at 25,000, with an additional 6,000 fighters stationed in Libya (Landay 2016). A 2016 Military Balance Report indicated that despite setbacks, and the attentions of an American-led air coalition that had been attacking ISIS in Syria since September 2014 (and in Iraq since earlier in the year), the jihadist organisation continued to resist and expand, surprising local and international audiences with its resilience, adaptability, and brutality.

The Legitimacy of the Islamic State: Normalizing the Salafi-Jihadist Ideology

Do the institutions and the 'rules of the game' that the Islamic State practices and enforces garner 'normative approbation,' or legitimacy? Brunzel's analysis indicates that the Islamic State's foot soldiers may not be well versed in its ideology upon joining, but that its leadership is comprised of hardened adherents to Salafi-Jihadist ideology (Brunzel 2015). Recruits reportedly take two-week seminars before being assigned to their battalions (Weiss 2015a). Those who defect from rival factions are rung through three-month re-indoctrination boot camps (Weiss 2015b). In Raqqa, men with prior experience in Islamic education are provided training in order to be placed within the administration as teachers, prayer leaders, and imams, as the first issue of *Dabiq*, the Islamic State's English language publication, suggests.

In addition to providing some social services, law enforcement, and medical care, the Islamic State is beginning to institute a school curriculum informed by its radical brand of Salafi-Jihadism. A document obtained by *Niqash* reports that pre-teens learn arithmetic through war scenarios: 'If the Islamic State has 275,220 heroes in a battle and the unbelievers have 356,230, who has more soldiers?' (*Daily Beast/Niqash* 2015). In a recent PBS documentary, journalist Najibullah Quraishi visits an Islamic State school in Afghanistan where children learn Jihadist ideology, review military tactics, and practice combat drills. Teachers showcase online videos on 'how to kill people, how to behead, and how to become suicide bombers' (*PBS Newshour* 2016). In Raqqa, the Islamic State recently opened twelve schools for boys and twelve schools for girls, including courses for teenagers and adults with officially sanctioned curriculums (Khatib 2015).

Preference falsification and small sample sizes render reliable data on local support difficult to secure, but defectors report un-Islamic behaviour, in-group fighting, and low standards of living (Neumann 2015). Conceivably, the longer the Islamic State 'lasts,' the more likely that it is able to consolidate the institutions of state, and the more likely local populations could be normalized into its systems of governance and indoctrination.

The Functionality of the Islamic State: Towards a Trans-National Caliphate?

Providing an alternative to the Westphalian order requires that the Islamic State offers a model that benefits other 'states,' whether materially or ideologically. One of the indirect aims of the Islamic State is to overturn the Westphalian model by introducing a global caliphate in the region. Rather than beginning with a monolithic, contiguous entity that expands outwards from its territory in Syria-Iraq, the Islamic State seeks to carve out 'statelets,' or *wilayat*, within preexisting (Westphalian) state entities that, ostensibly, the Islamic State aspires to join together at a later date. Insofar as this model depends on taking over smaller blocks of territory within weak or ungoverned areas, the functionality of their model thus relies on its exportability, the dysfunctionality of weak states, and the delegitimization of Westphalian order.

Salafi-Jihadist groups gain easy access to what is believed to be the Islamic State's three-step strategy. Released online in 2004, the 248-page document entitled *The Management of Savagery* instructs readers to first pull western militaries into a 'stage of vexation and exhaustion,' followed by 'the administration of savagery,' and, finally, 'the establishment of the Islamic State' (Atwan 2015: 153–165). One ISIS cleric avers that the book is already 'widely circulated among provincial ISIS commanders and some rank-and-file fighters as a way to justify beheadings as not only religiously permissible but recommended by God and his prophet' (Weiss and Hassan 2015: 41).

Though refusing to recognize the sovereignty of other states, the Islamic State goes to great lengths to legitimise its own by projecting itself as *the* Islamic alternative to Western hegemony (Nielson 2015). Following the annexation of a swath of land across the Iraq-Syrian border, the fourth issue of *The Islamic State Report* (2016: 1) declared that,

> Years after the [Sykes-Picot] agreement, invisible borders would go on to separate between a Muslim and his brother, and pave the way for ruthless, nationalistic tawaghit [idolaters] to entrench the ummah's division rather than working to unite the Muslims under one imam carrying the banner of truth. Each taghut [idolater] in the lands of the Muslims was satisfied having his own piece of land to rule over and, in some cases, a grandiose title he assigned himself, such as Ghaddafi's "King of the Kings of Africa". This was in spite of that same ruler's humiliated position as a kafir [non-Muslim] puppet.

In the twelfth issue of *Dabiq*, captured-photojournalist John Cantlie was named as the purported author in an article quoting a United States Brigadier General as saying:

> The Islamic State meets all requirements ... to be recognized as a state," he said. "It has a governing structure, it controls territory, a large population, is economically viable, has a large and effective military and provides governmental services such as health care to its population. Dealing with it as if it were a terrorist movement is a non-starter. It is a State and if the West

wants to defeat it, it must accept either: 1) The Islamic State is enough of a threat to world or regional peace that the West is willing to go to war with it, or 2) The costs of a war are too great and the West must plan to contain the Islamic State and ultimately negotiate with it as a sovereign State (*Dabiq* 2015, 49).

In addition to the 43 organizations across Africa, Asia, Australia, and Europe that pledged allegiance or support to Baghdadi (*IntelCenter* 2015), its foreign fighters hale from over 100 nations worldwide in what the United Nations has deemed both 'an immediate and long-term threat' (Burke 2015). Returning fighters pose significant regional security risks as conveyer belts for the Islamic State's ideology and for the implementation of its local terror plots. According to Zelin, 'its wilayat in Libya and Sinai are following the same methodology on the ground and in the media as the Islamic State's wilayat have in Iraq and Syria' (Zelin 2015: 25). Libya is crucial, since its oil wealth could provide additional resources to maintain and expand the Islamic State's territorial claims and strongholds in self-proclaimed wilayats across the African continent (Dyer 2016).

Salafi-Jihadism is a continent-wide security concern that claims tens of thousands of lives across Africa annually (*The Economist* 2015). The acceptance of the pledge of allegiance by Nigeria's Boko Haram in March 2015 — a group responsible for over six thousand deaths in Northern Nigeria in 2014 alone (Karimi and Almasy 2016) — is further indication that its overall strategy of taking over unsecure and ungoverned areas is succeeding. If seized, co-opted, and/or monopolized by a network of Islamic State wilayats, ancient trade routes across the Sahel could pose a major obstacle to stemming the flow of arms and funds to Islamic State-aligned Jihadist groups across Africa and into Asia and Europe (Caulderwood 2015). An overturned Westphalian 'order' is just as, if not more, likely to emanate in the long run from an epicentre on the African continent as it is from the 'Caliphate' in Iraq-Syria.

Conclusion

The current 'order' is marked neither by the Westphalian 'idea' of absolute nation-state sovereignty nor by the post-Westphalian imaginary of global democracy. On the one hand, globalization renders the Westphalian state porous. On the other, cosmopolitanism remains the privilege of social minorities. States are the primary holders of power over and within the *international* system, yet a hierarchy exists among them, and loose networks of political and economic elites comprise a class that preserves an uneven distribution of power within and between them. A vision of liberal internationalism that aims at promoting democracy, human rights, and free markets through international laws and institutions occupies this uneasy interregnum through a more or less universal consensus reached by state leaders that no viable alternative is available despite the many apparent problems with maintaining an 'order' that is capable of being so dis-orderly. This consensus garners only partial legitimacy, however, and both within and across states a polarization is emerging that contests the legitimacy of a system that proposes democracy while aiding to contravene its substantive theoretical commitments to 'freedom and equality.'

Many among Arab, Muslim, and post-colonial communities harbour understandable resentment towards those states that practiced and continue to maintain relationships of dependency and uneven development between what, for simplicity's sake, is often referred to as the 'global North' over the 'global South.' Oftentimes, perpetuating these relationships thwarts economic equalities and political liberalisation. On the one hand, the economic policies advocated by international financial institutions beginning in the 1980s led to the withdrawal of social security with severe forms of privatisation that restricted social movements for human rights while enriching the political and economic elite across the MENA region and widening domestic economic inequalities (Hanieh 2013). On the other hand, selective military interventions (Libya, Syria, Iraq) in the name of 'democracy' further destabilized the security of the region, while continued support for dictatorships proved Western commitments to democratic transformations to be empty rhetoric.

'The reluctance of politicians to use the word "state,"' Napoleoni argues, 'springs from the fear of accepting, if only with a word, the claim of the Islamic State to be not a terrorist organization, but a legitimized war of conquest and internal consensus' (Napoleoni 2014: xi). The Islamic State's territorial claims over large areas of Iraq and Syria; its ability to exploit weak and failed states to secure footholds across the African and Asian continents; and the 'lone wolf' and pre-meditated attacks in Australia, Belgium, Canada, France, and the United States make the Islamic State a veritable security threat to regional and international populations. Yet, neither its terrorist nor insurgency tactics make the Islamic State particularly unique in the annals of political violence.

Its challenge to international order arises from the fact that it 'rejects the central principles and institutions of the international society and outlines an alternative way to organizing the world that is not based on states' (Mendehlson 2015: 10). The possibility for the Islamic State to threaten (and not only challenge) the (post-)Westphalian international order exists insofar as it can successfully establish the 'Caliphate' as both an empirical reality and ideational construct. As argued above, this involves imposing the 'Caliphate' on local populations (power) while garnering and maintaining support for its normative project (legitimacy) and continuously providing materially and ideologically visions of an alternative Islamic order (functionality). In other words, the Islamic State poses a challenge to international order by calling out the foundational principles and tenets upon which (post-)Westphalianism is based, starting — according to its own narrative — with the imposition of the Sykes-Picot Agreement of 1916 in formerly Ottoman Caliphal lands. It only becomes a veritable threat when the Islamic State is able to assert its model of statehood as a reliable competitor to the Westphalian state system. That project began with the erasure of the Sykes-Picot border, and it ends — again, according to its own narrative — with the extension of the 'Caliphate' *in toto*. The possibility of the Islamic State replacing (post-)Westphalia is well-nigh impossible, and its ability to pose an actual threat to international order is highly unlikely insofar as a clear majority of the world's states are invested in the 'order' that liberal internationalism and its primary backers support.

Nonetheless, the threshold between a 'challenge' and a 'threat' is tenuous, and diffusion effects are unpredictable especially in regions wrought by weak and failed states with sizeable unstable or 'ungoverned' spaces. Thus, while cautioning against the self-fulfilling prophecy of the 'clash of civilizations' that replaced the Cold War as the next worst threat against 'Western' interests, it is important at the same time to acknowledge the regional insecurity that the continued presence of the Islamic State signifies alongside some of the underlying causes of the Islamic State's rise, including the grievances of its leadership and cadre of militants and supporters. In this regard, Salafi-Jihadism generally, and the Islamic State in particular, will likely remain a challenge to regional, if not international, order, for the foreseeable future. The rise of the Islamic State indicates a high level of disaffection with the current 'order,' as well as some support for an alternative, dystopian post-Westphalian order based on so-called 'Islamic' (read: Salafi-Jihadist) values. While not diametrically opposed or locked into some Manichean dualism, liberal internationalism and the Islamic State's model of the 'Caliphate' nonetheless represent competing universalisms.

As Hayman and Williams (2006: 531) propose:

> Maintaining a norm system in the face of multi-faceted opposition may produce two polar outcomes. Either the system realises its ultimate form by a process of incremental strengthening or its opponents succeed in dissolving the

mortar of its foundations. Alternatively, an uneasy balance emerges between the two, whereby a new, but inherently unstable, position is adopted containing in it a delicate and shifting relationship aspects of both establishment and oppositional principles. This requires rendering malleable the establishment principle that the established teleology has petrified.

Putting the onus on Muslims alone to 'fill' the 'ungoverned spaces,' as quoted at the outset of this chapter, overlooks the role of international actors as either directly or indirectly responsible for the outbreak of increasingly violent and capable generations of Salafi-Jihadists. It is, after all, the uneven and incoherent application of the admixture of Westphalian and post-Westphalian 'order' that produced the structural conditions upon which the Islamic State capitalized to produce a proto-state in the first place (Nuruzzaman 2015). The central grievances expressed by the Islamic state and its supporters indicate a keen awareness of regional and international injustices based upon a history of colonialism, corrupt Arab leaderships, and continued Western support for them — militarily, economically, politically, or all of the above. While the brand of violence they use to oppose these grievances are brutal and anathema to regional and international peace, it is important to recognize that their critique of the international order and its imbalances is not mistaken. It should therefore come as no surprise that in the face of a secular world order, religion was brought back as a central organizing principle with Salafi-Jihadists as the 'couriers of religious logic' (Mendelsohn 2012).

Remedying the advance of the Islamic State will undoubtedly require military measures. Bearing in mind that bombing the populations under Islamic State control may produce more rather than less radicalism, halting the ideological advance of the Islamic State will require, as Hayman and Williams are cited above, that we 'realise the ultimate form of the system by a process of incremental strengthening.' One might then consider countering the Islamic State's ideology with a consistent application of our own. In this scenario, delegitimizing the Islamic State's dystopian post-Westphalian 'order' requires that the international community (re)formulate and actively practice a coherent doctrine in which the pillars of global democracy and liberal internationalism are prioritized above and beyond realpolitik. We might start, as this chapter suggests, by targeting the most vulnerable people residing in the so-called 'ungoverned spaces' most inclined to produce the territorial, material, and human resources capable of further empowering the Islamic State and its Salafi-Jihadist kin. We might also consider the cadre of foreign fighters hailing from the diverse community of nations as an indication that 'a "clash of civilisations" between Islam and the West is woefully misleading' (Atran 2015). Expounding on the Islamic State's fighters, Atran (2015) avers:

[v]iolent extremism represents not the resurgence of traditional cultures, but their collapse, as young people unmoored from millennial traditions flail about in search of a social identity that gives personal significance and glory. This is the dark side of globalization. Individuals radicalise to find a firm identity in a flattened world. In this new reality, vertical lines of communication between the generations are replaced by horizontal peer-to-peer attachments that can cut across the globe.

Countering the Islamic State's ideology thus requires a better understanding of its adherents' grievances. This includes acknowledging the connections between the destruction wrought by a history of colonialism, illegal and ill-conceived patterns of foreign military intervention, the continued support for dictatorial regimes through direct or indirect military armaments, and the deleterious promotion of neoliberal economic policies that further dependency relationships and thwart local and regional forms of economic sustainability and cooperation. All of these contribute to the self-fulfilling prophecy of 'clashing civilizations' and world (dis)orders that serve to perpetuate the legitimacy, power, and functionality of the counter-order upon which the Islamic State bases its religious, political, and moral claims. Conceiving of non-military medium-term and long-term solutions to the Islamic State's challenge means not only looking forward to consider how the international community can buttress domestic and regional advancements in democracy and stability through 'incremental strengthening' of commitments to the utopian variant of Westphalia. It also means reflecting back upon the historical prioritization of stability over democracy endemic to Westphalia's shifting and uneven conceptualization and application.

References

Acharya, A. (2007). State Sovereignty after 9/11: Disorganized Hypocrisy. *Political Studies* 5(2): 274-296.

Acharya, A. (2015, June 25). How the two Big Ideas of the post-Cold War Era failed. *The Washington Post*. Available at: https://www.washingtonpost.com/news/monkey-cage/wp/2015/06/24/how-the-two-big-ideas-of-the-post-cold-war-era-failed/

Albert, M. (2006). *Identities, Borders, Orders: Rethinking International Relations Theory*. Minneapolis: University of Minnesota Press.

Allinson, J. (2016). *The Struggle for the State in Jordan: The Social Origins of Alliances in the Middle East*. London: IB Tauris.

Atran, S. (2015, December 15). Isis is a Revolution. *AEON*. Available at: https://aeon.co/essays/why-isis-has-the-potential-to-be-a-world-altering-revolution

Atwan, Abdel Bari. 2015. *Islamic State: The Digital Caliphate.* Oakland: University of California Press.

Back to School in Mosul. (2015, October 29). *The Daily Beast.* Available at: http://www.thedailybeast.com/articles/2015/10/29/back-to-school-in-mosul-the-isis-curriculum.html

Bilger, A. (2014, May 22). ISIS Annual Reports Reveal a Metrics-Driven Military Command. *Institute for the Study of War*. Available at: http://www.understandingwar.org/backgrounder/ISIS-Annual-Reports-Reveal-Military-Organization

Brunzel, C. (2015). From Paper State to Caliphate: The Ideology of the Islamic State. *Center for Middle East Policy at Brookings Analysis Paper* 19: 1-42.

Burke, J. (2015, May 26). Islamic State Fighters Drawn from Half the World's Countries, says UN. *The Guardian*. Available at: https://www.theguardian.com/world/2015/may/26/islamist-fighters-drawn-from-half-the-worlds-countries-says-un

Caulderwood, K. (2015, June 6). Drugs and Money in the Sahara: How The Global Cocaine Trade is Funding North African Jihad. *International Business Times*. Available at: http://www.ibtimes.com/drugs-money-sahara-how-global-cocaine-trade-funding-north-african-jihad-1953419

Dryzek, J. S. (2012).Global Civil Society: The Progress of Post-Westphalian Politics. *Annual Review of Political Science* 15: 101-19.

Dyer, J. (2016, January 6). The Islamic State's Next Target: Libyan Oil. *Vice News*. Available at: https://news.vice.com/article/the-islamic-states-next-target-libyan-oil

Falk, R. (2002). Revisiting Westphalia, Discovering Post-Westphalia. *The Journal of* Ethics 6(4): 311-352.

Faulconbridge, G. and Saul, J. (2015, December 15). Islamic State Oil is Going to Assad, Some to Turkey, U.S. Official says. *Reuters*. Available at: http://www.reuters.com/article/us-mideast-crisis-syria-usa-oil-idUSKBN0TT2O120151210

Gerstein-Ross, D. (2015, February 9). How Many Fighters Does The Islamic State Really Have? *War on the Rocks*. Available at: http://warontherocks.com/2015/02/how-many-fighters-does-the-islamic-state-really-have/

Hanieh, A. (2013). *Lineages of Revolt: Issues of Contemporary Capitalism in the Middle East*. Chicago: Haymarket Books.

Hayman, P.A. and Williams, J. (2006). Westphalian Sovereignty: Rights, Intervention, Meaning and Context. *Global Society* 20(4): 521-541.

How the Islamic State Indoctrinates Afghan Children. (2015). *PBS Newshour*. Available at: http://www.pbs.org/newshour/bb/how-the-islamic-state-indoctrinates-afghan-children/

Ikenberry, G. J. (2010). The Three Faces of Liberal Internationalism. In: Alexandroff, A.S. & Cooper, A.F. eds.. *Rising States, Rising Institutions: Challenges for Global Governance.* Baltimore: Brookings Institution Press. 17-47.

Ikenberry, G. J. (2014). The Logic of Order: Westphalia, Liberalism, and the Evolution of International Order in the Modern Era. In: Ikenberry, G. J. ed.. *Power, Order, and Change in World Politics*. Cambridge: Cambridge University Press. 83-106.

Jihafrica. (2015, July 18). *The Economist*. Available at: http://www.economist.com/news/middle-east-and-africa/21657801-biggest-threat-african-peace-and-prosperity-comes-dangerous

Joyce, R. (2011). Westphalia: Event, Memory, Myth. In: Johns, F., Joyce, R. & Pahuja, D. eds. *Events: The Force of International Law*. New York: Routledge. 55-68.

Karimi, F. and Almasy, S. (2016, February 14). Boko Haram Attacks Kill at Least 30, Locals Say. *CNN*. Available at: http://edition.cnn.com/2016/02/13/africa/boko-haram-attack-nigeria/

Kayaoglu, T. (2010). Westphalian Eurocentrism in International Relations Theory. *International Studies Review* 12: 193-217.

Keene, E. (2002). *Beyond the Anarchical Society: Grotius, Order, and the Anarchical Society*. Cambridge: Cambridge University Press.

Khatab, S. (2002). *Hakimiyya* and *Jahiliyya* in the Thought of Sayyid Qutb. *Middle Eastern Studies* 38(3): 135-170.

Khatib, L. (2015, June 29). The Islamic State's Strategy: Lasting and Expanding. *Carnegie Middle East Center Paper*. Available at: http://carnegie-mec.org/2015/06/29/islamic-state-s-strategy-lasting-and-expanding-pub-60511

Klein, A. and Waked, A. (2016, January 25). Report: Islamic State, Al Qaida, Muslim Brotherhood Discuss 'Mega Merger' in Libya. *Breitbart*. Available at: http://www.breitbart.com/jihad/2016/01/25/report-islamic-state-al-qaida-muslim-brotherhood-discuss-mega-merger-in-libya/

Krasner, S. D. (1999). *Sovereignty: Organized Hypocrisy*. Princeton: Princeton University Press.

Kreuder-Sonnen, C., and Zangl, B. (2014). Which post-Westphalia? International Organizations Between Constitutionalism and Authoritarianism. *European Journal of International Relations* 21(3): 568-594.

Landay, J. (2016, February 4). New U.S. Intelligence Reports Say Islamic State Weaker. Available at: http://www.reuters.com/article/us-mideast-crisis-fighters-idUSKCN0VD2ZO

Lynch, M. (2010). Islam Divided Between Salafi-jihad and the Ikhwan. *Studies in Conflict & Terrorism* 33: 467-487.

Lynch, M. (2015, March 17). Introduction. *POMEPS Studies 12: Islamism in the IS Age*. Available at: http://pomeps.org/wp-content/uploads/2015/03/POMEPS_Studies_12_ISAge_Web.pdf

Mecham, Q. (2015, March 17). How Much of a State is the Islamic State? *POMEPS Studies 12: Islamism in the IS Age*. Available at: http://pomeps.org/wp-content/uploads/2015/03/POMEPS_Studies_12_ISAge_Web.pdf

Mendelsohn, B. (2012). God vs. Westphalia: Radical Islamist Movements and the Battle for Organizing the World. *Review of International Studies* 38: 589-613.

Mendelsohn, B. (2015, July 22). The Jihadist Threat to International Order. *POMEPS Studies 15: Islam and International Order*. Available at: http://pomeps.org/wp-content/uploads/2015/07/POMEPS_Studies_15_Islam_Web.pdf

Moghadam, A., Berger,R. and Beliakova, P. (2014). Say Terrorist, Think Insurgent: Labeling and Analyzing Contemporary Terrorist Actors. *Perspectives on Terrorism* 8(5): 1-17.

Napoleoni, L. (2014). *The Islamist Phoenix: The Islamic State and the Redrawing of the Middle East*. New York: Seven Stories Press.

Neumann, P. R. (2015, September 18). Victims, Perpetrators, Assets: The Narratives of Islamic State Defectors. *The International Centre for the Study of Radicalization and Political Violence.* Available at: http://icsr.info/wp-content/uploads/2015/09/ICSR-Report-Victims-Perpertrators-Assets-The-Narratives-of-Islamic-State-Defectors.pdf

Nichols, M. and Irish, J. (2015, December 17). U.N. Security Council Puts Focus Sanctions Focus on Islamic State. *Reuters*. Available at: http://www.reuters.com/article/us-mideast-crisis-islamic-state-un-idUSKBN0U030P20151217

Nielson, R. A. (2015, March 17). Does the Islamic State Believe in Sovereignty? *POMEPS Studies 12: Islamism in the IS Age*. Available at: http://pomeps.org/wp-content/uploads/2015/03/POMEPS_Studies_12_ISAge_Web.pdf

Nuruzzaman. M. (2015). The Challenge of the Islamic State. *Global Affairs* 1(3): 297-304.

Revkin, M. and McCants, W. (2015, November 20). Is ISIS Good at Governing? *Brookings*, 20 November. https://www.brookings.edu/blog/markaz/2015/11/20/experts-weigh-in-is-isis-good-at-governing/

Schmidt, S. (2011). To Order the Minds of Scholars: The Discourse of the Peace of Westphalia in International Relations Literature. *International Studies Quarterly* 55: 601-623.

Tatuianu, S. (2013). *Towards Global Justice: Sovereignty in an Interdependent World*. Asser Press: The Hague, Netherlands.

Tibi, B. (1990). The Simultaneity of the Unsimultaneous: Old Tribes and Imposed Nation-States in the Modern Middle East. In: Khoury, P.S. & Kostener, J. eds. *Tribes and State Formation in the Middle East*. Berkeley: University of California Press. 127-152.

The Military Balance 2016. (2016, February 9). *The International Institute of Security Studies*. Available at: https://www.iiss.org/en/publications/military%20 balance/issues/the-military-balance-2016-d6c9

Weiss, M. (2015, November 18). Inside ISIS Torture Brigades. *The Daily Beast*. Available at: http://www.thedailybeast.com/articles/2015/11/17/ inside-isis-torture-brigades.html

Weiss, M. (2015, November 16). Confessions of an ISIS Spy. *The Daily Beast*. Available at: http://www.thedailybeast.com/articles/2015/11/15/ confessions-of-an-isis-spy.html

Weiss, M. and Hassan, H. (2015). *ISIS: Inside the Army of Terror*. New York: Regan Arts.

Zelin, A. (2015, March 17). The Islamic State's Model. *POMEPS Studies 12: Islamism in the IS Age*. Available at: http://pomeps.org/wp-content/ uploads/2015/03/POMEPS_Studies_12_ISAge_Web.pdf

10

'What Goes on in the Coffin': Border Knowledges in North American Literature

ASTRID M. FELLNER & SUSANNE HAMSCHA

In *Survival*, Margaret Atwood laconically notes that 'a whole book could be written exploring the coffin-funeral syndrome in Canadian literature' (Atwood 2012: 232), whose central experience, she argues, is death and whose central mystery is that of 'what goes on in the coffin' (ibid.: 230). The 'Great Canadian Coffin,' as she calls it, bespeaks a silence and inaction, a failure to articulate a conflict or a crisis, to which death is offered as a pragmatic solution. The coffin is thus quite literally dead weight, a box that contains complicated and unresolved (hi)stories; as they are kept encased and hidden from view, these uncomfortable (hi)stories linger beneath the surface of the Canadian cultural landscape. But, as Atwood explains, they occasionally come to the fore in the shape of the archetypal casket '*with the lid off*' (ibid.: 252, emphasis in the original). The open coffin implies knowledge, 'genuine knowledge' even, which one can only gain through the comprehension of the meaning of death (ibid.: 253). In that sense, the coffin encloses fundamental truths, albeit truths that cannot be adequately represented or articulated and that, therefore, remain somewhat of an enigma.

Atwood's thoughts on the 'Great Coffin' as a Canadian literary tradition bring to mind two of the most notable appearances of coffins as containers of unspeakable knowledge in North American literature. In his 1542 account in *La Relación*, Alvar Núñez Cabeza de Vaca recounts the peculiar discovery of several boxes holding unknown bodies painted with deerskin, which subsequently were destroyed. In Herman Melville's novel *Moby-Dick* (1855), the narrator, Ishmael, becomes the lone survivor of a shipwreck as he holds on to the coffin of Queequeg, a Polynesian harpooner and Ishmael's friend. In both cases, the coffin figures as a symbol for fundamental knowledge about life and death; however, it is knowledge that neither de Vaca nor Ishmael can properly interpret and make sense of. In this essay, we want to re-read de Vaca's account of the boxed bodies and Ishmael's rescue by the coffin as instances of 'border thinking' in order to recover what we call a *cripistemology of the coffin*. We understand the coffin as a metaphor for subjugated knowledges that have been buried deep down in national cultural imaginaries and that resurge as haunting presences. This resurgence constitutes a crisis of knowledge, a *cripistemology* that builds on alternative forms of knowing, which lurks in canonical cultural texts and sits at the heart of cultural self-definition but that is generally disabled by traditional Western paradigms of thought.

A Cripistemology of the Coffin

The colonisation and settlement of the North American continent is a story of cultural imperialism, violence, and destruction. Recent interventions in the field of Native studies have argued that the conquest of Native peoples and the nationalist enterprise that entailed their sexual colonization can be understood as 'terrorizing' acts which produced a 'colonial necropolitics that framed Native peoples as queer populations marked for death' (Morgensen 2010: 106). As Scott L. Morgensen convincingly argues, the European colonizers applied their modern, Western frames of references to the practices and traditions of Native peoples, dismissing them as primitive and savage in order to be able to supplant them with their own, supposedly more 'advanced' cultural practices (ibid.).[1] Feminist and queer interventions in Native studies have theorized the complicity of terror and violence in producing a biopolitics that frames Natives as subjects of death and settlers as subjects of life; however, by approaching the project of colonialization through the lens of a 'necropolitics', to use Achille Mbembe's (2003) term, one runs the risk of re-enacting those acts of extinction and of perpetuating the silencing of indigenous voices. Rather than focus on the terrorizing acts, we want to shift attention to that which has been supplanted by those acts: what are the indigenous forms of knowledge and frames of reference that the colonizers sought to eradicate?

---

[1]   Morgensen (2010) specifically focuses on the colonizers' regulation of indigenous gender and sexuality, arguing that the project of colonization produced a 'settler sexuality,' by which he means a white national heteronormativity that forms the pinnacle of sexual modernity. However, a similar observation can be made regarding the supplementing of indigenous conceptions of disability by a modern understanding of healthy and anomalous bodies, as Kim Nielsen (2013) has shown, which is why Morgensen's argument can be expanded beyond the dimension of gender and sexuality.

As Birgit Brander Rasmussen has shown, one of the most crucial dividing lines between colonizer and colonized was writing, a practice that has often been equated with alphabetism and, therefore, excluded indigenous forms of recording (hi)stories and knowledge. Within the logic of the colonial project, literacy signified civilisation and its absence primitivism. Literary inquiry, Brander Rasmussen (2012: 4) argues, needs to acknowledge the 'agency, knowledge, and ... existence of indigenous perspectives recorded in non-alphabetic texts' in order to contest 'the monologues of colonial agents' and heighten 'our understanding of the reciprocity of the colonial encounter.' As 'literacy' and 'writing' are part of a colonizing discourse, the 'whole complex of cultural meanings' as well as 'dynamics of dominance' are disrupted if one broadens 'the definition of writing in the Americas beyond a particular semiotic system—the alphabet' (ibid.). The inclusion of non-alphabetic texts in literary analysis transforms indigenous people from mute bystanders into active, literate subjects. Consequently, a vast archive of indigenous knowledge is uncovered that has for the longest time been enclosed and buried in the depths of the cultural imaginary.

Shifting the analytical focus towards non-alphabetic texts constitutes a metaphorical opening of the coffin in which indigenous knowledges are encased. The subjugated knowledges, that thus come to the fore as images, affects, gestures and other embodied practices, are 'genuine' records, to invoke Atwood once again, which cannot be integrated into traditional patterns of articulation and meaning-making. Following their own logics and traditions, these non-alphabetic texts require their own explanatory framework to be deciphered. Elizabeth Hill Boone and Walter Mignolo call these forms of knowledge 'alternative literacies', which, as Brander Rasmussen (ibid.: 10) explains, have 'the potential to radically disrupt a colonial legacy maintained by narrow definitions of writing and literacy.'

We suggest that the crisis of Western knowledge brought about by the resurgence of subjugated knowledges produces a cripistemology of the coffin. A cripistemology draws on disability and queer epistemologies, which encourage us to question what we think we know about identity categories and how we make sense of our environs around and through them. 'Crip,' as we understand it, is a critical positionality akin to 'queer,' which as such is marked by radical disorientation and disalignment from normative discourses and practices. While 'crip' is an offspring of disability studies (just as 'queer' is a child of gender and sexuality studies), it can be used powerfully to analyse critically the quick dismissal of a wide range of bodily expressions, gestures, and practices as unusable and defective. As Johnson and McRuer explain, their coinage of the concept 'cripistemology' was inspired by a discussion centred on questions of 'knowing and unknowing disability, making and unmaking disability epistemologies, and the importance of challenging subjects who confidently "know" about "disability", as though it could be a thoroughly comprehended object of knowledge' (Johnson and McRuer 2014: 130). Johnson and McRuer's take on disability is similar to Atwood's conception of death: the genuine knowledge both disability and death bear is nearly impossible to comprehend, unless one sheds dominant conventions and tries to find meaning in the practices and gestures that are so readily dismissed.

As it emerges in that liminal space between knowing and unknowing, between meaning and enigma, cripistemology evokes Walter Mignolo's notion of border thinking as 'thinking from another place, imagining an other language, arguing from another logic' (Mignolo 2000: 313). Even though Mignolo does not call for a replacement of existing epistemologies, his suggestion that 'border thinking' refers to an 'epistemology of and from the border' requires the acknowledgment that such a border epistemology necessarily entails disorientation, disalignment, and a thinking beyond Western paradigms (Mignolo 2000: 52). Border thinking presupposes a divorcing from hegemonic epistemology, that is, from the idea of 'absolute knowledge,' and thus serves as the paradigmatic reading strategy for non-alphabetic texts. A cripistemology of the coffin thus tries to merge the critical stances of border thinking and crip theory with provocative interventions in Native studies to invoke the coffin as a metaphor for an alternative literacy that is not only prevalent in Canadian literature but in North American literature at large. The coffin contains uncomfortable knowledges and (hi) stories that have continuously been repressed and dismissed as idolatrous or insignificant but that also continue to resurface and haunt the cultural imaginary. A cripistemological framework allows us to analyse the resurgence of indigenous knowledges from a liminal position and to recognize the confusion and disorientation they generate as an important critical inquiry which calls dominant, Western paradigms of knowledge fundamentally into question.

Bodies in Boxes and Undecipherable Marks

In North American literature, subjugated knowledges may resurge as tangible objects, such as coffins and boxes, which emblematize the presence of the non-alphabetic, indigenous text in Early America. At first glance, Alvar Núñez Cabeza de Vaca's exploration narrative entitled *La Relación* (1542), for instance, may reflect the inability of many early texts to recognize indigenous forms of knowledge and the failure to acknowledge their validity as an alternative textual medium. Upon closer look, however, one can see that the text taps deeply into the archive of indigenous knowledge, engaging in what

Brander Rasmussen (2012: 10) has termed 'colonial dialogization.'[2] In fact, several scholars have commented on Cabeza de Vaca's hybrid self — the coming together of his Spanish heritage and his acquisition of Native American culture — and many have been fascinated by the text's careful representation of New World alterities.[3] In this first-hand account of his odyssey through North America, Cabeza de Vaca relates his experiences of shipwreck and captivity, opening up a narrative space in which Native epistemology and alternative literacies coexist with Western cultural and narrative forms. His numerous identitarian changes from conquistador to captive to missionary and his transformation into a Spaniard who has gone Native, wandering 'lost and naked' (de Vaca 1993: 28) through North America, give rise to a dialogic text that is organized around cultural encounters between different groups of people, voicing 'a conflict between ideas of empire and an epistemic conflict between two ideas of knowledge as they arose in the geopolitical dialectic between European expansionism and centralizing monarchy' (Bauer 2003: 33–34).

One instance is particularly interesting. In Chapter 4, Cabeza de Vaca recounts the peculiar discovery of several boxes containing unknown bodies covered with painted deerskin. This is how he writes about the incident:

> There we found many merchandise boxes from Castile, each containing the body of a dead man. The bodies were covered with painted deerskins. This seemed to the Commissary to be a type of idolatry, and he burned the boxes with the bodies. We also found pieces of linen and cloth and feather headdresses which seemed to be from New Spain. We also found samples of gold (de Vaca 1993: 35).

Upon the commissary's request, Cabeza de Vaca and his comrades burned the boxes and destroyed the local knowledge the bodies bore. Considering the bodies to be evidence of primitive idolatry, the Spaniards deemed the knowledge they embodied threatening and sacrilegious at most, but certainly not relevant and worth preserving. These boxes, which apparently were merchandise boxes from Castile but whose meaning is impossible to comprehend, emblematize the presence of Native knowledge in the text. Cabeza de Vaca mentions these coffins, but he fails to provide an

---

[2]   Michael Holquist has explained the dialogization process in the glossary to Bakhtin's *The Dialogic Imagination* as 'A word, discourse, language or culture undergoes "dialogization" when it becomes relativized, de-privileged, aware of competing definitions for the same things. Undialogized language is authoritative or absolute' (Holquist 1981: 427).

[3]   See, for instance, Molloy (1987) and Bruce-Novoa (1993).

interpretation, choosing not to go into more details concerning this act of destruction of local knowledge. The assemblage of these bodies in boxes therefore constitutes a form of cripistemology, representing the 'non-alphabethic, indigenous text in the colonial world, as well as the possibility for recovery and resurgence of subaltern literacies, texts and knowledges' (Brander Rasmussen 2012: 15–16). We cannot decipher the content, because it is divorced from its original environment. As a result, as Bruce-Novoa (2011: 28) has stated:

> The denunciation Cabeza de Vaca cannot speak, that resounds in its silence — and like Antigone, cries for redress — is the destruction, not just of the bodies, but of the entire assemblage. It was the Indians' manipulation of bodies, boxes, deerskins and the materials used to draw on them — paint, dies, beads, blood, we do not know — this fusion of elements, European and Native, focused on the ultimate question of life everywhere: Death, or at least the effort to render significant death's presence in the form of bodies turned cadavers … it was all this and more that vanished before given a chance to "speak," a chance to be appreciated as a sign within its own code of signification.

Cabeza de Vaca's act of self-fashioning in his account almost obliges him to leave out details concerning the spectacle of the boxed bodies (Fellner 2009: 51). His reference to this enigmatic assemblage of bodies, however, gives the painted deerskins the status of undeciphered writing. Serving as markers of alterity, these containers of indigenous knowledge represent an alternative system of meaning, which despite never being fully reconstructable remain present in American literature. Figuring prominently in the archive of Early American literature, boxes and coffins therefore point to the 'possibility of coeval commensurability' (Brander Rasmussen 2012: 138) between alphabetic and indigenous forms of writing.

Probably the most famous coffin in American literature is Queequeg's coffin. The appearance of this coffin in Herman Melville's novel *Moby-Dick* is peculiar, as it becomes a symbol of life and rebirth in the course of the story and sheds more obvious associations with vanishing and death. *Moby-Dick* ends with the shipwreck of the *Pequod* and its crew of which the novel's narrator, Ishmael, is the lone survivor. As the *Pequod* sinks, Ishmael is drawn into the vortex, when suddenly the 'vital center' of the 'black bubble' bursts upward and disgorges a coffin, which Ishmael clings to until he is rescued (Melville 1992: 625). The coffin that becomes Ishmael's lifebuoy is the strange casket Queequeg, a Polynesian harpooner, had built when he thought that he was dying of fever and that he used as a chest for his belongings after his recovery. The casket seems strange to Ishmael and the rest of the crew because of the 'hieroglyphic marks' carved onto it, which none of them are able to decipher.

The marks on Queequeg's coffin remind us of the marks on the skin of the white whale, which Ishmael compares to 'ancient hieroglyphs' one would find on the 'walls of pyramids,' mysterious and unintelligible, and to Native forms of writing inscribed on the American landscape along the Upper Mississippi. In other words, Melville likens Polynesian, Egyptian, and Native American scripts as heritage of civilized cultures and implicitly criticizes the colonization and the disappearance of Native knowledge.[4] Both the coffin and the whale are thus sites of inscription, bearers of non-alphabetic texts that Ishmael desperately seeks to decipher, as he is haunted by thoughts about the seemingly lost knowledge. As Ishmael tells his readers, the inscription on Queequeg's coffin is an exact copy of the 'twisted tattooing on his [Queequeg's] body,' which, he learns, actually comprise 'a complete theory of the heavens and the earth, and a mystical treatise on the art of attaining truth' (ibid.: 524). Queequeg's tattoos, like the markings on the whale's skin, are 'a riddle to unfold,' a fundamental truth whose meaning continues to elude Ishmael.

Ishmael's attempt to comprehend the mystery of Queequeg is centred on the mark with which he signed onto the *Pequod* and which is carved onto the lid of the coffin. Queequeg's signature mark is the only non-alphabetic sign included in Ishmael's narrative, that is, in the printed text of *Moby-Dick*, which resembles a heraldic cross. As Matthew Frankel has argued, the mark symbolizes the 'cultural misapprehension' Queequeg is subject to, as it signifies Queequeg's very own unintelligibility (Frankel 2007: 135). Brander Rasmussen similarly suggests that Ishmael's assertion that even Queequeg cannot read his own marks and tattoos ascribes illiteracy to Queequeg and emphasizes Ishmael's failure to imagine that what he is looking at might be an indigenous system of writing (Brander Rasmussen 2012). At the same time, however, Melville lets Queequeg's hieroglyphic markings stand as signifiers of 'alterity and anteriority,' as testament to the presence of other, earlier literary cultures that are not pressed 'into the service of a nationalist narrative' (ibid.: 112) but recognized as 'a different but equally legitimate literary heritage' (ibid.: 113). We thus read *Moby-Dick* as a meditation on legitimate cultural and literary heritage, as Ishmael struggles to accept his

---

[4]   On this point, see also Brander Rasmussen, who suggests that Melville insinuates 'that Native American petroglyphs represent an equally ancient and important writing system awaiting recognition and decipherment' as Egyptian hieroglyphs (Brander Rasmussen 2012: 122).

inability to make sense of Queequeg's hieroglyphic marks and constantly searches for ways to attain the truths inscribed on the harpooner's skin and coffin. The hieroglyphs on the coffin 'encode Queequeg's interpretation of the whiteness of the whale,' and if Ishmael learns to read those signs, he will understand not only Queequeg, but also the whale and finally himself (Powell 2000: 176).

As he reveals at one point in his narrative, Ishmael's own skin is covered with tattoos. For lack of any other medium on which he could record the 'valuable statistics' of the measurements of the Sperm Whale's skeleton, Ishmael had them tattooed onto his right arm (Melville 1992: 492). Similar to Queequeg's body, Ishmael's body is turned into a text, albeit a decisively *Western* text, as his skin is inscribed with Western measurements and thus Western systems of knowledge. When he covers his right arm with the statistics of the whale, Ishmael remarks that he wants the other parts of his body to remain blank for a poem he is still composing. Frankel suggests that the prospect for further and more extensive tattoos relates to Ishmael's admiration of Queequeg's whole-body ornaments, 'thereby revealing a desire to revisit in corporeal terms the "living contour" of his departed friend' (Frankel 2007: 138). Ishmael seeks to compensate the impossibility of accessing the knowledge Queequeg's body contains 'by approximating as best he can what it would be like to live in Queequeg's skin' (ibid., 139). As Queequeg is likened to the white whale in Ishmael's narrative, his approximation to Queequeg's body would, inevitably, also entail an approximation to the whale's body. All three of them would bear strange markings and tattoos representing systems of knowledge that complement and challenge one other at the same time.

As long as Queequeg's tattoos and the markings on the coffin cannot be decoded, his narrative, the text that he has composed on his skin and the coffin's surface, remains true and cannot be adequately translated and articulated in Ishmael's narrative. Queequeg's tattooed body will never resurface 'whole and complete to allow its codex to be deciphered in its entirety, glorious and direct' (Bruce-Novoa 2011: 39). It turns out that Ishmael's limited memory is the only source of information of Queequeg's narrative that the reader has, even though his mark and the strange engravings on his coffin, which would in all likelihood produce a more accurate picture, are right in front of his eyes. Untranslatable as they are, however, they prove to be enduring, yet obscure, evidence of an indigenous presence without which Ishmael — and, by extrapolation, an Anglo-American tradition[5] — would quite literally not exist.

---

[5]   Particularly in Cold-War-receptions of *Moby-Dick*, Ishmael has been stylized as the 'canonical (idealized) essence of the American nation', that is, as a cultural figure that seems to embody something quintessentially 'American' (Spanos 1995: 34). In Ishmael,

Conclusion

As the coffin stands for Queequeg's absence, 'the body no longer present,' the Polynesian seems to readily represent the 'vanishing primitive' who falls victim to colonial enterprise (Bruce-Novoa 2011: 39). However, even though he perishes in the shipwreck, he remains a haunting presence in American culture. His coffin weathers all storms and enables Ishmael's survival, which implicitly places Queequeg's narrative right at the centre not only of *Moby-Dick* but of American literature at large. Queequeg's coffin serves as a reminder of 'a sense of shared destiny,' a reminder that Western/alphabetic and indigenous/non-alphabetic systems of knowledge are 'mutually interconnected and enabling' (Brander Rasmussen 2012: 138). The indigenous knowledge inscribed on the coffin remains obscure, but the coffin's resurgence and transformation into a lifebuoy promises the survival of Queequeg's narrative. Perhaps his inscriptions will never be deciphered, never translated into alphabetic text, but Queequeg's knowledge of the 'heavens and the earth' has been recorded and remains intact with the coffin serving as proof of an indigenous presence that cannot be compromised.

The central mystery in Canadian literature and culture, as Margaret Atwood has noted, is 'what goes on in the coffin' (Atwood 2012: 252). As a container of unspeakable knowledge, the coffin does not only figure prominently in Canadian texts but also in the United States-American imaginary, as our contribution has shown. This is not to challenge Atwood's claim that the question as to what goes on in the coffin dominates particularly Canadian literature, but to suggest that more consideration should be paid to the significance of coffins, burial grounds, and bone ashes in North American literature at large, as the repression and resurgence of indigenous knowledges is frequently negotiated through these motifs. From William Bradford's *Of Plymouth Plantation* (1606–1646) and Thomas Jefferson's *Notes on the State of Virginia* (1785) to Henry David Thoreau's *Walden* (1854) the residue of the indigenous population haunts Anglo-American writers and constitutes an unspeakable presence in 'classic' literature. Our analysis of Cabeza de Vaca's *La Relación* and Melville's *Moby-Dick* has shown that indigenous knowledges prove to be incommensurate with Western systems of meaning making and thus remain inaccessible to European colonizers. Most importantly though, both texts testify to the fact that indigenous knowledges are a central, constitutive pillar of the North American imaginary. They exhibit the presence of alternative forms of writing in the

---

this interpretation suggests, Anglo-America finds a representative type, an ideal form that seems to articulate a coherent national narrative. Even though more recent readings of *Moby-Dick* discuss Ishmael's manifold ambiguities, he has remained somewhat of a stock-character in American cultural productions (Hamscha 2013).

archive, yet they also highlight the violence and the processes of exclusion which have made indigenous knowledges invisible to North American literary studies.

References

Atwood, M. (2012) *Survival: A Thematic Guide to Canadian Literature*. Toronto: House of Anansi Press.

Bauer, R. (2003) *The Cultural Geography of Colonial American Literature*. Cambridge: Cambridge University Press.

Brander Rasmussen, B. (2012) *Queequeg's Coffin: Indigenous Literacies and Early American Literature*. Durham: Duke University Press.

Bruce-Novoa, J. (1993) Shipwrecked in the Seas of Signification: Cabeza de Vaca's *La Relación* and Chicano Literature. In: Herrera-Sobek, M. ed. *Reconstructing a Chicano/a Literary Heritage: Hispanic Colonial Literature of the Southwest*. Tucson: University of Arizona Press.

Bruce-Novoa, J. (2011) Unpacking America's Boxed Gifts: From Cabeza de Vaca to Donald Duck. In Fellner, A. M. ed.. *Body Signs: The Body in Latino/a Cultural Production*. Vienna: LIT.

Fellner, A. M. (2009) Performing Cultural Memory: Scenarios of Colonial Encounter in the Writings of John Smith, Cabeza de Vaca, and Jacques Cartier. In Hebel, U. J. ed.. *Transnational American Memories*. Berlin and New York: de Gruyter.

Frankel, M. C. (2007) Tattoo Art: The Composition of Text, Voice, and Race in Melville's *Moby-Dick*. *ESQ* 53(2): 114–147.

Hamscha, S. (2013) *The Fiction of America: Performance and the Cultural Imaginary in Literature and Film*. Frankfurt/Main: Campus.

Hill Boone, E. (1994). Introduction. In: Hill Boone, E. & Mignolo, W.D. eds. *Writing Without Words: Alternative Literacies in Mesoamerica and the Andes*. Durham: Duke University Press. pp. 3-26.

Holquist, M. (1981). Glossary. In: Holquist, M. ed. *The Dialogic Imagination: Four Essays by M.M. Bakhtin*. Austin: University of Texas Press. pp. 423-35.

Johnson, M. L. and McRuer, R. (2014). Cripistemologies: Introduction. *Journal of Literary and Cultural Disability Studies* 8(2): 127-147.

Mbembe, A. (2003) Necropolitics. *Public Culture* 15(1): 11–40.

Melville, H. (1992) *Moby-Dick, Or: The Whale*. New York: Penguin Books.

Mignolo, W. D. (2000) *Local Histories/Global Designs: Coloniality, Subaltern Knowledges, and Border Thinking*. Princeton: Princeton University Press.

Molloy, S. (1987). Alteridad y reconocimiento en los *Naufragios* de Alvar Núñez Cabeza de Vaca. *Nueva Revista de Filología Hispánica* 35(2): 425-49.

Morgensen, S. L. (2010). Settler Homonationalism: Theorizing Settler Colonialism Within Queer Modernities. *GLQ* 16(1-2): 105-131.

Nielsen, K. E. (2013). *A Disability History of the United States*. Boston: Beacon Press.

Powell, T. B. (2000) *Ruthless Democracy: A Multicultural Interpretation of the American Renaissance*. Princeton: Princeton University Press.

Spanos, W. V. (1995). *The Errant Art of* Moby-Dick: *The Cold War, and the Struggle for American Studies*. Durham: Duke University Press.

de Vaca, C. and Nuñez, A. (1993) *The Account, Alvar Nuñez Cabeza de Vaca's Relación*. Translated by M. A. Favata and J. B. Fernández. Houston: Arte Público.

11

The Informal Colonialism of Egyptology: From the French Expedition to the Security State

CHRISTIAN LANGER

Introduction: Egyptology as a Product of Colonialism

The academic discipline of Egyptology emerged in Europe in the late eighteenth and early nineteenth centuries as Europeans appropriated the knowledges of the Middle East. This article shows how this discipline has been part of coloniality ever since its creation, and how it has subsequently been utilised by Egyptian elites to stabilize their own position.

Whereas Arabic scholars had earlier tried to make sense of ancient Egyptian remains, the creation of modern, European-dominated Egyptology coincided with the French expedition or rather invasion of Egypt in 1798. The French military tried to disrupt the British trade route to India (Said 2003) and to acquire colonies in Africa and Asia (Burleigh 2007). The French forces also counted scholars among them. Their mission was to explore Egypt in every conceivable way — to chart its landscapes and monuments. The result was the first scientific survey of Egypt — at least in a European sense. Arabic scholars had been studying ancient Egyptian sites in their own way for centuries.[1] This survey prompted the decipherment of the hieroglyphic script, and the ability to read and understand the Egyptian languages. From 1809, the findings of the expedition were published in the *Description de l'Égypte* by the French *Commission des sciences et arts d'Egypte*. In other words, the genesis of western Egyptology went hand in hand with European imperialism,

---

[1]   For more information on indigenous Egyptology prior to the French invasion, see Okasha El Daly (2005) and Louise L. Wynn (2007).

i.e., colonialism, in the Middle East (Wynn 2007). This also coincides with the creation of modern *Orientalism* (Said 1994; 2003).[2] Since then Europe, or rather the West, has had the hegemony over the study of ancient Egypt.

However, according to Walter Mignolo, *Orientalism* was but the second stage in the creation of modernity or rather the colonial world system understood as epistemological domination by the 'West' along with the subsequent degradation of non-western knowledges and perspectives. In other words, the *local* European history turned into a narrative of global history. Other *local* histories became subaltern. The first step commenced with the colonisation of the Americas, the self-conception of European powers as the 'West' during the course of the sixteenth century as a result, and the subsequent division of the world by the papacy into a western and an eastern hemisphere. *Orientalism* merely resulted out of *Occidentalism* (see Mignolo 2012).

In effect, the production of Egyptological knowledge was firmly based on the colonial matrix of power (or coloniality) and, as a result, knowledge about ancient Egypt was colonial from the start. Coloniality goes beyond mere formal colonialism in that also knowledge is colonised (Quijano 2000; Mignolo 2007). In that sense, Egyptological knowledge was very much a part of the colonial matrix of power in its early days, both as a means and as a target of Western policy in the Middle East.

Interestingly, the creation of Western Egyptology coincided with a power shift within the colonial matrix of power. Its centre shifted away from the Iberian Peninsula to France and Britain during the Enlightenment in the late eighteenth century — the second phase of modernity according to Mignolo (2012). The creation of Egyptology also coincided with the first permanent presence of European powers in the Middle East since the Crusades (1095– 1291). The colonisation of the Americas helps explain this coincidence. France had lost its colonies in Canada, Acadia, and Newfoundland to Great Britain in the French and Indian War (1754–1763) and the Seven Years War (1756–1763) (Anderson 2000). Unable to compete with Britain, Portugal, and Spain in the Americas, the only accessible non-colonised regions lay in India and the Middle East — especially since Africa had not been opened up for European exploitation yet apart from the coastal regions on the way to the Indian subcontinent. Great Britain was already present in India. This led

---

[2]   Orientalism means the construction of 'oriental' societies as backward and barbarian who, as such, have been considered the anti-thesis to an enlightened, civilized 'West.' For instance, orientalist thought includes the narrative that Middle Eastern people are not ready for democracy and human rights, that only autocracy can make their societies work. However, not only Arab people are orientalised. This rather includes all people of (former) European colonies around the world.

France to attempt to interrupt the British trade routes to India by capturing Egypt and Palestine. France had been pondering an invasion of Egypt since 1774 (Burleigh 2007). This coincides with the loss of the French possessions in continental North America. As Captain Joseph-Marie Moiret of the French expedition stated, 'This new colony would reimburse us for the loss of those that the wiliness of the English had stolen from us in the New World' (quoted after Cole 2007: 18).

Contrary to what was taking place in the Americas, where it was easy for colonial powers to largely destroy the visible and immaterial Amerindian heritage (see Mignolo 1995), the colonial forces of Europe chose to engage the Middle Eastern heritage in a different way. During the Crusades, European powers had tried to transform the Middle East in their own image directly via the Crusader States (Tyerman 2006). Centuries later it was the attempt to transform it by claiming and controlling Middle Eastern heritage. The French campaign realised old European plans to capture Egypt during the Crusades (ibid.). During this time, European empires constructed Egypt as a precursor to Western civilisation and as their natural appendix. French scholars assisted in portraying contemporary Egypt as barbaric and in need of liberation from Mamluk rule (Abul-Magd 2013). Joseph Eschasseriaux, a legislator in the commission to explore the possibility of French colonies in Africa, wrote,

> What finer enterprise for a nation which has already given liberty to Europe [and] freed America than to regenerate in every sense a country which was the first home to civilization and to carry back to their ancient cradle industry, science, and the arts, to cast into the centuries the foundations of a new Thebes or of another Memphis. (quoted after Cole 2007: 16).

Hereby, France established the intellectual encounter with the ancient heritage of Egypt and put itself in the tradition of the 'once great' ancient Egyptian civilisation. Its mission was to restore the country to its former greatness as a semi-autonomous colony (Said 2003). The Amerindian nations could never have been considered a legitimate part of European heritage. With Egypt's ancient links to Greece, Rome, and the Christian Bible, this would be different. This *mission civilisatrice* would provide the overall narrative of the French campaign in Egypt (Laurens 1987). The colonial encounter with Egypt prompted the creation of Egyptology. The Spanish had no interest in the Middle East and were fully occupied with the commercial circuits in the Americas and their access to the Chinese circuit through the Philippines (Mignolo 2012).[3] Spain was looking west, not east (Dussel 1998).

---

[3]   At the time, the economic centre of the world lay in China with Western Europe at

Thus it was not necessary for Europeans to engage and appropriate its ancient heritage until the French invasion.

By 1900, Britain, France, Germany, Italy, the United States of America, and other European countries were competing for Egyptian antiquities and access to archaeological sites. (Reid 1985; 2015). Europeans even pressed for the genesis of the Egyptian antiquities service and the *Egyptian Antiquities Museum* in Cairo (Reid 2002; Gady 2007). The Egyptian Antiquities Museum has been commonly known as the Egyptian Museum to foreign tourists since the late nineteenth century. The equalisation of ancient Egypt with the 'true' Egypt is demonstrated by this linguistic twist. Islamic Egypt is thus not regarded as properly Egyptian by Western audiences (Riggs 2013). The *Grand Egyptian Museum*, which is currently under construction and will also solely house ancient Egyptian objects, will continue this colonial tradition.

Modern Egyptology was an academic discipline conceived by Europeans for Europeans. Europe had appropriated Egypt's ancient heritage (Blakey 1994). Egyptian Egyptologists played virtually no role until the emergence of Egyptian nationalism and eventual formal independence from British domination in the 1920s. They were discouraged from pursuing the exploration of their own ancient heritage both by Islamic tradition and the Western archaeological or rather colonial agenda (Elshakry 2015; Reid 2015) and usually relegated to the role of anonymous archaeological labourers (Quirke 2013; Doyon 2015). Only recently, the importance of the indigenous workforce was highlighted in a project on the British Egyptologist William Matthew Flinders Petrie by Stephen Quirke (2010) and by Joanne Rowland (2014).

Furthermore, the academic languages of the discipline came to be English, French, and German, which reflected the power relations of the time within the modern/colonial world system; every other language was marginalised. In other words, the West was in complete control of the discipline and the production of its knowledge until at least the early twentieth century. This Western domination of Egypt's heritage had some peculiar results.

By the late nineteenth century, pharaonic Egypt had become a projection screen of monarchist values and a European sense of cultural and racial superiority. For example, Petrie's Egyptological research was crucial in

---

the fringes of the regional commercial circuits. Mignolo sees this as the reason for Iberian interest in China and their attempts to reach it directly by sea. As a result of the colonization of the Americas, the global economic centre shifted to the Atlantic (Mignolo 2012). The Crusades, as a quest to capture Jerusalem, appear as a European attempt to connect with the economic centre in Asia (Dussel 1998).

lending historic evidence to the Eugenics Movement (Sheppard 2010; Challis 2013). The myth of 'Eternal Egypt' was also created at the time. The European monarchies felt threatened by the advent of new social movements seeking to abolish them (Moreno García 2015). This myth sees the ancient Egyptian monarchy remain virtually unchanged for nearly 3,000 years; ever conservative and ever paternal. Juan Carlos Moreno García explained what he once called a 'reactionary utopia' (Moreno García 2009) very well by saying:

> Ancient Egypt became a lost paradise and an enchanted land of mystery, with Egyptologists playing the role of zealous keepers and unique interpreters of pharaoh's achievements, a position ultimately threatened by "materialist" approaches or by exigent intellectual agendas (Moreno García 2015: 52).

Yet, this 'reactionary utopia' has not only hampered the Egyptologists' comprehension of ancient Egypt so far, but also strongly affected the population of modern-day Egypt for it has helped legitimise authoritarian rule in the country.

The very term 'Egyptology' itself solely limits Egypt to its ancient past and marginalises its Coptic or Islamic periods (Reid 1985).[4]

From Western Colonialism to Informal Colonialism

Egypt controls the economically important Suez Canal. Furthermore, the country is the centre of the Arab World and home to the single largest Arabic-speaking population. Due to this geostrategic importance, Egypt has attracted the interest of colonial powers for centuries. From the sixteenth century until 1882 the country was part of the Ottoman Empire and governed by a Turkish minority (Hunter 1984; Winter 1992). The year 1922 saw the independence of Egypt from British colonial rule on paper; however, Britain exerted some control over the country until 1954. In 1952, the Egyptian monarchy was overthrown in a United States-backed coup of so-called 'Free Officers' (Kandil 2014). Two years later, formal colonialism came to an end in Egypt, when the last remnants of foreign rule were dispelled (Selak 1955). However, even after abandoning monarchy and gaining formal independence, the Egyptian elite co-opted the colonial structures put in place by the former colonisers in

---

[4]   On the curriculum of Egyptology, see Quirke (2010). Contrary to widespread belief, Egyptology does not research Egyptian history after Late Antiquity. Islamic and modern Egypt are not part of the curriculum.

order to fortify its own power (Kandil 2014).[5] Also, the country was not free of foreign influence and intervention. It soon became entangled in the Cold War between the West and the Soviet Union — the climax of which was the Suez Crisis in 1956 when Israel, Britain, and France invaded Egypt over the nationalisation of the Suez Canal, supposed Egyptian support for anti-colonial insurgents in French Algeria, and arms deals with the Soviets — only to be stopped by diplomatic efforts by the Soviet Union, United Nations, and United States (ibid.).

Initially under Soviet influence during the reign of Gamal Abdel Nasser (1954–1970), Egypt was part of the United States' sphere of influence since the signature of the *Camp David Accords* in 1978, receiving financial aid including $1.3 billion per year for the military from 1987 onwards (Sharp 2015). Close cooperation between the United States and the Egyptian military continued after the coup of July 2013, which saw the military formally back in power and turned the *January 25 Revolution* of 2011 into a failed one.[6] Since then the military regime has resorted to both physical and systemic violence to impose order and stability onto a profoundly divided Egyptian society. For political and economic reasons, Western leadership has turned a blind eye to the events in Egypt after the revolution of 2011. What might be the role of Egyptology in this informal colonialism?[7]

Appropriating Authority through Informal Colonialism

Ancient Egyptian heritage is important to Egypt in terms of the national tourism industry, which is one of the largest income generators for the country after the Suez Canal. Yet, apart from the economic significance, it is utilised in another way. The Egyptian elites utilise the myth of 'Eternal Egypt' to legitimise a strong, paternal, and traditionalist state governed by the military. In effect, today's elite profits ideologically from the attitude of nineteenth and early twentieth century Egyptology (Carruthers 2015; Omar 2015). The idea

---

[5]   For instance, this holds true for the secret police apparatus which was installed by the British colonial administration prior to 1952. The Egyptian surveillance structures are the most striking example. Subsequently, the Nasserist government expanded the existing structures — especially the internal intelligence services — in order to consolidate its rule. This was advised by the administration of the United States (Kandil 2014). In that sense, there is a direct continuity between the modern Egyptian security apparatuses and those established by colonial powers.

[6]   On the military coup of 2013, see Kandil (2014). For further reading on the revolution of 2011, consult Korany and El Mahdi (2014).

[7]   Informal colonialism is to be understood as a colonial system in which local elites are politically independent in domestic policies but act as agents in the interests of an external 'Big Brother' should the scenario arise (Gallagher and Robinson 1953; Osterhammel and Jansen 2012).

of an 'Eternal Egypt' is very much kept alive by modern-day Egyptology. Moreno García explains how Egyptology has mainly been devoted to art history, developing an elitist and romanticising attitude, alienating it from the social sciences in the process. Non-professional amateur societies help maintain a nostalgic vision of ancient Egypt — alongside museums and the entertainment industry (Moreno García 2015).

With the latter capitalising on 'Eternal Egypt,' it becomes apparent that Egyptology is still a captive of its own past. So, even in the present, the 'reactionary utopia' of 'Eternal Egypt' is reproduced — or maybe even amplified — by the very discipline that should have deconstructed it by now via the utilisation of self-critique and self-reflection. Connected to this is the neoliberalisation of the discipline throughout the industrialised countries. Only because of the privatisation of research it became necessary for researchers to collect third-party funds in order to conduct research. However, as implied by Moreno García, the conservative past might be piggybacking on the funds (Moreno García 2015). This might be exemplified by the *Qatar Foundation* — privately owned by high-ranking members of the Qatari elite who have also been involved with the Qatari government — which funds the Qatar branch of the *University College London*. Its purpose is the study of Middle Eastern heritage of which ancient Egypt forms a part.[8] Qatar has also been accused of funding the Islamic State of Iraq and Syria (Blanchard 2014; Dettmer 2014; Cockburn 2015) — which recently has taken to destroying Middle Eastern heritage — and of being one of the greatest opponents of the so-called *Arab Spring*. Third-party funding bears the possibility of influencing research on the part of the funder. This means that research could be used to support the Qatari elite's conception of the Middle East. The adherence to a 'reactionary utopia' makes it easy to oppose liberation from any kind of oppression in the Middle East or elsewhere.

Ancient Egyptian Iconography as Instrument of Self-Legitimation in Elite Discourse

In fact, ancient Egypt plays a prominent role in the public imagery. For instance, obelisks from the New Kingdom (c. 1550–1069 BCE), Egypt's imperial age, are plainly placed in squares in and around Cairo. Some obelisks contain rhetorical inscriptions praising the king's authority and dominion over different areas and peoples of the world known to Egyptians in the Late Bronze Age (Habachi 1977). Especially since the French expedition, obelisks have become a symbol of imperial power. Obelisks, both ancient and modern, have been erected in modern imperial centres around the globe

---

[8]   As of March 2016, the *Qatar Foundation* has withdrawn its financial support to archaeological missions in both Egypt and Sudan.

(Curran et al. 2009). These representatives of Egyptian autocracy are joined by a monumental statue of the New Kingdom's King Ramses II, also known as 'the Great,' which was relocated to a square in front of the central station of the Egyptian capital shortly after the revolution of 1952. This action represented a link between ancient and revolutionary Nasserist Egypt, implying the renaissance of ancient glory in modern Egypt (Carruthers 2014).

However, the most striking application of ancient Egyptian iconography in public imagery is modern. The outer walls of Egyptian barracks, for example, are decorated with reliefs depicting the 'glorious' history of the Egyptian military through the ages. The sequence begins with a New Kingdom style battle relief, showing the mighty king in his chariot, riding down and shooting foreign enemies with his bow. The relief then progresses with battle scenes up to modern times. In this fashion, the Egyptian military is set in the tradition of ancient Egypt's imperial age, glorifying strong and swift action as well as strong individual leadership. This supports the narrative that Egypt had always been governed by strong authority (ibid.; Lampridi 2011).

A more recent adaptation of ancient iconography was employed in a campaign to promote the Egypt Economic Development Conference in March 2015 (*The Cairo Post* 2015). The ancient Egyptian *Ankh*, a symbol for life, was chosen as its logo. The *Ankh* was artistically integrated into fields, construction sites, coral reefs, and the Suez Canal, implying a link between ancient Egypt and modern Egypt's economic elite, or rather that free enterprise ensures the continuation of Egypt's long history. The modern adaptation of ancient iconography continued in the summer of 2015 at the opening ceremony of the New Suez Canal.[9] During the opening concert, a performance of Giuseppe Verdi's opera *Aida* took place. Auguste Mariette, the leading figure of the European administration of Egyptian antiquities in the mid-nineteenth century, was integral in devising the opera's plot (Busch 1978) and, thus, in the creation of its idealised vision of ancient Egypt. In effect, the Egyptian elite decided to commemorate the opening of the canal with an orientalising piece conceived by Europeans. This demonstrates the co-optation of colonial Western narratives by Egyptians for their own purposes.

Another example is a twelve-hour concert at the Giza pyramids to celebrate the new millennium. In the process, the Eye of Horus was projected onto one side of the Great Pyramid as a light image. The Egyptian government cancelled its plans to lower a light-emitting, golden pyramid capstone by a helicopter beforehand after concerns had emerged that this might be a Zionist-Masonic plot to infiltrate the country. Zahi Hawass later defended the

---

[9]   The performance starts at about the 48-minute mark using the following link: https://www.youtube.com/watch?v=Yyut0C7TVHc.

plans saying that it re-enacted a 'pharaonic national ritual' and a project of national unity (Wynn 2008).

Not only does ancient Egypt serve a political purpose in the public imagery, it is also used for rhetorical purposes in political speeches. For instance, Gamal Abdel Nasser was imagined as 'the first Egyptian ruler to come from the soil of this homeland in two thousand years' by Hosni Mubarak (Lampridi 2011: 232). Under Anwar as-Sadat's presidency (1970–1981), Nasser's pan-Arabism that sought to unite all Arab peoples was abandoned in favour of Egyptian nationalism. Egypt was constructed as the most important and oldest Arab nation given that its existence dates back seven millennia. In fact, this heritage was imagined as the very reason that Egyptians were the most precious of all Arab peoples (ibid.).

The reference to a distant, supposedly glorious past in order to generate legitimacy has been utilised by authoritarian governments throughout modern history. Prominent examples include Greece under the Metaxas regime and the military junta, Nazi Germany, Ba'athist Iraq, and Fascist Italy. Governments in these countries created legitimacy by referring respectively to ancient Greece and the Byzantine era (Kokkinidou and Nikolaidou 2006), Germanic prehistory (Arnold 1990), ancient Babylon and prominent figures of Islamic history (Isakhan 2013), and the Roman Empire (Munzi 2006). In this sense, one could regard the ideological exploitation of the distant past as a trademark of authoritarian governments. Consequently, the analysis of the way the Egyptian elite has engaged their distant past can help unmask the Egyptian government as authoritarian.

Ancient Egypt also has the potential to be instrumentalised by the opponents of the political elites. Adel Iskandar and Yasmin El Shazly portrayed activists of the *January 25 Revolution* as the direct continuation of ancient Egyptian workers who made fun of New Kingdom royalty using satirical graffiti (Iskandar 2013; El Shazly 2014). In this sense, activists can also utilise ancient iconography as can be seen from the work of (post)revolutionary street artists (for examples, see Hamdy & Karl 2014; Morayef 2016).

Ultimately, Egyptian heritage is a contested space — an ideological battleground between the different stakeholders within Egyptian society as well as scholars and politicians from abroad. The coloniality of Egyptology has made the country's ancient heritage a borderland where *local* histories meet and converge.[10] At stake is the interpretational sovereignty over the past of a people. The ancient heritage of Egypt is where the 'colonial difference'

---

[10]   Borders are not only physical divisions, but also psychological and racial classifications as well as divisions of gender or sexuality (see Mignolo 2012).

emerges.[11] In this sense, the Egyptian people are *dwelling in the border* — in the borderland and the according existential experience that colonialism has created.[12] *Dwelling in the border* is the necessary prerequisite to taking on colonial difference and engaging in *border thinking*. Border thinking is a different way of thinking that recovers subaltern knowledges and perspectives to counter hegemonic knowledge. Mignolo (2012: 85, emphasis in original) states that it

> is the key concept of border thinking: *thinking from dichotomous concepts rather than ordering the world in dichotomies*. Border thinking, in other words, is, logically, a dichotomous locus of enunciation and, historically, is located at the borders (interiors or exteriors) of the modern/colonial world system.

Border thinking helps make visible the cracks in the imaginary of the modern/colonial world system (ibid.; see also Mignolo in this volume). For instance, such cracks become apparent through the study of how Egyptian elites have co-opted Western narratives of their own past.

Co-optation of Western Narratives

The study of ancient Egypt is an example of *Chakrabarty's Dilemma*. *Chakrabarty's Dilemma* refers to the circumstance in which scholars from marginalised or (formerly) colonised countries, in order to study their own history, need to refer to European historiography. This leads them to reproduce European narratives in some way since Europe still appears as the academic hegemon (Chakrabarty 1992; Mignolo 1999; 2012). Egyptian scholars, if they are serious about studying their own heritage, will eventually feel compelled to leave Egypt to study or conduct research at a Western university. An exception from this rule may be the *American University in Cairo*, which is basically a Western-style university and a place of education

---

[11]   'The colonial difference is the space where coloniality of power is enacted. It is also the space where the restitution of subaltern knowledge is taking place and where border thinking is emerging. The colonial difference is the space where *local* histories inventing and implementing global designs meet *local* histories, the space in which global designs have to be adapted, adopted, rejected, integrated, or ignored. The colonial difference is, finally, the physical as well as imaginary location where the coloniality of power is at work in the confrontation of two kinds of local histories displayed in different spaces and times across the planet' (Mignolo 2012: xxv, emphasis in original).

[12]   On dwelling in the border, see Mignolo (2012). On the existential experience of border-dwelling, see Anzaldúa (1987).

for the Egyptian elite at Tahrir Square in the centre of Cairo. Western Egyptological institutions remain the epistemological powerhouses of the discipline. Therefore, any Egyptian Egyptologist will develop a double-consciousness based on colonial disciplinary knowledge; regardless of whether they are studying for their first degree or a PhD. This also includes writing scholarly works in the imperial languages of the discipline (see, also, Wynn 2007). Again, Egyptians are *dwelling in the border*.

In this respect, it might be premature to celebrate the advent of indigenous Egyptology beginning in the twentieth century. While the direct administration of the Egyptian heritage by Egyptians may be a sign of decolonisation (Walker 2012), it is only superficial. The reign of Zahi Hawass as Minister of State for Antiquities Affair, before he was ousted in the wake of the *January 25 Revolution*, has demonstrated that even Egyptians readily reproduce the myth of 'Eternal Egypt' and the colonial epistemology it embodies. Hawass became known for continuing the commodification of Egyptian heritage, mainly for economic reasons (Walker 2012; Elshahed 2015; Shenker 2016). However, other dimensions, such as the Arab-Israeli conflict, factor into contemporary local approaches in Egyptology as well. Thus, discoveries such as the tombs of workmen were used in an attempt to disprove Israeli narratives concerning the construction of the Giza pyramids by Israelite slaves. Moreover, the construction of the same pyramids was retroactively constructed as 'the national project' of ancient Egypt, providing unity and an identity, and was likened to conscription in modern Egypt more than once by Hawass (Wynn 2008). Wynn argued that this narrative legitimizes the appropriation of labour of the lower classes of Egyptian society. In the wake of the *January 25 Revolution*, Hawass — still in office at the time — also stated that Egypt has 'always needed a strongman; without one you have chaos. Things change, but I am the only one who understands this country's history, who can truly see the past' (Shenker 2016: 120). Here, by implying that Egypt's ancient history had any bearing on modern society and that it is in some way ingrained in the DNA of Egyptians, Hawass basically co-opts an orientalist narrative of his own country and its population. One could say that the Egyptian elite has been 'occidentalising' itself by co-opting Western elites through informal colonialism and as a result 'orientalising' its own population. This implies that, in terms of decolonisation, it is simply not enough to replace Western rule with an Egyptian rule using colonial knowledge produced in the West to stabilize and enact its own authority. Or, to paraphrase, it is not enough to replace external colonialism with informal internal colonialism.

As shown above, a regime of informal colonisation instrumentalises the Egyptian heritage. Moreover, the Egyptian tourism industry has been mainly directed at foreign, and predominantly Western, tourists (Mitchell 2002; Doyon 2013). As such, it largely satisfies the image of ancient Egypt that is expected by Western audiences, i.e., the myth of 'Eternal Egypt' outlined above. This is made especially clear by the evocation of the eighteenth-century dynasty king Tutankhamun (c. 1332–1323 BCE) and the story of the discovery of his tomb in 1922. Furthermore, there is a difference in the treatment of foreigners and Egyptians when it comes to access to ancient sites and museums. For instance, there are geographically separate entrances for both groups to the Giza plateau — the entrance for Egyptians is four kilometres away from the pyramids while the one for foreign tourists is much closer. This was justified by Hawass, alleging that Egyptians behaved disrespectfully toward their ancient heritage (Shenker 2016). Fanon, based on his observations in the Algerian War of Independence (1954–1962), indicated that the tourism industry of (formerly) colonised countries would focus on Western audiences as the target group when he wrote that,[13]

> the national bourgeoisie identifies itself with the Western bourgeoisie, from whom it has learnt its lessons ... The national bourgeoisie will be greatly helped on its way to decadence by the Western bourgeoisies, who come to it as tourists avid for the exotic, for big game hunting, and for casinos. The national bourgeoisie organizes centers of rest and relaxation and pleasure resorts to meet the wishes of the Western bourgeoisie. Such activity is given the name of tourism, and for the occasion will be built up as a national industry (Fanon 1963: 153).

The discovery of Tutankhamun's tomb also provided a link for Egyptian nationalism (Mitchell 2002; Mondal 2003; Reid 2015) and the evocation of a once great nation as a precursor of contemporary Egypt. This ideology of *Pharaonism* saw the creation of national monuments that combined ancient and modern Egyptian iconography (Hassan 1998). As a result, Egyptology, both past and present, does offer the Egyptian elite an ideological legitimisation for authoritarian government. This confirms the prevalent internal colonisation of the Egyptian heritage.

Conclusions and Outlook

What has become apparent is that the study of a country's past and cultural heritage has a direct relevance to international relations. It bears the power to colonise local histories and ideologically legitimise governments.

---

[13]   Lynn Meskell (1998) has already noted the connection between tourism and colonialism.

From formal to informal colonialism, Western Egyptology provides Egyptian ruling elites with a legitimising ideological narrative of paternalist rule. It is for this reason that the auto-critique and decolonisation of Egyptology is an imminently political act.

While the wealthy elites of Egyptian society instrumentalise Egypt's heritage for political and economic purposes, it may seem as if the working poor are merely being exploited to maintain a system of informal colonial-style elite rule. For those not part of the elite, however, this instrumentalisation may also be central to making a living in the tourism industry. While decolonising Egyptology might be an urgent issue for Egyptian academics, who often belong to the upper and middle class, this might not necessarily be the case for lower class Egyptians depending on the commodification of this heritage for their living.[14] However, in considering such aspects of economic necessity, one must be careful not to create apologies for the status quo. This would mean that the current system be maintained so as not to threaten the material survival of the working poor through any overall changes to the informal colonial identification of Egypt with the ancient Egypt of Western-style Egyptology. In that case, any decolonial approach, not unlike current contemporary Western foreign policy, would find itself stuck in the dilemma between radical political critique and the wish for social, political, and economic stability in a post-colonial globalized world order.

The future will show whether Western and Egyptian Egyptologists are willing and capable of performing serious self-critique and self-reflexion in order to tackle this dilemma. Beyond being a formal problem concerning the coloniality of knowledge production within the academic discipline of Egyptology, ancient Egypt describes a trope with profound political and economic implications for contemporary Egypt. As this chapter has shown, elite rule in Egypt is performed through informal colonialism that is based on the co-optation of Western colonial narratives. Ending its ideological legitimisation is thus inseparable from the decolonisation of Egyptology.

* The author would like to thank Anna Carastathis (University of the Aegean), William Carruthers (European University Institute), Kyra Gospodar (Free University of Berlin), Walter D. Mignolo (Duke University), Juan Carlos Moreno García (Paris-Sorbonne University), Stephen Quirke (University College London), Thais Rocha da Silva

---

[14] It has been argued that archaeological missions fulfil a role of charity since they provide labourers in rural areas with an increased chance for material survival (Quirke 2010). However, this narrative of philanthropy should perhaps rather be seen in the overall context of the modern/colonial world system. There, narratives of philanthropy help maintain or reorganise the very system they seem to critique. For more information, see Negri and Hardt (2000), Badiou (2001) Cohen et al. (2008), and Weizman (2011).

(University of Oxford), Sebastian Weier, Marc Woons (University of Leuven), and Justin Yoo (King's College London), and a colleague from Egypt (who for reasons of safety has to remain unnamed) for their insights, comments, and suggestions.

References

Abul-Magd, Z. (2013). *Imagined Empires: A History of Revolt in Egypt.* Berkeley: University of California Press.

Anderson, F. (2000). *Crucible of War: The Seven Years' War and the Fate of Empire in British North America, 1754-1766.* New York: Vintage Books.

Anzaldúa, G. (1987). *Borderlands/La Frontera: The New Mestiza.* San Francisco, CA: Aunt Lute Books.

Arnold, B. (1990). The Past as Propaganda: Totalitarian Archaeology in Nazi Germany. *Antiquity* 64:464-478.

Badiou, A. (2001). *Ethics: An Essay on the Understanding of Evil.* London: Verso Books.

Blakey, M. L. (1994). American Ethnicity and Nationality in the Depicted Past. In: Gathercole, P. & Lowenthal, D. eds.. *The Politics of the Past.* London: Routledge. 38-48.

Blanchard, C. M. (2014). *Qatar: Background and U.S. Relations.* Congressional Research Service RL31718. Available at: http://www.fas.org/sgp/crs/mideast/RL31718.pdf.

Burleigh, N. (2007). *Mirage: Napoleon's Scientists and the Unveiling of Egypt.* New York: Harper Collins.

Busch, H. (1978). *Verdi's Aida: The History of an Opera in Letters and Documents.* Minneapolis, MN: University of Minnesota Press.

Carruthers, W. E. (2014). *Egyptology, Archaeology and the Making of Revolutionary Egypt, c. 1925-1958.* PhD diss., University of Cambridge.

Carruthers, W. E. (2015). Introduction: Thinking about Histories of Egyptology. In: Carruthers, W.E. ed.. *Histories of Egyptology: Interdisciplinary Measures.* New York: Routledge. 1-15.

Chakrabarty, D. (1992). Postcoloniality and the Artifice of History: Who Speaks for 'Indian' Pasts?. *Representations* 37:1-26.

Challis, D. (2013). *The Archaeology of Race: the Eugenic Ideas of Francis Galton and Flinders Petrie*. London: Bloomsbury.

Cockburn, P. (2015). *The Rise of Islamic State: ISIS and the New Sunni Revolution.* London: Verso Books. EPUB edition.

Cohen, M. A., Küpçü, M. F. & Khanna, P. (2008) eds.. The New Colonialists. *Foreign Policy* 164:74-79.

Cole, J. (2007). *Napoleon's Egypt: Invading the Middle East.* New York: Palgrave Macmillan.

Curran, B. A., Grafton, A., Long, P. O. and Weiss, B. (2009). *Obelisk: A History.* Cambridge, MA: Burndy Library.

Description de l'Égypte, ou Recueil des observations et des recherches qui ont été faites en Égypte pendant l'expédition de l'armée française: publiée par les ordres de Napoléon Bonaparte (1994). Köln: Benedikt Taschen.

Dettmer, J. (2014). U.S. Ally Qatar Shelters Jihadi Moneymen. Available at: http://www.thedailybeast.com/articles/2014/12/10/rich-little-qatar-big-ugly-ties-to-terror.html.

Doyon, W. (2013). Egyptology in the Shadow of Class. In: Piacentini, P, Orsenigo, C. & Quirke, S. eds.. *Forming Material Egypt: Proceedings of the International Conference London, 20-21 May, 2013*. Egyptian and Egyptological Documents, Archives, Libraries 4. Milan: Pontremoli Editore. 261-272.

Doyon, W. (2015). On Archaeological Labor in Modern Egypt. In: Carruthers, E.C. ed.. *Histories of Egyptology: Interdisciplinary Measures*. New York: Routledge. 141-156.

Dussel, E. (1998). Beyond Eurocentrism: The World-System and the Limits of Modernity. In: Jameson, F. & Miyoshi, M. eds.. *The Cultures of Globalization*. Post-Contemporary Interventions. Durham, NC: Duke University Press. 3-31.

El Daly, O. (2005). *Egyptology: The Missing Millennium*. London: UCL Press.

El Shazly, Y. (2014). The Origins of the Rebellious Egyptian Personality. In: Hamdy, B. & Karl, D. eds.. *Walls of Freedom: Street Art of the Egyptian Revolution*. Berlin: From Here To Fame Publishing. 6-8.

Elshahed, M. (2015). The Old and New Egyptian Museums. In: Carruthers, W.E. ed.. *Histories of Egyptology: Interdisciplinary Measures*. New York: Routledge.255-269.

Elshakry, M. (2015). Histories of Egyptology in Egypt: Some Thoughts. In: Carruthers, W.E. ed.. *Histories of Egyptology: Interdisciplinary Measures*. New York: Routledge. 185-197.

Fanon, F. (1963). *The Wretched of the Earth*. New York: Groove Press.

Gady, É. (2007). Champollion, Ibrahim Pacha et Méhémet Ali: aux sources de la protection des antiquités égyptiennes. In: Goyon, J-.C. & Cardin, C. eds. *Proceedings of the Ninth International Congress of Egyptologists – Actes du Neuvième Congrès International des Égyptologues: Grenoble, 6-12 septembre 2004*. Orientalia Lovaniensia Analecta 150. Leuven: Peeters. 767-775.

Gallagher, J. and Robinson, R. (1953). The Imperialism of Free Trade. *The Economic History Review, New Series* 6(1): 1-15.

Gange, D. (2015). Interdisciplinary Measures. In: Carruthers, W.E. ed.. *Histories of Egyptology: Interdisciplinary Measures*. New York: Routledge. 64-77

Habachi, L. (1977). *The Obelisks of Egypt: Skyscrapers of the Past*. New York: Charles Scribner's Sons.

Hamdy, B. and Karl, D. (2014). *Walls of Freedom: Street Art of the Egyptian Revolution*. Berlin: From Here To Fame Publishing.

Hassan, F. A. (1998). Memorabilia: Archaeological Materiality and National Identity in Egypt. In: Meskell, L. ed. *Archaeology Under Fire: Nationalism, Politics and Heritage in the Eastern Mediterranean and the Middle East*. London: Routledge. 200-216.

Hunter, F. R. (1984). *Egypt Under the Khedives 1805-1879: From Household Government to Modern Bureaucracy*, Pittsburgh, PA: University of Pittsburgh Press.

Isakhan, B. (2013). Heritage Destruction and Spikes in Violence: The Case of Iraq. In: Kila, J.D. & Zeidler, J.A. eds. *Cultural Heritage in the Crosshairs: Protecting Cultural Property during Conflict*. Leiden: Brill. 219-247.

Iskandar, A. (2013). *Egypt in Flux: Essays on an Unfinished Revolution.* Cairo: The American University in Cairo Press.

Kandil, H. (2014). *Soldiers, Spies, and Statesmen: Egypt's Road to Revolt.* London: Verso Books. Second edition.

Khalil, A. (2011). *Liberation Square: Inside the Egyptian Revolution and the Rebirth of a Nation.* New York: St. Martin's Griffin.

Kokkinidou, D. and Nikolaidou, M. (2006). On the Stage and Behind the Scenes: Greek Archaeology in Times of Dictatorship. In: Galaty, M.L. & Watkinson C. eds.. *Archaeology under Dictatorship*. New York: Springer. 155-190.

Korany, B. and El-Mahdi, R. (2014). *Arab Spring in Egypt: Revolution and Beyond*, Cairo: The American University in Cairo Press.

Lampridi, A. (2011). Egypt's National Interest: A 'Sociology of Power' Analysis. PhD diss., Barcelona: Universitat Autònoma de Barcelona. Available at https://ddd.uab.cat/pub/tesis/2013/hdl_10803_117451/al1de1.pdf.

Laurens, H. (1987). *Les origines intellectuelles de l'éxpedition d'Égypte: l'orientalisme islamisant en France (1698-1798).* Istanbul: Editions Isis.

Meskell, L. (1998). Archaeology Matters. In: Meskell, L. ed.. *Archaeology Under Fire: Nationalism, Politics and Heritage in the Eastern Mediterranean and the Middle East*. London: Routledge.1-12.

Mignolo, W. D. (1995). *The Darker Side of the Renaissance: Literacy, Territoriality, and Colonization*. Ann Arbor, MI: The University of Michigan Press.

Mignolo, W. D. (1999). I am where I think: Epistemology and the Colonial Difference. *Journal of Latin American Cultural Studies: Travesia* 8(2): 235-245.

Mignolo, W. D. (2007). Delinking: The Rhetoric of Modernity, the Logic of Coloniality and the Grammar of De-Coloniality. *Cultural Studies* 21(2): 449-514.

Mignolo, W. D. (2012). *Local Histories/Global Designs: Coloniality, Subaltern Knowledges, and Border Thinking.* Princeton: Princeton University Press. Second edition.

Mitchell, T. (2002). *Rule of Experts: Egypt, Techno-Politics, Modernity*, Berkeley: University of California Press.

Mondal, A. A. (2003). *Nationalism and Post-Colonial Identity: Culture and Ideology in India and Egypt*, New York: Routledge.

Morayef, S. (2016). Pharaonic Street Art: The Challenge of Translation. In: Baker, M. *Translating Dissent: Voices From and With the Egyptian Revolution.* London: Routledge. 194-207.

Moreno G. & Carlos, J. (2009). From Dracula to Rostovtzeff or: The Misadventures of Economic History in Early Egyptology. In : Fitzenreiter, M. ed. *Das Ereignis: Geschichtsschreibung zwischen Vorfall und Befund. Internet-Beiträge zur Ägyptologie und Sudanarchäologie 10.* London: Golden House Publications. 175-198.

Moreno G. & Carlos, J. (2015). The Cursed Discipline? The Peculiarities of Egyptology at the Turn of the Twenty-First Century. In: Carruthers, W.M. ed.. *Histories of Egyptology: Interdisciplinary Measures.* New York: Routledge. 50-63.

Munzi, M. (2006). Italian Archaeology in Libya: From Colonial Romanità to Decolonization of the Past. In: Galaty, Michael L. & Watkinson C. eds.. *Archaeology Under Dictatorship.* New York: Springer. 73-107.

Negri, A. and Hardt, M. (2000). *Empire.* Cambridge, MA: Harvard University Press.

Omar, H. (2015). The State of the Archive: Manipulating Memory in Modern Egypt and the Writing of Egyptological Histories. In: Carruthers, W.E. ed.. *Histories of Egyptology: Interdisciplinary Measures*. New York: Routledge. 174-184.

Osterhammel, J. and Jansen, J. C. (2012). *Kolonialismus: Geschichte, Formen, Folgen*. Beck'sche Reihe Wissen. München: C. H. Beck. Seventh revised edition.

Quijano, A. (2000). Coloniality of Power, Eurocentrism, and Latin America. *Nepantla. Views from the South* 1(3): 533-580.

Quirke, S. (2010). *Hidden Hands: Egyptian Workforces in Petrie Excavation Archives, 1880-1924*. London: Duckworth.

Quirke, S. (2013). Exclusion of Egyptians in English-directed Archaeology 1882-1922 under British Occupation of Egypt. In: Bickel, S., Fischer-Elfert, H.-W., Loprieno, A. & Richter, S. eds. *Ägyptologen und Ägyptologien zwischen Kaiserreich und Gründung der beiden deutschen Staaten: Reflexionen zur Geschichte und Episteme eines altertumswissenschaftlichen Fachs im 150. Jahr der Zeitschrift für ägyptische Sprache und Altertumskunde. Zeitschrift für Ägyptische Sprache und Altertumskunde Beihefte 1*. Berlin: Akademie Verlag. 379-405.

Reid, D. M. (1985). Indigenous Egyptology: The Decolonization of a Profession? *Journal of the American Oriental Society* 105(2): 233-246.

Reid, D. M. (2002). *Whose Pharaohs? Archaeology, Museums, and Egyptian National Identity from Napoleon to World War I*. Berkeley: University of California Press.

Reid, D. M. (2015). *Contesting Antiquity in Egypt: Archaeologies, Museums & the Struggle for Identities from World War I to Nasser*. Cairo: American University in Cairo Press.

Riggs, C. (2013). Colonial Visions: Egyptian Antiquities and Contested Histories in the Cairo Museum. *Museum Worlds: Advances in Research* 1:65-84.

Rowland, J. (2014). Documenting the Qufti archaeological workforce. *Egyptian Archaeology* 44: 10-12.

Selak, C. B. (1955). The Suez Canal Base Agreement of 1954. *The American Journal of International Law* 49(4): 487-505.

Sharp, J. M. (2016). *Egypt: Background and U.S. Relations*. Congressional Research Service RL33003. Available at: http://www.fas.org/sgp/crs/mideast/RL33003.pdf.

Shenker, J. (2016). *The Egyptians: A Radical Story.* London: Allen Lane.

Sheppard, K. L. (2010). Flinders Petrie and Eugenics at UCL. *Bulletin of the History of Archaeology* 20(1): 16-29.

Said, E. W. (1994). *Culture and Imperialism.* New York: Vintage Books.

Said, E. W. (2003). *Orientalism.* New York: Vintage Books. Twenty-fifth anniversary edition.

The Cairo Post. 2015. Economic Conference Chooses 'Key of Life' as Symbol. Available at: http://thecairopost.youm7.com/news/140850/culture/economic-conference-chooses-key-of-life-as-symbol.

Tyerman, C. (2006). *God's War: A New History of the Crusades*. London: Penguin Books.

Walker, A. (2012). Indigenous Egyptology: How the Egyptian People Reclaimed Their Cultural Heritage. Available at: https://www.academia.edu/3658678/Indigenous_Egyptology_How_the_Egyptian_People_Reclaimed_their_Cultural_Heritage.

Weizman, E. (2011). *The Least of All Possible Evils: Humanitarian Violence from Arendt to Gaza.* London: Verso Books. EPUB edition.

Winter, M. (1992). *Egyptian Society under Ottoman Rule, 1517-1798*. New York: Routledge.

Wynn, L. L. (2007). *Pyramids & Nightclubs: A Travel Ethnography of Arab and Western Imaginations of Egypt, from King Tut and a Colony of Atlantis to Rumors of Sex Orgies, Urban Legends about a Marauding Prince, and*

Blonde Belly Dancers. Austin: University of Texas Press.

Wynn, L. L. (2008). Shape Shifting Lizard People, Israelite Slaves, and Other theories of Pyramid Building: Notes on Labor, Nationalism, and Archaeology in Egypt. *Journal of Social Archaeology* 8(2): 272-295.

12

Fugitivity Against the Border: Afro-pessimism, Fugitivity, and the Border to Social Death

PAULA VON GLEICH

Fugitive Beginnings

Flight generally entails borders. Whether prison walls, plot boundaries, or borders between states, being fugitive implies that borders have been and/or are still to be overcome. One might assume that flight ends when the borders that stood between the captive and their freedom have been successfully crossed. Enslaved African Americans frequently fled their enslavers and legal owners in North America to gain freedom by, for instance, crossing the demarcating lines between slave plantation and the wilderness or the Mason-Dixon Line, the Ohio River, and the borders to Canada and Mexico into 'free' territory. However, with legislation such as the *Fugitive Slave Acts*, a fugitive slave remained retrievable property even in the supposedly 'Free North' so that freedom for a fugitive slave in nineteenth century North America was only a constrained form of freedom, if the term applies at all. But what if the 'social death' (Patterson 1982) that enslavement brought over 'people racialised as Black' (Coleman 2014: n.p.) has been never-ending as the Afro-pessimist Frank B. Wilderson III (2010) has suggested? And if so, how can we conceptualize Black social life that has undoubtedly endured despite social death in such a framework?

I assume that Afro-pessimism — in theorizing a structurally incommensurable demarcation between non-blackness and Blackness, civil life and social death, and between 'the inside [and] outside of civil society' (Wilderson, von Gleich, and Spatzek 2016: 15) — tacitly implies an epistemological border concept that continues to have very real (i.e., fatal) consequences for people racialized as Black in the United States of America and beyond since the transatlantic slave trade began.[1] Based on this understanding of Afro-pessimism as theorizing a structurally *a priori* incommensurable, absolute, and antagonistic demarcation, the border concept I consider in Afro-pessimist thought appears decidedly different from well-known conceptualizations of permeable borders as epistemological zones of dialectic cultural contact and conflict developed in American cultural and literary studies over the last thirty years. I argue that the concept of fugitivity is more suitable — than those concepts of borders as zones — when it comes to conceptualizing enduring Black social life in the face of anti-blackness as a constant struggle against social death. It is my contention that the 'Black border' in Afro-pessimism and the concept of fugitivity taken together might help convey very abstract and theoretically elaborate Afro-pessimist arguments, as figures of thought. They also make apparent the potential relations and tensions between the Afro-pessimist structural analysis of Blackness and fugitivity's focus on the level of experience and performance, shedding light on the paradox of Black social life in social death.

This chapter begins with a summary of Afro-pessimist arguments in order to show how a border concept could be entertained in this radical trajectory of contemporary Black Studies in the US. Second, I compare and contrast the proposed 'Black border' with Mary Louise Pratt's concept of the 'contact zone' (Pratt 1991; 2008) as an example of a well-known conceptualization of a liminal border space. Third, I examine the ways in which fugitivity might be able to address both Black social life and accept basic Afro-pessimist assumptions condensed in the suggested border concept by drawing on Tina M. Campt's engagement with the concept of fugitivity in *Image Matters: Archive, Photography, and the African Diaspora in Europe* (2012). It is in this manner that I encourage readers to think of fugitivity as a constant struggle against the 'Black border' without, however, ever dismantling the border or arriving at the other side that bodes civil life inside civil society only for the 'non-black.' Thus, I propose that the concept of fugitivity carries with it the potential of linking analyses of fugitive experiences and performances with an

---

[1]   In this chapter, I use the term *Blackness* to refer to the ongoing structural positionality that has been assigned to 'people racialised as Black' in the United States of America. The term *Afro-pessimism* references the radical trajectory of U.S. Black Studies that has theorized this position, most influentially in the work of Frank Wilderson (2010). Afro-pessimism is also influenced, for instance, by Frantz Fanon (2008), Saidiya Hartman (1997; 2007), Orlando Patterson (1982), Hortense Spillers (1987), and Sylvia Wynter (1994; 2006). It differs from the pessimist perspective on the future of Africa under the same name. For a more elaborate discussion of Afro-pessimism and the challenges it poses (not only) to European and to German American Studies, see Weier (2014).

Afro-pessimist structural analysis of the position of Blackness.[2]

The Black Border of Afro-Pessimism

Afro-pessimism takes as one central starting point the observation that a specific form of racism has targeted people racialized as Black in the United States since slavery, through the Black Codes, forced prison labour, and Jim Crow segregation all the way to today's 'New Jim Crow' and the 'neo-slavery' of the Prison Industrial Complex (Alexander 2012; also James 2005; Blackmon 2008). Taking up Lewis Gordon's claim that we live in an 'antiblack world' (Gordon 1995), Afro-pessimism assumes that U.S. society is fundamentally built on and structured by this anti-blackness which has made it possible to arbitrarily enslave, imprison, harm, and kill people racialized as Black for centuries. Anti-blackness is therefore understood as inherent to U.S. society and entails violence which Wilderson describes as 'ontological and gratuitous' (Wilderson 2003: 229) or 'metaphysical' violence (Douglass and Wilderson 2013: 122) directed against people racialized as Black not contingent on any prior transgression (see Wilderson 2010: 17–18).[3]

In his ground-breaking film study *Red, White, and Black: Cinema and the Structure of U.S. Antagonism* from 2010, Wilderson focuses on the structural positions of people racialized as Indigenous, white, and Black inside and outside of U.S. civil society. Rather than the experiences and performances of those three groups of people, he is concerned with the *structures* that have assigned them different positions with respect to civil society and have constituted U.S. civil society as fundamentally white supremacist and anti-black. In accord with Saidiya Hartman's contention that today is the 'afterlife of slavery' (Hartman 2007: 6), Wilderson argues, first, that 'Black' still means 'Slave' (Wilderson 2010: 7) or 'prison-slave-in-waiting' (Wilderson 2007: 18). Second, he contends that 'white' refers to the 'senior ... partners of civil society' (Wilderson 2010: 38). Third, Wilderson describes other groups of people subordinate to the 'white' but who fall out of the category of 'the Black,' such as immigrants of colour and to some extent Native Americans as 'the junior partners of civil society' (ibid.: 28).[4] In this argument, the white

---

[2]   Parts of this essay are indebted to deliberations on Afro-Pessimism and a more detailed analysis of Wilderson's work in von Gleich (2015; 2016).

[3]   The often-arbitrary cases of fatal police violence against unarmed African American men, women, and children are painful reminders of this violence that has disproportionately targeted and killed people racialized as Black in the United States. Some of the more recent cases, involving Sandra Bland, Michael Brown, Eric Garner, Freddie Gray, Tamir Rice, and Walter Scott, have been widely covered in U.S. public and social media because of social justice movements such as #BlackLivesMatter. On state violence and policing, see, for example, Martinot and Sexton (2003).

[4]   In *Red, White, and Black*, Wilderson ascribes the structural position 'Red' to

'senior partners' are located at the centre of civil society, their 'junior partners' at its inside margins, and Black people are positioned 'outside of Humanity and civil society' (ibid.: 55).

Wilderson explains the locating of Blackness at 'the outside of Humanity and civil society' with Patterson's description of social death in slavery as 'generally dishonored,' 'open to gratuitous violence,' and 'void of kinship' (Wilderson 2010: 10–11; see, also, Patterson 1982). On this basis, Wilderson supposes that it is not legitimate to analogize between Black people who are positioned as socially dead outside of civil society and non-black people who are positioned civilly alive inside civil society. All attempts would fall prey to what he calls the 'ruse of analogy,' 'erroneously locat[ing] Blacks in the world — a place where they have not been since the dawning of Blackness' as well as mystifying and erasing the 'grammar of suffering (accumulation and fungibility or the status of being non-Human)' that Blackness entails in this argument (Wilderson 2010: 37). This is also why Wilderson describes the relation of Blackness to the world and 'the Human' (who is defined as not Black) as 'antagonistic' (ibid.: 5, 26), while the 'junior partners' have a dialectic and agonistic relation to civil society that leaves room for negotiation, no matter how small this room and the chances to have claims admitted might be.[5]

Wilderson's argument that the relation between Blackness and the world should not be understood as a resolvable conflict but as an incommensurable antagonism inextricably linked with the constitution of the white, male, 'Western' subject makes Afro-pessimism one of the most challenging and radical trajectories of U.S. Black Studies in recent years. If we consider this complex argument in relation to border conceptualizations, however, we may conceive of the antagonistic demarcation — between Blackness as social death outside of civil society and non-blackness as civil life inside civil society — as a distinct border concept not previously analysed as such. In fact, Wilderson uses the metaphor of a fortress built around civil society against Blackness to make the argument that 'Anti-Blackness manifests as the monumentalization and fortification of civil society against social death' (Wilderson 2010: 90). The structural bordering also becomes apparent when

---

Indigenous people in the United States as distinct not only from the positions of the 'White' and 'Black,' but also from the 'junior partners' (see Wilderson 2010: 29–30, 48–50). In a recent interview, he slightly revised this assumption when he explained that 'In some ways, American Indians are a liminal category, and in other ways they are more profoundly on the side of "junior partners" and antagonistic to Blacks' (Wilderson, von Gleich, and Spatzek 2016: 14).

[5]   Wilderson argues that in the liminal case of Indigenous peoples, the object of negotiation would be land and in the case of migrants of colour it would be 'immigrant rights' (Wilderson 2010: 3).

Wilderson explains that gratuitous violence 'against Blacks' lives' is necessary 'to actually produce the inside-outside [of civil society]' (Wilderson, von Gleich, and Spatzek 2016: 15). The border that demarcates the inside from the outside defines what 'humanness' and the subject concept mean by delimiting 'the Human' — or 'the genre of Man' (Wynter and Thomas 2006: 24) — from the 'non-Human' at the expense of the subjectivity of people racialized as Black by, in other words, ostracizing them beyond the realm of 'the Human.' This epistemological demarcation is absolute because it has not allowed any kind of movement across the border and no relation between the two sides other than as a structural antagonism with respect to Blackness.

The absoluteness of this border is also reflected by the ways in which it is supposed to have withstood any attempts to change its position and structure since its erection as part of the transatlantic slave trade. The changes that have taken place in the United States, for instance through the Civil Rights and Black Power movements, do not figure in the 'conceptual framework' (Wilderson 2010: 10, 57) and on the level of abstraction Wilderson calls for in his work. In fact, from an Afro-pessimist perspective, those endeavours have not fundamentally changed the structural positionality of Blackness outside of civil society other than as what Jared Sexton (2011: 5) has called 'permutations.' Since the socially, culturally, and historically important changes have taken place on the level of experience and performance, Wilderson and Sexton would argue that they have not disconnected Blackness from 'Slaveness' on a structural level (Wilderson 2010: 11). According to this argument, the constitutive nature of the demarcation of Blackness as 'Slaveness' from 'humanness' for civil society makes any form of change inside civil society seem futile in terms of structure. To align it with the register of the border, the changes have happened within civil society and have therefore not effectively dismantled the epistemological border structure that has enclosed civil society and demarcated it from Blackness understood as the outside of civil society — or, more precisely, making Blackness civil society's outside.

Contact Zones and the Border to Social Death

Having established the 'Black border' between Blackness as social death outside of civil society and non-blackness as civil life inside, one may wonder in what ways the concept differs from other border concepts developed in American cultural and literary studies, such as Mary Louise Pratt's 'contact zone' (1991; 2008), Gloria Anzaldúa's 'borderlands' (1989), Homi K. Bhabha's 'third space' (1994), and Walter Mignolo's 'border thinking' (2000). Indeed, at first glance the 'Black border' exhibits commonalities with all four. All seem to use spatial tropes to conceptualize the relation of differently racialized people and their (im)possibilities in terms of dwelling and thinking as well as communicating within a specific epistemological space. Relations between these groups are rooted in colonialism and slavery, and their ongoing legacies are still affected by these origins. While some concepts, such as Pratt's 'contact zone,' construct borders as generally contingent, dialectic, and permeable, the 'Black border' I consider in Afro-pessimism appears absolute, antagonistic, and impermeable with respect to Blackness. In order to illustrate this, let me briefly compare and contrast the two.

The contact zone is well known within and beyond cultural and literary studies for its conceptualization of a space of cultural contact across asymmetrical power relations in the long aftermaths of colonialism, the transatlantic slave trade, and slavery in the Americas and the Caribbean. First coined in her essay 'Arts of the Contact Zone' and further developed in her study of European eighteenth and nineteenth century travel writing in *Imperial Eyes: Travel Writing and Transculturation*, Pratt (2008: 4) defines contact zones as 'social spaces where disparate cultures meet, clash, and grapple with each other, often in highly asymmetrical relations of domination and subordination — like colonialism, slavery, or their aftermaths as they are lived out across the globe today.' Pratt conceptualizes (post-)colonial cultural contact and communication between the (former) colonizers and the (former) colonized and enslaved (ibid.). As she shows in her analysis of Guama Poma's writing, Pratt understands this contact as a form of forced conversation on unequal grounds in which 'the subordinate peoples' find ways to talk back and self-represent through 'transculturation' and 'autoethnography' (Pratt 1991: 36). In this way, the contact zone takes on the issue of resistance to subjugation and the role knowledge production and dissemination plays in this context. It therefore refers less to a specific geographical location and more to an improvised interpersonal and epistemological space for communication and interaction in the (post-)colonial world. The space the two parties enter is hierarchically structured, but it still leaves room for 'the subordinate' to negotiate with 'the dominant' and therefore also presupposes (a limited form of) agency on the side of the former.

Juxtaposing the contact zone with the border concept proposed here, the term *contact* already implies a relation that the 'Black border' seems to forbid with its assumption of a structural antagonism between Blackness and the world. By foregrounding the possibility of negotiation in a highly asymmetrical space, Pratt assumes that even though different groups of people do not possess the same position of or to power, they can still enter, live in, communicate across, and occupy the socio-symbolic space of the contact zone. Thus, it seems not too far-fetched to compare the position of 'the subordinate' in the contact zone with the position of Wilderson's non-black 'junior partners' located at the inside margins of U.S. civil society. From this point of view, contact zones could be found within civil society as spaces where Wilderson's 'junior' and 'senior' partners negotiate across asymmetrical power relations, whereas Blackness positioned as 'Slaveness' would provide the basis for these negotiation processes by enclosing civil society with the 'Black border.'[6]

Fugitivity against the Border

But how can we grapple with Black sociability that happens against all odds on the other side of the border, where social death seems to deny Blackness any leeway for negotiation in or with civil society? If we look at the 'Black border' that condenses the Afro-pessimist arguments outlined above, there seems to be no place in Afro-pessimism or on the 'Black border' to apprehend the everyday lives of Black people and their battles and negotiations in the United States other than to consider them as being 'permutations.' This is because they figure on the level of experience with which Wilderson's conceptual framework seems hardly concerned. Nonetheless, scholars such as Saidiya Hartman and Fred Moten — whose work appears closely related to but arguably different from Afro-pessimism as developed by Wilderson — have attempted to mutually address Black sociability and the structural position of Blackness in the 'afterlife of slavery.' Interestingly, both draw — to different extents — on the long history of Black fugitivity to do so (see Hartman 2007; Moten 2009).

In a similar vein, the historian Tina M. Campt also draws on the concept of fugitivity in her landmark monograph *Image Matters* (2012) to examine the ways in which Black diasporic photography participated in community and identity formation in a hostile environment that negated Blackness. In her study of vernacular photography of Black German families (1900–1945) and portrait photography of 'African Caribbean migrants to postwar Britain' (1948–1960), Campt addresses the broad question of 'how do black families and communities in diaspora use family photography to carve out a place for themselves in the European contexts they come to call home?' (Campt 2012: 14). Campt puts the concept of fugitivity to direct use in her analysis of 'snapshot' photographs of the lives of Afro-German families in Nazi-Germany. Her image analyses reveal the ways in which the 'fugitivity of these photos lies in their ability to visualize a recalcitrant normalcy in places and settings where it should not be' (ibid.: 91). The images practice a form of fugitivity by displaying and thereby (re)creating spaces of private refuge for Black German subjects in Nazi Germany. Consequently, in her preceding discussion of definitions of the term *fugitive*, Campt explicitly includes those who 'cannot or

---

[6]   For a more elaborate consideration of a border concept in Black feminist and Afro-pessimist interrogations of the category of 'the Human,' see von Gleich (2016).

do not remain in the proper place, or the places to which they have been confined or assigned' (ibid.: 87). Thus, for Campt, the images challenge us 'to see in [them] everyday practices of refusal, resistance, and contestation' (ibid.: 112) of and against 'the very premises that have historically negated the lived experience of Blackness as either pathological or exceptional to white supremacy' (Campt 2014: n.p.).

Admittedly, relating Afro-pessimism concerned predominantly with the structural positionality of Blackness in the United States to a concept of fugitivity developed with respect to vernacular photography of Black diasporic life in Europe seems quite a stretch — not only across different levels of abstraction but also across diverse geographies and histories. Nevertheless, when we juxtapose the 'Black border' in Afro-pessimism being proposed here with Campt's concept of fugitivity, we may imagine fugitivity as conceptualizing the 'lived experience of Blackness' as constant practices of 'refusal' to accept and to remain within the structurally ostracized position of social death. Fugitivity could then be understood as a constant running up against 'Slaveness' that — instead of successfully crossing or overcoming the 'Black border' — still remains on the outside of civil society where social death is located. In fugitivity, Black freedom as the supposed end of social death may be expressed and experienced, for instance through photography, but only as 'Fugitive Dreams' as the title of Hartman's last chapter of *Lose Your Mother* suggests (Hartman 2007: 211), without ever reaching a position from where to lay claims to civil society that has defined freedom as 'not Black/not Slave' for hundreds of years. In this way, fugitivity as a figure of thought enables us to accept the structural antagonism Afro-pessimism poses as well as reflect on the strategies and expressions of Black survival, perseverance, and sociability in an anti-black world, with the latter being unaccounted for in Afro-pessimism and exemplarily analysed in Campt's work.

Yet by imagining fugitivity as running up against social death, I cannot help but fall back on the assumption of some form of Black agency in relation to the 'Black border' and the civil society it encloses, a 'capacity' that the concept of social death problematizes in Wilderson's framework (Wilderson 2010). No matter how tentatively I weigh my words to describe flight and the struggle to survive social death, the concept of fugitivity still demises to the fugitive some 'capacity' to act as a subject or agent. The question of agency — obviously inseparable from Black social life and arguably incommensurable with social death — appears as a central fault line when attempting to grapple with Black sociability and social death across the levels of structure and experience.

The supposed agency attached to the concept of fugitivity appears, however, reasonably different from the constrained agency of 'the subordinate' that the concept of the contact zone adopts. While Pratt would deem it possible to negotiate with and self-represent against Wilderson's white 'senior' partners towards change, the fugitive practices of refusal and the 'stealing away' of the socially dead assume a more indeterminate form of agency. In fact, an Afro-pessimist analysis of the structures that position Blackness as social death outside of civil society implies an utter lack of symbolic agency in relation to that society. Within this framework, fugitivity might merely comprise the capacity to flee and struggle against the border between social death and civil life, without causing more than reverberations of the otherwise intact border structure. Moreover, under the auspices of Afro-pessimism, the fugitive's running up against the border of social death from outside civil society is not a matter of choice but rather appears as the crux of Black social life doomed to social death. Understood in this way, Black sociability entails the capacity to survive, live, and struggle, using Campt's words, in places 'where it should not be' (Campt 2012: 91) and by extension seems almost congruent with fugitivity in social death.

However, fugitivity may conceptually account for fugitive experiences and performances as Black social life only as long as the 'Black border' remains intact and still positions Blackness outside of civil society and the world as 'Slaveness.' Consequently, Afro-pessimism would deem crushing the 'Black border' between 'Blackness-as-Slaveness' and 'humanness' as its ultimate ambition. Since Wilderson renders imagining Black freedom against the backdrop of today's 'afterlife of slavery' in this 'antiblack world' problematic, he maintains with Frantz Fanon that the world — built on the demarcation of Blackness from 'humanness' — would have to come to an end for Blackness to entail something other than social death (Wilderson 2010; Fanon 2008).[7] In other words, the antagonistic border regime of white supremacy and its junior partners that I suggest Wilderson points out could only be overcome if said epistemological border structure would be completely demolished.

Fugitive Conclusions

Interpreting central Afro-pessimist assumptions as a border concept might not only help us to better understand Afro-pessimism. It also enables us to see how the premises of Afro-pessimism condensed in the 'Black border' differ from other well-known border concepts such as Pratt's 'contact zone.' When we conceptualize it as a border, the theoretical demarcation Afro-pessimism

---

[7]   For a differently accentuated view on the ongoing endeavour of creating new encompassing concepts of 'the Human' in and through Black Studies, especially Black feminism, see Weheliye (2014).

offers between non-blackness and Blackness, freedom and 'un-freedom,' and white social life inside civil society and Black social death outside of it appears insurmountable and absolute in its demarcation. The 'Black border' does not seem to allow for any dialectic relation between the two sides other than as a structural antagonism that disregards the level of experience. Fugitivity as elaborated by Campt might make it possible to account for Afro-pessimist assumptions about social death and reflect on the persevering 'lived experience of Blackness.' In this way, fugitivity might be understood as a running up against the absolute and impermeable border between social death and civil society that nonetheless remains intact. Consequently, fugitivity refers to a struggle for the transformation from 'Slaveness' to freedom that is not within actual reach but sought after as/in flight.

The challenge thus becomes thinking fugitivity together with Afro-pessimism because the former inevitably devolves a rudimentary 'capacity' to act in this world onto the fugitive that Afro-pessimism would call into question. This 'capacity,' however, has not entailed choice or triggered structural change, but has paradoxically warranted no more and no less than the enduring social life of the socially dead. In an Afro-pessimist framework, true agency would presumably mean bringing about the end of the world, or 'the freedom dream of a blackened world in which all might become unmoored, forging in struggle, a new people on a new earth' (Sexton 2010: 223). To pay heed to the potential realisation of this 'freedom dream' in the form of the end of the world while focussing on fugitive acts of refusal against social death within this world presents another important challenge of thinking fugitivity and Afro-pessimism together.

Instead of overriding the structural antagonism that locates Blackness outside of civil society and condemns it to social death and 'Slaveness,' I propose that we should instead consider how the Afro-pessimist argument and the concept of fugitivity together might bear the potential of regarding both social death and the enduring sociability of Blackness. My hope, for want of a better word, is that fugitivity might indeed function as a figure of thought that enables us to better appreciate fugitive practices of survival and resistance in the face of social death, but only if we also bear in mind the momentous challenges this fugitive thought experiment, which certainly needs further testing, abides. Ultimately, the question Black Studies has frequently addressed for centuries recurs: What does it take to dismantle the border erected between people defined as humans and people condemned to 'non-humanness' and to forge a new and truly all-encompassing concept of 'the Human'? Wilderson's answer, echoing Frantz Fanon, is as old as the question posed: 'the end of the world' as we know it.

References

Alexander, M. (2012) *The New Jim Crow: Mass Incarceration in the Age of Colorblindness.* 2nd ed. New York: New Press.

Anzaldúa, G. E. (1987) *Borderlands: The New Mestiza.* San Francisco: Aunt Lute Books.

Bhabha, H. K. (1994) *The Location of Culture.* London: Routledge.

Blackmon, D. A. (2008) *Slavery by Another Name: The Re-Enslavement of Black Americans from the Civil War to World War II.* New York: Anchor Books.

Campt, T. M. (2012) *Image Matters: Archive, Photography, and the African Diaspora in Europe.* Durham: Duke University Press.

Campt, T. M. (2014, Oct. 7.) *Black Feminist Futures and the Practice of Fugitivity.* Helen Pond McIntyre '48 Lecture held at the Barnard Center for Research on Women, Barnard College/Columbia. Available at: http://bcrw. barnard.edu/videos/tina-campt-black-feminist-futures-and-the-practice-of-fugitivity/

Coleman, N. A. T. (2014, Apr. 25). The Atlantic Ocean is not the Only Black Sea. *Futures of Black Studies: Historicity, Objectives and Methodologies, Ethics conference, University of Bremen.*

Douglass, P. and Wilderson, F.B. (2013). The Violence of Presence: Metaphysics in a Blackened World *Black Scholar* 43(4): 117–123.

Fanon, F. (2008). *Black Skin, White Masks.* London: Pluto Press.

von Gleich, P. (2015). African American Narratives of Captivity and Fugitivity: Developing Post-Slavery Questions for *Angela Davis: An Autobiography. Current Objectives of Postgraduate American Studies* 16.(1): n. p. Available at: http://copas.uni-regensburg.de/article/view/221/318

von Gleich, P. (2016). How Black is the Border? Border Concepts Traveling North American Knowledge Landscapes. In: Klöckner, C., Knewitz, S. & Sielke, S. eds. *Knowledge Landscapes North America.* Heidelberg: Winter. pp. 191-210.

Gordon, L. (1995). *Bad Faith and Antiblack Racism.* Atlantic Highlands: Humanities Press.

Hartman, S. V. (1997). *Scenes of Subjection: Terror, Slavery, and Self-Making in Nineteenth-Century America.* New York: Oxford University Press.

Hartman, S. V. (2007). *Lose Your Mother: A Journey Along the Atlantic Slave Route.* New York: Farrar, Straus and Giroux.

James, J. ed. (2005). *The New Abolitionists: (Neo) Slave Narratives and Contemporary Prison Writings.* Albany: State University of New York Press.

Martinot, S. and Sexton, J. (2003). The Avant-Garde of White Supremacy. *Social Identities: Journal for the Study of Race, Nation and Culture* 9(2): 169–181.

Mignolo, W. D. (2000). *Local Histories/Global Designs: Coloniality, Subaltern Knowledges, and Border Thinking.* Princeton: Princeton University Press.

Moten, F. (2009). The Case of Blackness. *Criticism* 50(2): 177–218.

Patterson, O. (1982). *Slavery and Social Death: A Comparative Study,* Cambridge: Harvard University Press.

Pratt, M. L. (1991). Arts of the Contact Zone. *Profession*: 33–40.

Pratt, M. L. (2008). *Imperial Eyes: Travel Writing and Transculturation.* London: Routledge.

Sexton, J. (2010). African American Studies. In: Rowe, J.C. ed. *A Concise Companion to American Studies.* Malden: Wiley-Blackwell. 210-228.

Sexton, J. (2011). The Social Life of Social Death: On Afro-Pessimism and Black Optimism. *Intensions* 5: 1–47.

Spillers, H. J. (1987). Mama's Baby, Papa's Maybe: An American Grammar Book. *Diacritics* 17(2): 65–81.

Weheliye, A. G. (2014). *Habeas Viscus: Racializing Assemblages, Biopolitics, and Black Feminist Theories of the Human.* Durham: Duke University Press.

Weier, S. (2014). Consider Afro-Pessimism. *Amerikastudien/American Studies* 59(3): 419–33.

Wilderson, F. B. (2003). Gramsci's Black Marx: Whither the Slave in Civil Society? *Social Identities* 9(2): 225–40.

Wilderson, F. B. (2007). The Prison Slave as Hegemony's (Silent) Scandal. In. James, J. ed. *Warfare in the American Homeland: Policing and Prison in a Penal Democracy.* Durham: Duke University Press, pp. 23–34.

Wilderson, F. B. (2010). *Red, White, and Black: Cinema and the Structure of U.S. Antagonisms.* Durham: Duke University Press.

Wilderson, F. B, von Gleich, P. and Spatzek, S. (2016). 'The Inside-Outside of Civil Society': An Interview with Frank B. Wilderson, III. *Black Studies Papers* 2 (1): 4–22. Available at: http://elib.suub.uni-bremen.de/edocs/00105247-1.pdf

Wynter, S. (1994). 'No Humans Involved': An Open Letter to My Colleagues. *Forum N. H. I.: Knowledge for the 21st Century* 1(1): 42–73.

Wynter, S. and Thomas, G. (2006). Proud Flesh Inter/Views: Sylvia Wynter. *ProudFlesh: New Afrikan Journal of Culture, Politics and Consciousness* 4: 1–36.

13

Interview with Juliane Hammer

Where do you see the most exciting research happening in your field?

The answer to this question depends a little bit on how I define my field. If it is the study of American Muslims, then the most exciting developments concern negotiations of race and culture in American Muslim communities. There is very challenging work taking place that explores the ways in which American Muslims at least since the turn of the twentieth century have been carving out spaces in a racially divided American society while attending to issues of social justice and equality within their own ranks. There are many ways in which American Muslims have actively participated in anti-racist struggles while others have attempted to attain whiteness and thus protection from a racist system that has excluded and marginalized them.

If I define my field as women and gender studies and especially the intersection of Islamic studies and gender studies then I would have to say that the most interesting developments pertain to a more serious, theoretically sophisticated, and intellectually critical application and exploration of gender as a category. There is so much research on Muslim women that it is necessary and important to take the next step and explore gender beyond women, to include men, but also to get away from gender binaries. Even further, the connection between gender and sexuality, which is often rhetorically advanced, is being taken seriously and has produced some of the most exciting new research.

In religious studies, my official discipline of teaching and research, we continue to debate questions of normativity, the need for public scholarship, and the continued significance of religion in people's lives as well as global and local politics.

How has the way you understand the world changed over time and what (or who) prompted the most significant shifts in your thinking?

Since growing up in East Germany, going through the German academic system by getting an MA and PhD in Islamic studies after German reunification, and then moving to the United States to teach and conduct research, my understanding of the world has shifted significantly and more than once. Somewhere in the process I realized that I have been an activist since I was a teenager: for me being an activist means feeling and being responsible for changing the world, however small the steps. I am also, and perhaps intrinsically linked to my activism, an intellectual, someone who not only studies society but sees the production of knowledge both as a responsibility and as a deeply political and public act.

The world I live in has changed so much in the past twenty-five years that it is sometimes hard to recognize it. Along with those sweeping changes — some positive and others very negative in my view — I have come across, learned from, and been changed by many people, including scholars, intellectuals, activists, and artists. I count among them (this is not an exhaustive list): Edward Said, James Baldwin, Tracy Chapman, Mercedes Sosa, Amina Wadud, Judith Butler, Saba Mahmood, Fatima Mernissi, Leila Ahmed, and many others. I have also been shaped by my own academic and activist contemporaries who continue to change and challenge my ideas and views.

Perhaps the most profound change to my view of the world has come through my two daughters who make it both urgent and significant to change the world into a safer, better place for them and to model rather than teach them that each of us matters and that what counts in the end is to have tried.

In what ways, through theory or method, can scholars of Islam integrate gender as a category of their work, outside of its current sanctioned place in work on and by Muslim women?

I'll start with the ways in which it is hard: scholarship on Muslim women was, beginning in the 1970s, an important corrective to existing work on Muslim societies as well as Muslim histories and texts in which men as the norm were largely taken for granted. However, this corrective came with a heavy price: it worked on the assumption that Muslim women are oppressed and in need of liberation, a claim that itself has problematic ties to European colonialism and the colonization of Muslim-majority societies. Once scholars moved on to Muslim women's agency and resistance to their oppression, there were more openings for critical scholarship but also for the inclusion of Muslim women's own scholarly perspectives and ideas.

It is hard to complain about these necessary historical steps. More recently, however, I have come to see the now seemingly obsessive focus on Muslim women, aided by global events and politics, as a serious impediment to critical analysis of how gender is constructed and negotiated in Muslim societies and communities, beyond the female-male gender binary and always in close proximity to questions of sexuality, sexual nature, and practice. Both benefit from the inclusion of more than women in our considerations. One way this has played out in my own work is by focusing on marriage and sexual practice, which are not always easy to research but by their very nature as topics require reaching beyond women's discourses and practices.

A key challenge I see in recognizing work on gender is that unless women or gender are mentioned in the title or abstract of a particular work, it is precisely in the organic inclusion of gender as a category that it becomes difficult to find such work and hold it up as gender work.

Lastly, in the study of gender among Muslims, the focus away from women and towards gender also raises important questions for activism as well as for the application of Euro-American and often universalized gender theory to Muslim contexts. Activists might need to insist on their focus on women in order to change the societies and communities they are working in and it takes additional theoretical work to show how changes in any society can only be achieved when both women and men are included as agents of change. In terms of theory, I wrestle with the question of what it means to apply gender theory that posits either gender or both sex and gender as constructed, and also pushes against a gender binary, in the face of communal realities and theological commitments that are left behind in the process. In other words, how can I question the gender binary or posit sex as constructed when many Muslims read the Qur'an, the Sunnah of the Prophet Muhammad, and their interpretive textual tradition as firmly representing a divine mandate for a male-female binary?

How do you wrestle with the Catch-22 of advocacy against gender violence within American Muslim communities in the context of the pervading colonial investment by Western powers and some feminist writing in saving Muslim women from Islam?

The short answer is that I wrestle with this Catch-22 every day of my life and how I approach it depends on the day as well as on my audience. I have come to realize that sometimes it makes sense to verbalize and thus call out into the open the fact that this predicament is a trap set by society and that I want to negotiate my way out of it. It helps to frame this verbalization as part of what miriam cooke has called 'multiple critique.' Many Muslim women scholars have used versions of this concept to say that it is both possible and necessary to critique capitalist 'western' societies for their marginalization and violation of Muslim communities and societies while also levelling a sustained critique towards our own Muslim communities and societies for their continued victimization and violation of women. It also helps to demand nuance; there is a difference between analysing and critiquing structures and systems in a society that oppresses and marginalizes women, including economic, political, cultural, social, and religious factors, and to claim that 'Islam' (itself a construct) oppresses Muslim women or that all Muslim men always oppress all Muslim women. It is more complicated than that and I insist on attending to that complicatedness.

Are there necessary limits to the exploration of diverse Muslim perspectives on gender with a commitment to what you call 'feminist normativity'? Why have you chosen to continue to self-identify with the term 'feminist' given the suspicion around this title in American Muslim communities?

I see my commitment to feminist normativity and my own identification as a feminist as an act of honest engagement. I was a feminist before I became a Muslim (at age 27) and my commitment to the full humanity of women and to critiquing patriarchy (that is what defines my feminism) has come with me into my Muslimness. I am also a white, European Muslim woman which carries with it a certain privilege to practice critiques of European and American feminisms as an insider to them and not as someone who has routinely and consistently been excluded from such discursive production. This exclusion is the case for women of colour who wrestle with the white, middle class, and Euro-centric narrative assumptions of feminism by finding space through designations such as womanism and mujerista feminism.

I do not embrace the term Islamic feminism because it carries normative baggage but I am comfortable calling myself a Muslim feminist. My contribution hopefully lies as much in challenging feminism to consider other ideas and perspectives and become less Euro-centric, secular, and white, while also allowing me to challenge the Muslim communities I am involved in to consider feminist critique. And yes, there are times when I experience limitations in my access to Muslim individuals and communities that reject my requests and also my arguments because I identify as a feminist. I see the greatest danger in not being able to access those who need to be challenged the most: Muslims who are at the other end of the spectrum with regards to gender roles and rights from where I position myself. Change will be difficult if I/we do not engage with that other side but it is very hard work to sustain conversations when the strategy of that other side is silencing and ignoring our ideas.

How does your work account for the extensive growth of queer theory as well as gender and sexuality studies beyond a gender binary? In what ways are these developments meaningful to work on communities that want to retain their theological interpretation of a gender binary in Islam?

Honestly, I am at the very beginning of a challenging road. I want to engage with cutting edge gender and sexuality theory and find some of it very compelling. One danger is the tendency of theoretical frameworks in these fields to deconstruct everything. Deconstructions comes before as well as after critique and I get that — if the system fails to be just and to provide everyone a good life, it needs fixing. However, deconstructing everything is also causing deep anxiety and uncertainty, especially for people who want to hold on to precepts and ideas because they make them feel safe. That is not an excuse but it accounts for the enormous resistance to much of post-modern theory. I want it to do work for me but I don't want to be expected to perform theory in one particular way. And because I see no boundary between my work and my life — I never stop thinking, analysing, critiquing, and changing — I also want to be certain about some things. I am relatively comfortable with ambivalence, perhaps also because I am a migrant and an intellectual exile, but I have a longing for both a community to belong to and ideas, beliefs, and perhaps material realities to hold on to. This ambivalence about questioning all categories and exploring their power in shaping but also breaking people's lives extends logically into my work with sex and gender as constructed categories. I find myself speaking to and about people who identify as men and women and being comfortable with that. This relative comfort is only broken when Muslims who do not identify as such or self-identify as queer come onto my radar and it is clear that their lives and experiences are anything but comfortable. I am always with the oppressed, always, and this commitment carries through here as a challenge to myself to be less invested in the gender binary and more open, not only when I see oppression directly, to theoretical work and community activism in that direction.

You do not identify as a theological writer yet are invested theologically in your academic work. With whom do you feel theological community as a scholar and how does that boundary extend when working on ethnographic projects beyond academia?

I am cautious about the word theology as applied to Muslims — it is after all a

Christian term for a very Christian activity, namely to contemplate what to believe about God. Muslims have ideas about that but perhaps it makes more sense to think in broader terms of interpretation of scripture, wrestling with discerning the will of God through ritual, as well as ethical and legal practice. I also teach at a public university, in a department of religious studies that has very little room for theological inquiry or religious normativity. My work on the various normative commitments that scholars in the humanities have and that cannot be avoided by scholars of religion(s) is an attempt to chip away at the rigid boundary between those supposedly analysing religion rationally and those who work prescriptively within their own religious tradition. There are many more ways to be insiders or outsiders to communities, systems, and traditions than to say I am Muslim and thus an insider or I am not a Muslim and thus an outsider. As discussed above, I identify as a Muslim feminist but that makes me an outsider to many Muslim communities regardless of what I claim to be myself. I am also a critical insider which puts me at the margins of some communities.

The question of religious more than theological community is a difficult one. I have already mentioned my longing to belong to a community. I have built relationships with other Muslim women scholars and activists and a few male Muslim allies and have decided that these connections are community for me. I do not want to compromise my commitments and ideas in order to be accepted. Many people are part of this network while others are intellectual and religious inspirations and foremothers to the struggle for non-patriarchal Muslim communities and societies in which people of all gender identities are accepted as equally human and only distinguished by their *taqwa*, their God-consciousness. I have also built relationships, often through my ethnographic work in Muslim communities with people who would disagree with my feminist commitments but who do have ethical commitments when it comes to respecting differing ideas and opinions. And especially in my work on Muslim efforts against domestic violence I have met many people who I feel connected to as part of Muslim communities in the struggle for ending domestic abuse. A shared cause can be the basis for a powerful and lasting connection. And perhaps it is here that I would qualify my religious commitments as deep ethical convictions and a foundational belief in God's intent for humans to strive for a just society for all.

If a textual focus on Muslim women theologians and activists helps to undo the reductive reading of women writers according to their personal biography, where is there space to still build with and from women's personal experience in order to develop a 'critical consciousness'?

That is a very good and challenging question especially considering that the significance of individual experience is both an important claim of some feminist theory and practice that has come back into focus in the work of some Muslim women scholars as well. On the one hand, it is important not to reduce the work of women, people of colour, LGBTQI people, or anyone who is perceived as different/other to their personal experience, thereby claiming that their lives are of no significance beyond them. This is particularly problematic when one refuses to see their oppression, marginalization, violation, and isolation as part of systems of exclusion and oppression. Refusing to recognize systemic structures of exclusion, hierarchy, and power differentials is a powerful tool for maintaining the status quo and for diminishing and crushing resistance to that status quo. Often, reducing scholars and activists to their biographies also takes on tones of psychoanalytical reduction and the imposition of constructed ideas of what it means to be mentally stable, healthy, or normal. If we can explain someone's feminist and/or anti-racist activism by finding instances of personal abuse, we absolve ourselves and the system that is our society from any responsibility for patterns of such abuse or negative personal experience. This also makes it possible to ostensibly distinguish between 'real' and 'felt' abuse. There is a long history in western societies of victim-blaming that is based on precisely this pattern, again, to absolve society and the state from the responsibility to affect change.

On the other hand, taking seriously the textual production of people, including Muslim women, claims and occupies spaces in areas of research, publishing, and teaching in which they historically had no place and were not recognized as full participants. They have agency in this process but also have to struggle to be recognized as scholarly and/or religious authority figures by building communities of interpretation and/or communities of shared methods and theories. The project of crossing borders — here the borders of academia, the borders of patriarchal interpretation, the borders of racist societies — comes full circle when scholars and activists acquire space to do their work and then insist that they will reconfigure the rules of scholarship and activism in the process. If Muslim women scholars write, publish, teach, and work in communities simultaneously, which is hard and can cause burn out, they can insist in those spaces that their experiences are part of who they are but that they cannot be reduced to them. Religiously speaking, I find it most compelling to think of personal experience as part of God's self-disclosure beyond revelation. As such, experience like revelation becomes both an opening and a command for interpretation and meaning-making.

In bringing an intersectional critique of normativity to scholarship, how do you incorporate and interrogate how race is discussed in the study of Islam in America? How does solidarity work being undertaken by Muslim women with other marginalized women, especially women of colour, move beyond assumptions of what Muslim activism looks like?

There are at least two questions here. The first about the intersectional nature of critique and constructive scholarship is one in which I still lean heavily on my thoughts and ideas about gender equality in order to approach a better understanding of race. This is especially challenging in the study of American Muslims because many American Muslims — particularly those who are not African American — have found it difficult to acknowledge the enormous power of American racism in shaping their lives but also their perceptions of racialized otherness. There is still a severe lack of solidarity with Black Muslims along with other Black communities in the United States. To change that, I have found it useful to point out the connections between anti-Muslim hatred and hate crimes and what is often called Islamophobia and racist discrimination and violence. In fact, I see 'Islamophobia' and anti-Black racism, as well as other forms of racism and racialization, as part of the same system. It is in the interest of that system that these overlapping and/or parallel ways of discrimination should not be recognized as connected.

Here is also where gender comes back in for me. Feminist critiques of patriarchy have the potential to recognize parallel systems of oppression even if feminist ideas have been, and continue to be, used to aid colonialism, capitalism, and thus racism. I find that in scholarship on American Muslims the problem is often that scholars either do gender well or they do race well — it is much harder to find scholars who can and will, in sophisticated and accessible ways, do both. I am striving to become more familiar with critical race theory and anti-racist activism in order to see race and address it even in those spaces where the communities I study do not.

How does the use of the concept or trope 'border' and its metaphorical logic help or block your thinking about gender, specifically in the context of feminism and Islam?

When I first got involved with the borderlands/border thinking project I was concerned that it would not be enough to think about borders between groups of people in my research between people in American society. I argued that there are borders within American society that are constructed and maintained along lines of religious as well as racial otherness, often at the intersection with gender. It is after all the paradox of American Islamophobia that the industry that produces and perpetuates images of Muslim women portrays them as both the 'reproducers' of a fifth column of dangerous Muslim terrorists while also arguing that Muslim women are oppressed by Muslim men and Islam and need to be saved by American society and especially American feminists. Muslim women have borne the brunt of hate crimes and harassment, so the anti-Muslim sentiments are enacted on their bodies and through that on their families and communities.

There is also a blurry line between Islam and racial otherness, sometimes expressed in terms of cultural otherness (which I think obscures the racialized nature of it) and the ways in which Muslims are told that they just cannot be American while also insisting on being Muslims. There is of course a geopolitical and global dimension to this perception, but it nevertheless demands of Muslims that they surrender their distinct Muslimness and become assimilated into an imagined mainstream. I think it politically prudent at this juncture in American history to demand acceptance because of difference and not in spite of it. It is not a matter of being tolerated or continuously having to prove sufficient similarity or sameness to be included, but quite the opposite.

I continue to be fascinated by the rather uneasy inclusion of religion as a category in the border thinking project. The dynamics of decolonizing the production and dissemination of knowledge takes on very interesting and different tones and shades when considered in the context of Muslim majority societies and Muslims in minority contexts like the settler colonial state that is the United States of America.

And to come back to feminism and Islam, my colleague Fatima Seedat in South Africa has recently written about the possibilities inherent in having the concepts Islam and feminism speak back to each other, so that Muslim feminists and those invested in gender justice can contribute and teach from within their Islam while also learning and taking ownership of the diversity of feminisms that exists and might be possible.[1] This is a very different idea from insisting that 'Islamic feminism' is a movement and a thing. Borders are conceptual in this way and I find it both inspiring and challenging to consider borderlands as spaces of opportunity. Even if a border is described as porous, a space of exchange rather than separation, it is still a border. It may just be that this borderlands thinking is the way of those without much power to make sense of their situation and claim agency from within those limitations. This thinking does makes the border real, though, and thus by recognizing it as an opportunity of sorts it still legitimates its existence.

And lastly on this question, the borders imposed by particular gender binaries

---

[1]   See Seedat (2013).

commonly found in Muslim discourses past and present make it difficult to apply some ideas from feminist theory without questioning the very foundations of one or the other. This is, for me, a productive space because I have come to a tentative peace with the ambivalence involved.

What is the most important advice you could give to young scholars of borders, borderlands and border thinking?

I take it this question implies that I am an older scholar. Hm. I would start by saying that like with any alternative approach to the academy there is risk involved, both on the level of career advancement and acceptance as a scholar and in the ways in which a concept like border thinking cannot be unthought. The intellectual project of the humanities rests on a set of Euro-centric assumptions *and* the academy is part of a capitalist system in which we produce things that can be sold. Both intellectually and financially it is risky to unravel the system that you are part of. That does not mean you should not do it. But you should both be aware of the risks and take them intentionally or postpone doing so, and I think I have learned as a feminist scholar in the academy that risk assessment and strategies to deal with that risk require both mentors and peers. The academy can be a lonely and deeply competitive place and transformational work is never to be achieved alone. Building networks like the one reflected in this volume, seeking validation and advice, and offering support are as important as advancing ideas. And lastly, I have found it liberating to see and occupy the academy as a transformative space in which subversion of the stated goals of higher education is possible even if not often welcomed by our administrators, donors, and politicians. There is enormous power in even reaching one student, one reader, one activist and help shift their way of thinking about the world.

This interview was conducted by Katherine Merriman

Recommended Readings

Ahmed, L. (1992). *Women and Gender in Islam: Historical Roots of a Modern Debate*. New Haven: Yale University Press.

Ali, K. (2016). *Sexual Ethics and Islam: Feminist Reflections on Qur'an, Hadith, and Jurisprudence*. Revised Edition. Oxford: Onworld.

Baldwin, J. (1998). *Collected Essays*. New York: Penguin.

Butler, J. (1990). *Gender Trouble: Feminism and the Subversion of Identity*. New York: Routledge.

Fatima S. (Fall 2013) Islam, Feminism, and Islamic Feminism: Between Inadequacy and Inevitability *Journal of Feminist Studies in Religion* 29(2): 25-45.

Hidayatullah, A. (2014). *Feminist Edges of the Qur'an* (New York: Oxford University Press, 2014)

Mahmood, S. (2015). *Politics of Piety: The Islamic Revival and the Feminist Subject.* Princeton: Princeton University Press.

Mernissi, F. (1987). *Beyond the Veil: Male-Female Dynamics in Modern Muslim Society* (Bloomington: Indiana University Press.

Mir-Hosseini, Z., Al-Sharmani, M. and Rumminger, J. eds. (2015). *Men in Charge? Rethinking Authority in Muslim Legal Traditions*. Oxford: Oneworld.

Said, E. (1978). *Orientalism*. New York: Random House.

Wadud, A. (2006). *Inside the Gender Jihad: Women's Reform in Islam*. Oxford: Oneworld.

Wadud, A. (1999). *Qur'an and Woman: Rereading the Sacred Text from a Woman's Perspective*. New York: Oxford University Press.

Note on Indexing

E-IR's publications do not feature indexes due to the prohibitive costs of assembling them. If you are reading this book in paperback and want to find a particular word or phrase you can do so by downloading a free PDF version of this book from the E-IR website.

View the e-book in any standard PDF reader such as Adobe Acrobat Reader (pc) or Preview (mac) and enter your search terms in the search box. You can then navigate through the search results and find what you are looking for. In practice, this method can prove much more targeted and effective than consulting an index.

If you are using apps (or devices) such as iBooks or Kindle to read our e-books, you should also find word search functionality in those.

You can find all of our e-books at: http://www.e-ir.info/publications

www.ingramcontent.com/pod-product-compliance
Lightning Source LLC
Chambersburg PA
CBHW060316030426
42336CB00011B/1076